From the Clinics to the Capitol

Reproductive Justice: A New Vision for the Twenty-First Century

EDITED BY RICKIE SOLINGER (SENIOR EDITOR),

KHIARA M. BRIDGES, LAURA BRIGGS, KRYSTALE

E. LITTLEJOHN, RUBY TAPIA, AND CARLY THOMSEN

From the Clinics to the Capitol

HOW OPPOSING ABORTION
BECAME INSURRECTIONARY

Carol Mason

UNIVERSITY OF CALIFORNIA PRESS

University of California Press
Oakland, California

© 2025 by Carol Mason

Cataloging-in-Publication data is on file at the Library of Congress.

ISBN 978-0-520-39703-3 (cloth)
ISBN 978-0-520-39704-0 (pbk.)
ISBN 978-0-520-39705-7 (ebook)

GPSR Authorized Representative: Easy Access System Europe, Mustamäe
tee 50, 10621 Tallinn, Estonia, gpsr.requests@easproject.com

34   33   32   31   30   29   28   27   26   25
10   9   8   7   6   5   4   3   2   1

For Martha

Contents

Illustrations

Introduction

Stormy Weather

Maybe it's the calm before the storm.

—DONALD TRUMP, October 6, 2017

Operation Rescue Redux

Westward I drove to Louisville, a steady rain graying everything outside. Traffic wasn't too bad on the interstate, and I had the phone telling me where exactly to go. Headed to a hotel just outside of the city, I was going out of sheer curiosity and for a distraction from my duties as department chair at University of Kentucky in Lexington. Two years into that administrative role and two years after my third book had come out, I was driving in this steamy summer storm, the windshield wipers splashing, to see some folks whose names I remembered from a while back. Mostly it was the name Matthew Trewhella that caught my attention in the stories about this upcoming gathering. I remembered him from back in the 1990s. I was headed to the hotel where Operation Save America had told its followers to stay during its revival of the "rescue" movement. Back in the day, thousands of abortion opponents would swarm reproductive health care centers to barricade the entrances and "rescue babies." Similarly, the aim in Louisville was to close down the last women's clinic in the state and to declare Kentucky the first state without any access to abortion.[1] It was the last week of July 2017.

Already that year there had been a few gathering storms, incidents and meetings that made me more than uneasy. To the southeast of me, in Pikeville, white supremacists had gathered publicly, a recruitment show for eastern Kentucky where they met resistance but there were no physical altercations.[2] On the West Coast, the alt-right, a disaffected community composed mostly of men fed up with women and organized largely online, had reclaimed the free speech movement on the campus of University of California, Berkeley.[3] The controversy over whether some of their speakers could make appearances in university spaces had erupted into street fighting. Donald J. Trump had been president for six months and was caging babies on the Southern border. Now the militant antiabortion "rescue" movement was being revived. What would it look like now? I had to go and see for myself. As I drove toward them, my mind reeled back to the 1990s.

In particular, I remembered going to Buffalo, New York, five months after Dr. Barnett Slepian had been murdered with a Russian-issued high-powered rifle by a sniper named James Kopp. Kopp had picked him off through the kitchen window of his house, a precise assassination right in front of the doctor's children's eyes. Years later Kopp was caught somewhere in France, indicating an international support system for the assassin. At trial, Kopp defended himself by comparing abortion to the Holocaust, a dubious line of defense that seemed especially hurtful and twisted given that Dr. Slepian was Jewish and had returned home from synagogue the evening he was murdered. Days after that murder, a pro-life reverend announced that "on April 19, 1999, there would be a Spring of Life reunion during a week-long Operation Save America action in Buffalo."⁴

Spring of Life? April 19? Rescue? What did all that mean?

The mention of the Spring of Life was referring to a 1992 action in which Operation Rescue (the group's original name) attempted to block entry to a clinic in the Buffalo area. The Spring of Life had hoped to replicate the success of the notorious Summer of Mercy, a forty-six-day siege on clinics in Wichita, Kansas, a year earlier, when thousands of abortion foes breeched barriers and fences in a mass attack. Planning this reunion on April 19 was a significant choice. April 19 is the anniversary of a series of violent events that sowed sympathy for anti-government rebels and apocalyptic believers. April 19 was the date on which the federal shoot-out with the Weaver family at Ruby Ridge, Idaho, happened in 1992 and the federal assault on the Branch Davidian compound in Waco, Texas, happened in 1993. In response to these armed conflicts, Timothy McVeigh executed a retaliatory bombing of the Alfred P. Murrah Federal Building in Oklahoma City on April 19, 1995.

Four years later, in 1999, there I was in Buffalo with a group of activists and a young filmmaker to witness this Operation Rescue reunion. We moved through the crowds of antiabortionists, some piously praying, others looking mean and menacing, and some leaders gleefully preaching to whomever would listen, including a wall of stone-faced cops. It was a tinderbox. A tall man wearing a skull mask told me how I, wearing the armor of a leather jacket, was going to hell. We knew what April 19 meant. We all feared something violent: another bombing, another sniper. But nothing erupted. At the end of the long day of supporting clinic workers and documenting the action and protests, we were just starting to let our guard down, trying to relax in the living room of someone I didn't know. We'd spread out our sleeping bags on the floor, ready to call it a day. We turned on the TV. There had been a mass shooting at a high school. Columbine, Colorado. There was the violence we'd been fearing. Little did we know that was the beginning of what has become regular mass shootings by young white men.

I had written about that 1999 trip to Buffalo in my first book, *Killing for Life,* so there was almost a nostalgic feel driving toward another Operation Rescue/Save America reunion, this time in Louisville, less than an hour's drive from my home of six years.[5] But my life was so different now, and I felt much older. Well into my fifties, I was a senior scholar whose job was to support the faculty, grad students, and undergrads. Diagnoses of arthritis and stenosis meant I wasn't going to sleep on anybody's living room floor. My youthful rage had dissipated through the decades. After getting my doctorate in the 1990s, I worked contingent positions for seven years before I landed my first tenure-track position. Every summer entailed finding extra money for health insurance because jobs didn't include it for non–tenure track faculty. At the time of the Buffalo trip, I had no idea if I would have a job in the fall. By the time I was driving to Louisville, however, I had been tenured twice and full professor for more than a decade. I had a mortgage, a wife, and a retirement account. I wore clothes from Talbots. My badass days (such as they were) were far behind me. What did I suppose I was going to do at this revival of rescue?

I wasn't sure. I got to the hotel and checked in, hoping to blend in with the other folks, some of whom looked older than I was. I wondered if their church paid them to get on a bus to pray around the clinic in the rain. I wondered about Matthew Trewhella, whose name I had typed plenty of times, explaining to readers that in the

1990s he had signed a statement that claimed killing physicians who provide abortions and murdering clinic workers were justifiable homicide. He also advocated organizing militias to oppose abortion. But I wasn't in Louisville because I was planning to write another book. I just wondered how visible the crossover of anti-abortionists, white supremacists, and other gun-toting militants was. For me, the crossover of these movements was obvious decades ago. I believe they emerged as parallel and sometimes intersecting movements. I believe that white nationalism had for decades been making inroads into the American imagination under the guise of opposing abortion. But most people don't see it that way. Most people think about antiabortionists as unrelated to the far right. I wondered if, now that Trump was riding high on right-wing populism, the antiabortionists would feel safer showing their alliances—in ideology and membership—with other militants. I just wanted to see.

After taking my bag up to my room, I returned to the vast hotel parking lot. I walked around in rainy twilight. There were a lot of cars and trucks from all over. Some vehicles were "truth trucks," vans or semis emblazoned with antiabortion imagery. Some of the imagery was predictable. There were lots of bloody pictures. One bloody "baby" the size of Godzilla adorned the side of what appeared to be a large moving van (figure 1).

The image was not one of the most typical—and its size? There was no verisimilitude there. What, then, was this bloody thing a sign for if not denoting the actuality of abortion? It is routine for antiabortion materials to exaggerate the size of prenatal organisms. A human egg, for example, is about the size of the period at the end of this sentence. This colossal monster seemed different from the pro-life visual politics of yesteryear. It advertised "death"

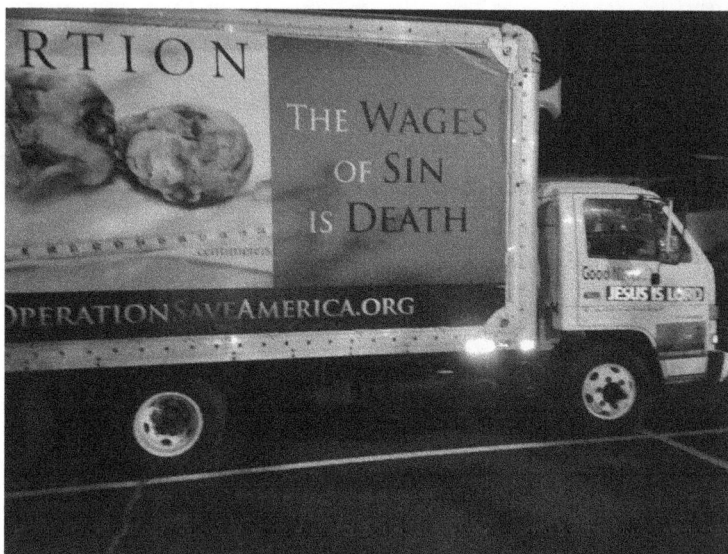

FIGURE 1. Unbelievably colossal carnage depicted on antiabortion truck in Louisville, 2017. Photo by author.

as the "wages of sin"—because those words appeared next to it on the truck. But it also could have been an advertisement of the "American carnage" that Donald Trump had weirdly invoked in his presidential inaugural address.

Some images were entirely new to me. Who was that cop pictured on the truth truck and what was the appeal of that? Why was the word "tyranny" so prominent? Some vehicles were personal cars. I noted bumper stickers, license plates, signs affixed to the sides of sedans or pickups. Most of these signs were run-of-the-mill antiabortion stuff. However, one small truck sported a collection of images that were peculiar to me. I took a picture of it.

On the side of a truck there was an image of a crying infant with syringes menacingly encircling it (figure 2). Below that image, a

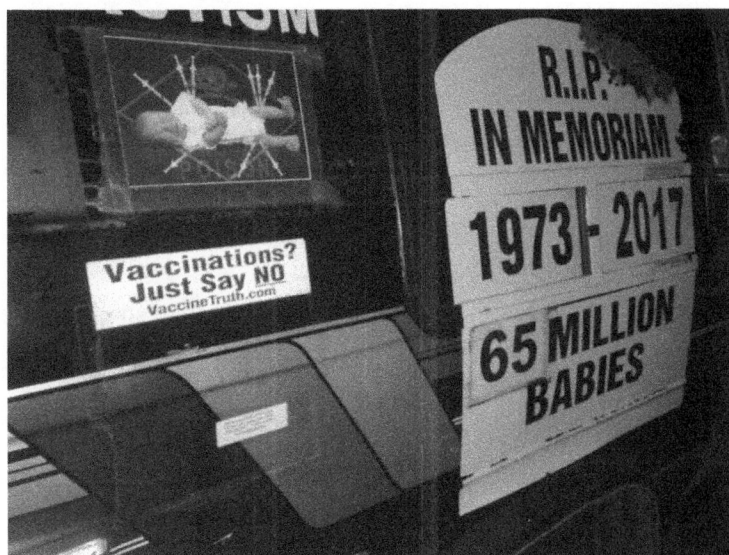

FIGURE 2. Truck espousing antiabortion and anti-vaccination message in Louisville, 2017. Photo by author.

bumper sticker read "Vaccinations? Just say NO." To the right of these two images—the anti-vaccination message and the white infant that appears to be attacked by hypodermic needles—is a tombstone that memorializes "65 million babies" who have died since 1973, that is, the date of the Supreme Court's decriminalization of abortion via the *Roe v. Wade* decision.

This was not run-of-the-mill antiabortion sentiment, although it certainly perpetuated the contempt for science that abortion foes use in slandering physicians and midwives as medical bottom-feeders. The "just say no" message was a repackaging of a slogan from the War on Drugs, a federal program originating during the Nixon administration that was very selective about whose drugs and which drug users were criminal. It was a racist selectivity that adversely affected communities of color, as studies have shown.[6] In displaying that "just say no" message alongside the white baby, the owner of the truck was shifting the history of the racist War on Drugs to a fear of the government's attack on the future of white people. I had heard about anti-vaxxers before, but I hadn't seen the movement against immunizations connected to the issue of abortion in this way. The side of the truck was equating the government-sanctioned health care efforts to make abortion and vaccinations accessible. The message seemed to be that the government and physicians that are stabbing the white child with vaccines are the same people committing mass murder through abortion.

On that rainy evening in July 2017, I couldn't see what was coming. I could not know that by 2020 LifeSiteNews would quote a Kazakhstan bishop who connected abortion and vaccines in the context of a pandemic he thought was pretext for a globalist coup. "This COVID situation was created not only to implement a new dictatorship and control of the population, but in some way to legalize abortion globally . . . so that the entire planet will be collaborating in the process of killing babies through the vaccine, which will use parts of aborted babies."[7] Vaccines may use stem cells, but these are not obtained through abortion. But the bishop did not know this. He went on to further assert that if COVID vaccines became mandated, "we will enter into the time of the apocalypse." In 2017, that apocalyptic tone was not reflected by the message on this anti-vax, antiabortion truck. But here was evidence that the anti-vaccination stance not only preceded the SARS COVID-19 pandemic, but also that some abortion opponents were already locked into that attitude. It was an anti-government (also known as anti-statist) attitude that connected opponents of abortion with opponents of vaccination.

It was also a direct reversal of how vaccinations and abortion rights were promoted and broadly received as things that were good for the nation in the 1960s. According to historian Leslie Reagan, the fight for abortion rights emerged alongside and in tandem with the fight to promote a German measles vaccine.[8] German measles, or rubella, was a public health crisis that was imperiling maternal and fetal health, often resulting in birth defects. Reagan's book *Dangerous Pregnancies* chronicles how the American public came to embrace vaccinations by envisioning unborn children as the future of the nation that needed to be protected. It was your duty as an American to get vaccinated so that unborn children would be safe from disease and disfigurement. Nationalism and ableism were thus part of the cultural logic involved in the public service campaigns to promote vaccinations, and, Reagan shows, securing the legal right to terminate a pregnancy was an extension—not a contradiction—of this idea of protecting the unborn. Furthermore, she shows how the campaigns for getting vaccinated and for abortion rights portrayed the unborn as white, so that middle-class, mainstream Americans were assured that these were the right things to do.

As I looked at the side-by-side anti-vaccine and antiabortion images on the truck in 2017, I remembered Leslie Reagan's excellent book and thought about how much the recognition of the public health benefits of immunization and abortion had been reversed. I thought about how Operation Rescue had been the beginning of antiabortion militancy on a large scale, and how it emerged alongside antiabortion arson, homicides, and bombs meant to maim people as well as blow up buildings. Over the last half of the twentieth century, opponents of abortion became increasingly radical, militant, apocalyptic, and anti-statist. I couldn't see the pandemic coming, but I felt this effort to revive the "rescue" movement was a variation on a theme that echoed the Pikeville gathering of white supremacists and the Berkeley battle with the alt-right that had happened earlier that summer. I wondered how the owners of this truck, and all the vehicles in the dark parking lot, thought opposing abortion fit into the growing prevalence of white nationalism, militancy, and authoritarianism.

Only a dozen days after my drive to Louisville, there was an attempt to bring together all sorts of right-wing actors. Legions of young white men held tiki torches aloft and chanted, "Jews will not replace us." It was a spectacular and spectacularly violent gathering. The August 11, 2017, Unite the Right rally in Charlottesville, Virginia, ended with the vehicular manslaughter of Heather Heyer. An Ohio man associated with the National Vanguard purposefully ran his Dodge Charger into a crowd of peace activists and killed her, injuring nineteen others.

After the Unite the Right rally, the National Vanguard changed its name to the Patriot Front. Other organizations regrouped. Charlottesville had not succeeded in uniting various aspects of the right, but another attempt came four years later, in the form of the January 6, 2021, insurrectionary attack on the Capitol building in Washington, DC. It was, to say the least, more successful than the rally. It was a larger, more inclusive, and scarier show of force. The media's coverage of the January 6 siege has largely left out the anti-abortion militants who were there at the Capitol and who have long perpetuated or advocated for domestic terrorism under the guise of saving babies. There have been plenty of media reports about white supremacists, militia groups, Christian nationalists, QAnon followers, and other militant conspiracists. What has received less attention is how abortion opponents overlap and intersect with these. All people who oppose abortion are not militants or white supremacists. It is important to acknowledge, however, how this underexamined element of the insurrection illuminates shared logics among a variety of right-wing revolutionaries, including antiabortionists who have become radicalized.

Plenty of antiabortionists were at the Capitol on January 6, although their presence has largely been ignored.[9] Antiabortionist John Brockhoeft, a clinic arsonist associated with the Army of God, joined other antiabortion militants such as Chad Estes and Bobby Lee. Dave Daubenmire said he had a crew of about 120 people with him. Reporters have identified others such as West Virginia politician Derrick Evans and Tayler Hansen, a proponent of Baby Lives Matter. Numerous representatives from other antiabortion organizations attended the Trump rally prior to the storming of the Capitol, including Abby Johnson, who wrote a book about leaving Planned Parenthood to become a career antiabortionist. As we will see in chapter 3, Johnson updated key narratives about why women can become alienated from the pro-choice movement and can profit, socially and financially, from joining the pro-life side.

On January 6, 2021, I was tracking the news with a paradoxical mix of incredulous fear and horrible recognition. I both couldn't believe it and had seen it all before. This kind of political combat was not only reminiscent of mass attacks on abortion clinics, but it was also the stuff of the right-wing fiction and nonfiction I had read over thirty years of research. Throughout the hours of rioting, my partner and I had two computers open to various news sources, the television tuned in to broadcast media, and our phones monitoring Twitter. When my wife called me into her office, I watched with her as people scaled the walls and entered the Capitol building. As the doors of the House chamber were nearly being breached, I swooned. I felt faint and had to sit down. The vision of so many right-wing narratives I had read were actually playing out. We were *that close* to a successful coup.

Later, after the riots had been quelled and Trump had told all the rioters they were "very special," I was texting with my sister. We grew up in West Virginia. She lives in Alaska now and votes Democrat. She was frustrated. She was perplexed by the events of the day, the break-in at the Capitol, and the hunting down of members of government. Reports of the police letting rioters into the Capitol building especially vexed her. She texted something to the effect of, *I just don't understand. I don't know why they would do that.* I looked at my phone and texted back: *I do.*

I fear my response came off as smug. I wasn't meaning to one-up my sister. I didn't realize it then, but in that exchange I was committing myself to sharing my understanding, with my sister and anybody else who didn't have the opportunity to read all that I've read throughout my career.

This book tells you what I know. I'm not intent on changing anybody's mind. My purpose is illumination, not conversion. My imagined reader is someone who has lived enough to have questions about how we got where we are today. A reader responding to my plan for this book suggested it would be helpful by making the links between race, reproduction, and the right "comprehensible for people outside the right-wing universe." I told him I am also writing this book to make right-wing movements *reprehensible* to the people *in* that universe. This book won't convert anyone who is deep in the far right, but those who are deep in the far right have families and loved ones who need intellectual and moral support. I want this book to be something that will help ease the pain of national gaslighting, which taught generations of Americans that a fertilized egg is the future of our country before it taught people that an election was stolen. I want the book to be something that some folks will read and say, "I *knew* I wasn't crazy; this connects so many dots that I encounter on a daily basis, but I just never put them together."

For decades white nationalism has been making inroads into the American imagination under the guise of opposing abortion, which has worked in tandem with right-wing populism. The purpose of this book is to elucidate the intersections of race, reproduction, and right-wing America. It's my hope that people will understand how ideas undergirding current manifestations of white nationalism and authoritarian populism became not only plausible to militants but also palpable to a more general public that accommodates it. Consider the two key concepts of this thesis.

Populism

What is populism? And how is it connected to opposing abortion? This connection was clear to me years ago but came into fierce focus as a result of that 2017 trip to Louisville. Along with antiabortion leader Rusty Thomas, head of Operation Save America, there was old-timer Matthew Trewhella. His work illuminates how fighting against abortion relies on and feeds populist ideas.

In the 1990s Trewhella caught the attention of the media and the FBI because he seemed to be advocating taking up arms against abortion providers.[10] While he said he wouldn't do it himself, he argued that murdering physicians and people who worked at clinics, such as receptionists, nurses, and security guards, was justifiable homicide. This wasn't his original idea. Trewhella could have been following the general sentiment that conservatives have voiced since Republican presidential candidate Barry Goldwater proclaimed in 1964 "that extremism in the defense of liberty is no vice! And let me remind you also that moderation in the pursuit of justice is no virtue!" But, more precisely, Trewhella was following the lead of antiabortionists such as Michael Bray, who wrote a book, *A Time to Kill* (1994), that spelled out the rationale in detail. Trewhella had signed a 1993 document called the Defensive Action Statement, which was written to condone the killing of Dr. David Gunn that year. The Defensive Action Statement served as an open letter informing the public that to oppose abortion meant rejecting man's law and living by God's law. According to the statement's interpretation of God's law, murdering people to protect the unborn was necessary and right. The man who penned the Defensive Action Statement proceeded to fatally shoot Dr. John Britton and his bodyguard, James Barrett, in 1994. In the 1990s seven people, including clinic workers and doctors, were murdered by antiabortionists inspired by this idea. In 2009, another physician who provided abortions was assassinated.

Flash forward to 2013: Trewhella self-publishes his own book that elaborates on the idea of obeying only God's law, *The Doctrine of the Lesser Magistrates: A Proper Resistance to Tyranny and a Repudiation of Unlimited Obedience to Civil Government.* Inspired by his interpretation of texts and discussions from the 1500s, Trewhella attempts to justify illegal action to oppose abortion by citing supposed precedents in American history. The doctrine argues that "when the superior or higher-ranking civil authority makes immoral/unjust laws or policies, the lower or lesser ranking civil authority has both a right and duty to refuse obedience to that superior authority. If necessary, the lesser authorities may even actively resist the higher authority."[11] According to Anna Rosensweig, an expert on early modern French literature, Trewhella bases his theory of defying laws in *Doctrine* on political writings and religious debates of the sixteenth century. Some of today's most cherished ideas about individual rights go back to some of the concepts and writings that Trewhella cites, but he misreads and decontextualizes those old writings in a way to legitimize breaking the law and revolting against the government. It is a more elaborate version of the general idea behind the Defensive Action Statement from the 1990s: the idea that Christians do not have to follow laws that don't mirror their beliefs. Because Trewhella has couched it in a centuries-old resistance theory, it has a ring of authority to it. In fact, many people are embracing it as authoritative text and as license to defy the law.[12]

Before coming to Louisville in 2017 to revive the rescue movement, in 2015 Trewhella traveled to eastern Kentucky to support a county clerk who refused to issue marriage licenses for gay couples following the Supreme Court decision in *Obergefell v. Hodges.* The county clerk, he said, should ignore the ruling because she was a lesser magistrate. As such she has a "duty" to "interpose on behalf of righteousness." Her doing so would help "abate the just judgment of God on our nation." He explained that if she would "stand in the gap" between God's law and the "tyranny" of "civil authority," "then God relents His judgment." But if she followed the law and her job description by issuing marriage licenses, she would bring wrath on the nation because God would "allow His righteous judgment to come upon the land."[13]

Two years after this showstopper, antiabortionist organizers brought a copy of Trewhella's book to Kentucky governor Matthew Bevin. They wanted the governor to "ignore *Roe*" as they wanted the county clerk to ignore *Obergefell.* In Rusty Thomas's words,

"Christians were remonstrating in Kentucky for months to encourage the state authorities to cross a line, be brave, and defy the lawless, corrupt, and unconstitutional ruling of Roe vs. Wade."[14] Trewhella and other organizers thus attempted to provide state officials with a rationale to defy, and to let the organizers defy, federal laws in order to oppose abortion by impeding access to the clinic.

Antiabortion leaders not only met with the governor of Kentucky but also addressed police as state officials, hailing them as lesser magistrates. Writing directly to law enforcement officers, leader Rusty Thomas argued that their loyalty as officials of civil government rests foremost with God. Thomas also appealed to officers' sense of being "targeted" as a result of recent campaigns to halt fatal police action against unarmed African Americans. With thinly veiled references to the Black Lives Matter movement, Thomas's open letter to police praised "THE THIN BLUE LINE that separates the criminal element from society." Thomas opined, "Anarchy runs rampant while government tyranny grows. Our nation stands in awkward amazement as violence, carnage, terrorism, and massacres are becoming a common everyday experience in our nation. To our horror, this violence has now targeted our law enforcement agencies."[15] In this appeal Thomas draws a distinct line between the police and the tyrannical federal government, presumably in hopes that police themselves would defy—or let the antiabortionists defy—federal law.

The "thin line" thinking emerged again when a group of Louisville high school journalists published a training slideshow used by the Kentucky State Police. The slideshow was titled "The Warrior Mindset." It privileged masculinity over policy, quoted Adolf Hitler several times, and advocated "ruthless" violence.[16]

One slide featured a quotation by Robert E. Lee alongside a photo of Southern secessionists wearing their gray Confederate States of America uniforms during the U.S. Civil War. That slide is titled "The Thin Gray Line." Like Thomas's invocation of the thin blue line, referring to the police, the police's invocation of the thin gray line, referring to seditious enemies of the United States, suggest an antagonism toward the federal government. Trewhella's and Thomas's outreach to the police to ignore federal authority when they were in Kentucky to shut down an abortion clinic seemed reasonable to them.

Lest you think that Trewhella's appeal to police and other "lesser magistrates" could work only on racist rubes or only in places such as Kentucky, let me disabuse you of the notion. His *Doctrine* has been used to justify opposing mask and vaccine mandates in Illinois and South Dakota, to praise Governor Ron DeSantis in Florida for his resistance to COVID precautions, to argue against counting mail-in ballots in Pennsylvania, and to prompt agitators from Moms for America to fight for "liberty" at school board meetings. This last appeal was issued by Michael Flynn, the former national security advisor, who has been promoting Trewhella's book as much as the conspiracy theories of QAnon. The *Doctrine* has also been cited as the authority upon which a county ordinance to suspend any federal law that obstructs an individual's constitutional rights was proposed.[17]

These attempts to justify and sanctify breaking the law exemplify populism. Right-wing populism can be examined as "an appeal to 'people' (usually white, heterosexual Christians) to rebel—against both liberal 'elites' from above and 'subversives' and 'parasites' from below—by engaging in a hardline brand of conservative politics."[18] Although populism is a mutating political concept, it has some recognizable, established conventions that current antiabortion rhetoric, such as Trewhella's, shares. Let's look at three such conventions, and then how they relate to what I saw in Louisville.

First, populism narrates *the people* as battling an evil, corrupt system. The people are victims of a merciless elitist system and, inevitably, are called to oppose it. Opposing it means proliferating an anti-elitist attitude that deems anything not of the people as no good. Thus, the second convention is celebrating the common and low culture at the expense of the elite. As Karen Lee Ashcraft explains, "flaunting the low" is neither "synonymous with the lower economic classes. Nor does it refer unilaterally to people who are disadvantaged or made 'lowly' by any manner of means. Instead, low refers to a cultural style that is cast off as inappropriate and unacceptable in the mainstream, disenfranchised from polite conversation and society."[19] Following Ashcraft, I don't demean the low, but I want to recognize how populists embrace anything that seems to belong to the people rather than the haughty elites. Moreover, "'flaunting the low' involves the public enactment of some kind of 'commonness' that is broadly eschewed. These days, it embraces political *in*correctness and takes pride in getting 'canceled.'"[20] Populism determines who the real folks are by celebrating common culture and by demonizing the elite.

Speaking of demonizing, a third convention is the denigration of anyone or any group that is perceived to be below common culture, below the low. They are depraved, lazy, diseased, or incompetent. Compared with *the people,* they are the disparaged Other—often immigrants, people of color, poor, queer, or trans. They are the folks who don't have the couth to keep clean, the commitment to learn the common language, the dignity to conduct themselves in normal ways. They are often demonized and blamed for why the people don't have more safety, money, or comfort. The racist aspect of such scapegoating has been around a long time, as a famous quotation from Lyndon B. Johnson attests: "If you can convince the lowest white man he's better than the best colored man, he won't notice you're picking his pocket. Hell, give him somebody to look down on, and he'll empty his pockets for you."[21] Some people recognize this racialized scapegoating as the psychological reward for staking a claim in being white and seeing oneself as separate from nonwhite folks who are scapegoated.[22] Populism demonizes these scapegoats as parasites who live off the hard work of the people or the overgenerosity of the government.

These three conventions—an antagonism between the virtuous people and the corrupt elite; a compulsion to celebrate and conform to commonness; and a demonization of those both above and below the people—were operating in the siege of Louisville.

In Trewhella's and Thomas's antiabortion version of populism, then, the antagonism is clearly between them, the people, and the federal government, which they portray as corrupt—even "tyrannical"—because it deviates from God's law. They presume no separation of church and state and consider the United States of America to be a God-created country that should be God centered as well. They demonize abortion provision as part of an evil federal government because of the Supreme Court's 1973 decision in *Roe v. Wade*. Their appeal to police as the "lesser magistrate" situates those officers in that righteously low status, which feeds a sense of antagonism with the corrupt elite of the federal government. Moreover, when Thomas casts aspersions about those in battle with the "thin blue line," he is using a dog whistle to demonize the Black Lives Matter protesters as a "criminal element." From this populist viewpoint of opposing abortion, Trewhella and Thomas narrate themselves and their followers as the people working against both a corrupt, evil, overpowering federal government threatening them from above and an anarchist criminal element threatening them from below.

Reproducerism

Moreover, Trewhella's championing the "lesser magistrates" offers a version of the populist storyline called producerism. In the classic sense, producerism presents the people as virtuous because they create goods and services; they work. Moreover, they work while others stationed above them—elite bureaucrats, professionals, experts—feed off the people's labor and productivity. Others stationed below the people—lazy losers who don't contribute to society—also don't deserve the benefits of goods and services produced by the people. The people perceive themselves as victims in the vise grip of this pair of parasitic groups, being squeezed from the top by elites and from below by the undeserving.[23] As the genuine producers of goods, services, and common wholesome culture, the people are victims who also are called to be warriors. Usually, this charge to lock horns with the elite is issued by a particular individual whose leadership is synonymous with fighting for the little guy, the forgotten man, the people. In the United States, Donald Trump has served that role of populist leader. We can further describe him as an authoritarian populist because he has embraced the idea of being a dictator, if only for a day. (Authoritarianism demands blind allegiance to a strongman or central figure and eliminates safeguards such as civil liberties, equal protection under the law, a system of checks and balances among different branches of government, and a democratic electoral system.) The producerist narrative that the Trump-influenced GOP spouts is that the people of MAGA are victims of a large bureaucratic government that taxes the people's good labor and disperses those funds to undeserving welfare cheats and foreigners who are taking over the country unless the people fight back and help Trump drain the swamp.

This producerist narrative circulates in antiabortion circles with a slight variation. Instead of describing the people as producers, the antiabortion version of the story narrates the people as reproducers. The reproductive people make babies for the country and are locked in an antagonism with the elite bureaucracy of the abortion industry, which prevents reproduction on a mass scale, and the others who won't or don't reproduce. Historically this list of non-reproducers included homosexuals, women who eschew motherhood, and anyone who doesn't honor parenthood as a natural priority. This *reproducerist* narrative, in which those opposing abortion appear as virtuous people who create children while others refuse to, deploys the conspiracist fears and demonizations that characterize populism. Reproductive health care is often referred to as an "abortion industry." As I demonstrate throughout this book, the so-called abortion industry is regularly depicted as a satanic or Jewish enterprise of global proportions working in cahoots with elitist governments. The people are called to combat the tyranny of the government-sponsored abortion industry. That was the message of Trewhella and Thomas in Louisville, as well as the cop depicted on the truth truck in the hotel parking lot. The fact that Thomas racialized that threat by indicating that the movement for Black lives is a criminal element threatening the people hints at how white nationalism is also part of the opposition to abortion.

White Nationalism

What is white nationalism? Nationalism prioritizes the nation—not international organizations, multinational agreements, or transnational coalitions—as the community we all should imagine as our starting and end points of government. Celebrating our nationhood, protecting our national interests, preserving our national culture all speak to this idea that the nation is how we imagine our community and how we know who we are. Nationalism presents the nation as our imagined community.[24] White nationalism imagines that community as built by and for white people, whose interests and culture are paramount. White nationalism is a racist outlook that privileges white people's lives above all others. How a country reproduces its citizenry is key to white nationalism. Figure 3 shows an artifact that crystalizes white nationalism's relationship to reproduction.

A sticker that was affixed to newspapers delivered in 2019 and 2020 features an image of a road sign used to alert motorists to watch for running immigrants crossing the road as they flee to America.[25] The image has a slash through it, indicated a prohibition of the caution it calls for. The message reads, "Send them back. They can't make White babies." This nativist sentiment is at once anti-immigrant and populist. It reflects and promotes the idea that white Americans make the right kind of babies and produce the babies that matter. This (re)producerism is rife with resentment of supposedly parasitical immigrants who ostensibly make babies who do not contribute to the growth and culture of American society. This is a clear example of white nationalism because it privileges white babies and white lives as what needs to be "made" while denigrating the offspring of immigrants as something detri-

FIGURE 3. Illustration of white supremacist sticker affixed to newspapers that asserts immigrants are unworthy of living in the United States because they don't (re)produce valuable children. Drawing by author-illustrator Rachel Elliott, used with permission.

mental to the nation. The group that created and circulated this message, the National Alliance, has for decades espoused a white nationalist ideology. They are militant racists who have, until Trump's presidency, considered the federal government as a hindrance to their goal of white nationalism.

According to Yotam Ophir and his coauthors, white nationalists use discussions of abortion to recruit people online. They oppose abortion for white women but not always for women of color. They justify this apparent contradiction in one of two ways. They believe nonwhite people are mentally and morally inferior and, consequently, should be encouraged not to reproduce by terminating pregnancies. They also believe that increased immigration is part of a plot to reduce the political power of white voters and to eradicate the demographic dominance of the so-called white race and Western civilization. This fear of so-called white genocide is often articulated as the great replacement conspiracy theory. Such themes proliferate on online platforms where white nationalists entice readers into a racist, revolutionary mindset that sees the federal government as the enemy.[26]

But white nationalism has also been imagined and promoted by nonmilitant people who work with the government. In "Trump's Angry White Women: Motherhood, Nationalism, and Abortion," Yvonne Lindgren shows how white women have opposed abortion in a way that promotes nationalism.[27] She examines the history of antiabortion argumentation and organizing. Synthesizing previous studies, she recognizes that there was a shift at the end of the 1970s. Before the shift, antiabortionists organized around the classically liberal terminology of "rights." They wanted to secure a "right to life" or "human rights" for the unborn. Some have argued that this focus on rights proves that the early defenders of prenatal life were politically progressive. Lindgren sees it instead as a rhetorical strategy that then shifted to a different rhetoric and mode of organizing, that of protecting a particular way of life. She writes that after the 1973 decision of *Roe v. Wade,* "the family values movement transformed opposition to abortion from the protection of fetal life to the protection of a *way of life.*"[28] I agree with her analysis; it mirrors what I argued in *Killing for Life* and it emphasizes protection. Protection becomes increasingly important as antiabortionism works in tandem with populist and nationalist movements.

Lindgren examines Phyllis Schlafly's conservative writings and speeches to demonstrate how the family values movement "linked opposition to abortion with protection of motherhood, family, and nation." A key aspect of those writings and speeches was to see abortion in the context of changing social norms that, according to Schlafly, disadvantaged white women by degrading their work and value as mothers of America's children. Those changing norms included creating childcare centers, increasing access to safe abortion and contraception, and desegregating educational spaces, which threatened to equate white and black girls and boys. By looking at the historical record, Lindgren sees how the end of the 1970s was a turning point during which antiabortionists won their first committedly pro-life president, Ronald Reagan. Lindgren's big contribution is explaining how this helped white people embrace not just patriotism and the love of one's national heritage, but nationalism as a political goal. She situates this amid examples of how other "nationalist movements have historically linked protection of nation and national culture with the protection and glorification of motherhood."[29] The United States antiabortion movement was "transformed into a powerful expression of white women's disaffection and nationalism," she asserts.[30] With this focus on the women strategists of the family values movement, Lindgren draws a bright, direct line from Phyllis Schlafly to Donald Trump, who met her in 2016, and who won the approval of 52 percent of white female voters that year to become president.[31]

Lindgren's focus on women, and especially her highlighting Schlafly (who has loomed large in the American imagination due to biographies and biopics of second-wave feminism and opposition to it), help us to see how nationalism is promoted through antiabortion rhetoric and organizing. It also adds to a growing body of work that examines women's roles in conservatism and right-wing movements. But her analysis steers us away from how white men in the United States feel they need protection too, whether they see themselves as fighting against abortion, for the nation, or for the white race. Or all three at once.

Why Now?

The sense that all these concerns are coalescing and need immediate attention to stave off certain calamity is a powerful feeling. Anticipating conflict has been an important feature of mobilizing against abortion, which is seen as a national sin and a revelation of depraved forces running amok—a sign that the world is coming apart. Antiabortion materials often promote not only a sense of political urgency and moral certainty but also a sense of being part of a larger, all-encompassing apocalyptic war. In *Killing for Life,* I explored how writings from the 1960s through the 1990s narrate antiabortion commitment to fight in this apocalyptic way, either in explicitly religious terms or on a more secular register. "Abortion: America's Armageddon" is a message that grew in intensity throughout the second half of the twentieth century and as we faced the start of a new millennium. Historically, a variety of religious and political groups in the United States have acted as if they are facing "the end times," and various forms of apocalyptic millennialism have shaped the American imagination as it has grappled with new technologies, new military threats, and new social formations.[32] I noticed how arguments and tactics against abortion became increasingly radical throughout the second half of the twentieth century, resulting in bombings and assassinations, and documented how an apocalyptic mindset and messaging fostered that radicalization. Moreover, *Killing for Life* recognized that apocalypticism was what militant and mainstream abortion foes shared with each other—and with right-wing groups like white power enclaves and "patriot" militias.[33] More than anything, there was sense of time running out or beyond regular clockwork—an apocalyptic and revolutionary (or *kairotic*) temporality—that a variety of factions on the right, including antiabortionists, organized white supremacists, and paramilitary groups, shared.[34] Their ideologies and aims might be different, but they were all amped up, preparing for a fight of world-ending proportions.

After *Killing for Life* appeared, soon after al-Qaeda attacked America on September 11, 2001, this apocalyptic sense of time mutated a bit. Antiabortion violence decreased in the wake of 9/11 because there was a pro-life president, but also because everyone now was familiar with terrorism—and it had become more apparent that that is what antiabortion violence was. As the twenty-first century moved into its second decade, the apocalyptic mindset remained but changed a bit. Jill Lepore recognized this in regard to the Tea Party movement, which emerged in response to the election of Barack Obama. She witnessed how Tea Party activists recalled the American Revolution in an odd way. As a historian she was concerned that their references to the Revolution did not reflect accurately the historical particularities of the 1700s. They read "founding documents" of our nation in a peculiar way—"in the same spirit with which religious fundamentalists read" and "as sacred texts" that deserved devout worship, not interpretation.[35] Moreover, she saw that references to the American Revolution functioned as what she called a "sacred past" in which accuracy and facts aren't important. This observation reminded me of what another scholar had observed: "History itself—the distinctiveness of its multiple stages—is irrelevant during a time of Manichean struggle."[36] What was important to these activists was the *idea* of revolution as an ongoing battle—a perpetual past and a cataclysmic fight against evil in which they were playing a part today.

Matthew Trewhella's influential *Doctrine of the Lesser Magistrates* also elides historical specificities, according to Rosensweig. She attests that "in Trewhella's writing there are no historical disjunctions, discontinuities, or differences, only an evangelical flattening of time that offers self-evident truths."[37] The sense of temporality imbued through Trewhella's writing conveys that same sense of perpetual-past-in-the-present, a time in which revolutionary action is ongoing and revolt against tyranny is ripe.

Likewise, Jeff Sharlet has documented this sense of revolutionary time and its apocalyptic feel in his book *The Undertow: Scenes from a Slow Civil War*.[38] He visits with insurrectionists and sympathizers of those rioters who broke into the Capitol on January 6, 2021, in an attempt to stop a peaceful transfer of power from the outgoing president, Donald Trump, to the winner of the election, Joseph Biden. Sharlet reports that these people are not only preparing for a revolutionary war, but that they are already engaged in it. And that's the major difference between the apocalyptic thinking of the twentieth century and this century: people now presume the apocalyptic or revolutionary conflict is already underway. They feel already victimized by evil, corrupt forces that—they suspect— want to subjugate them totally, and so they have become warriors for protection of their individual selves and for their way of life.

In ensuing chapters, examples of apocalyptic framing and revolutionary time emerge in contexts of people seeing themselves as victims and warriors.

What Lies Ahead

Picking up on the theme of protection, I proceed by showing how antiabortion rhetoric and actions depict white men and women in the United States as needing protection. As right-wing populism has grown in the United States and around the world, white men and women feel they are victims of corrupt elitists who are oppressing them from above, and of the parasites who can't or won't make the right kind of babies, oppressing them from below.

The terms "men" and "women" have in the past decade been weaponized by the right. A group called the Council on Biblical Manhood and Womanhood sponsored the "first-ever evangelical conference on transgender issues" in Louisville, Kentucky, in the fall of 2015. As I've written previously, this approach telegraphed the religious right's territorialization of "men" and "women" as the intellectual property and moral purview of Christian evangelicals, effectively sanctifying gender as a holy binary.[39]

After this conference, an onslaught of attacks against imagined and real transgender people ensued. So-called "bathroom bills" were introduced to politicize public toilets, in which white women and girls were portrayed as being victimized by racialized sexual predators.[40] Physical attacks on transgender people increased, with murders of them doubling from 2018 to 2022.[41] When outrage over bathrooms abated, it seemed that anti-trans stories of depravity and indoctrination became more frequent, more salacious, more titillating, and more extreme. Banning books and firing teachers ensued.[42] It got to a point where former President Trump was falsely telling parents that their children were being surgically operated on in schools.[43] Such stories were thus national news and, as baseless as they were, they normalized the notion that men and women are distinct, natural, and godly categories and that transgender people are therefore unnatural, unreal, or demonic. The right wields these exclusionary gender categories not only as a part of their worldview but also as a matter of strategy and political mobilization. Therefore, it is important to engage and understand how "men" and "women" work in writings, policies, and laws that may affect everyone but maintain the belief that all people are only, essentially, and exclusively male or female.

Consequently, I use trans-inclusive language when not directly examining right-wing logic and rhetoric. Sometimes, for example, I refer to "pregnant people" and, in so doing, recognize that not only cisgender women have the capacity to reproduce. Sometimes I use the term "reproducers," especially when discussing concerns about population. But mostly I use "women" and "men" to reflect the gendered imperative of right-wing movements because the words recognize a specific—if implicit—investment in a presumably naturally gendered binary. For the right, there is no blurring between men and women. Indeed, the right demonizes attempts to describe, explore, or research the complexities of gender as "gender ideology." This demonization is fueling right-wing militants, white nationalism, and populist movements across the globe. The antiabortion movement is a subset of these efforts and, in many ways, presaged its rhetoric and tactics.

What we call those tactics and how we classify movements and individuals who oppose abortion depend a lot on historical context. Language changes over time, reflecting shifts in argumentation, theological emphasis, organizational infrastructure, political alliances, strategic goals, and tactical objectives. Consequently, I use terms variously to reflect the type of abortion opposition I'm discussing. In doing so, I don't condone or lend legitimacy to these groups or ideas. For example, I sometimes refer to "right-to-life" organizations to emphasize the kind of rights-based arguments they use. More often I use "pro-life," which I consider to be the dominant, nationalist discourse that emerged with the New Right and the Reagan revolution, marked by the founding of the

American Life League in 1979. Most often I refer in general to organized opposition to abortion as simply "antiabortion." When it comes to antiabortionists whose convictions and ambitions drive them to illegal activity such as clinic violence and homicide, I refer to them as "radicals" or "militants," as well as by their groups' names. When I discuss their concern with "the unborn," I use that phrase to refer to an imagined collectivity representing the future rather than a person in a womb whose value and rights are exalted beyond all others.' Indeed, the unborn has crossover appeal for other militants who are envisioning their own kind of future.[44]

I use the term "far right" to refer to these visionaries because, as Cynthia Miller-Idriss notes, it is the best option for describing an array of "ideologies, individuals, and groups [who] espouse beliefs that are antidemocratic, antiegalitarian, white supremacist, and embedded in solutions like authoritarianism, ethnic cleansing or ethnic migration, and the establishment of separate ethnostates or enclaves along racial and ethnic lines. The entire far right spectrum," she continues, "does not share belief in all of these elements equally." "Far right" is therefore a useful but imperfect term that has become more prevalent as right-wing populism has increased its influence in the U.S. and abroad.[45]

The relationship among far-right groups and the antiabortion movement – including its most mainstream aspects -- is what this book is about. The ensuing chapters, organized into two parts, look specifically at how abortion opposition narrates white women and white men as victims in need of protection and as warriors called to take arms against their perceived enemies.

Part 1, "Victims," explains how narratives of whiteness circulated through both transnational and local antiabortion campaigns, portraying white people as victims worthy of protection and feeding the idea that they are imperiled. I begin by examining how white women are portrayed in terms of victimhood in transnational contexts and then turn to how white men are increasingly and strategically being represented as victimized too, especially at the local level.

Chapter 1 expands the discussion of protection from previous studies that focus mostly on the United States. As with other right-wing movements worldwide and historically, U.S. antiabortion rhetoric redeploys colonial and civilizational narratives about white women as victims. To understand the political and cultural influence that right-wing movements gain when they play the woman card, I trace the transnational traffic among antiabortion personnel, funds, and tactics. I focus on three countries where national identity is especially bound up with whiteness and where abortion has been particularly contested: Ireland, Russia, and the United States. The World Congress of Families (WCF) gets special attention here. As a Russian/U.S. collaboration, the WCF has promoted the idea that white people are losing a demographic contest to avoid extinction. They believe that opposing abortion, immigration, and homosexuality not only protects women but also the white race and Western civilization. They are emboldened to protect women as property rather than as human beings. These beliefs fuel international efforts to support populist parties in elections around the world.

Once we've taken a broad transnational look, I zoom in closer to home. To write chapter 2, I looked around me: at campus antiabortion activism, at local newscasts, at websites of regional organizations. What I saw was an escalation in the counterintuitive use of civil rights rhetoric to fuel racist, populist beliefs that white *men* as well as women are facing not only a precarious future but also an embattled present. Chapter 2 returns us to my home region. I examine the Ohio-based antiabortion group Created Equal to demonstrate the tactic of co-opting African American history to depict white men as victims in need of protection. Looking at four examples of filmic media produced by or about Created Equal, I argue that today's antiabortion visual politics don't operate the way they used to. Now the visual politics hinge not on the accuracy of the images but on who gets to look at them, display them, and own them. Questions of consent and property come into play in a heightened and racialized way. Representations of abortion as Black genocide and white antiabortionists as Freedom Riders are used as an occasion in real time and space to invite conflict. In these provoked physical altercations, white men do not prevail but are instead shown as victimized.

But playing the victim—or actually feeling like a victim—has a flip side. We must look, too, at people's responses to those feelings of racialized victimhood. We must see what makes them not only want to fight but also to engage in actual sabotage, murder, and combat. Part 2, "Warriors," presents narratives of whiteness in the form of antiabortion and militia writings. These writings radicalized readers to become anti-statist militants, to take up arms against those they saw as oppressing them from above, the elitists, and from below, the parasites. Again, I break this into writings by men and women, reflecting the gendered imperative of the movement itself.

Chapter 3 compares writings of notable female antiabortionists. Looking at primary materials from the 1970s onward, I show how women's writing reflects the political currents that took the American right from Cold War conspiracism and apocalyptic fundamentalism to anti-statist terrorism and Tea Party populism. This chapter features work by women heralded as leaders in an increasingly radicalized movement—Mildred Jefferson, Joan Andrews, Norma McCorvey, Shelley Shannon, and Abby Johnson. Understanding them illuminates how white women become militants, martyrs, and MAGA moms ready to wage war against the federal government.

In chapter 4 we consider how paramilitary patriots, white supremacists, and antiabortionists emerged in sometimes parallel and sometimes intersecting movements. Close examinations of two men—clinic bomber Eric Rudolph and publisher Paul deParrie—help us map the organizational and argumentative links among antiabortionists and the far right. Writings by both men prefigure today's antiabortion "abolitionism" and Make America Great Again populism, demonstrating how the strategy of leaderless resistance continues to shield movement influencers from legal liability for terrorist acts.

In the conclusion I apply what I've presented in previous chapters to the current situation. Roughly a year after the January 6, 2021, insurrection, the Supreme Court heard the case of *Dobbs v. Jackson* and eliminated the constitutional right to terminate a pregnancy. It also thwarted the doctrine of stare decisis—the practice of honoring legal precedents. Two summers after *Dobbs,* the Supreme Court ruled on *Trump v. United States* in a way that gave presidents immunity for their actions in office. These two decisions opened the door to authoritarian rule, and the 2024 election ushered in an administration capable of making it happen.

If the rain I drove through on the way to Louisville portended anything in 2017, I could not guess it was the COVID-19 pandemic. And although I was curious about the old antiabortionists I was driving there to check out, I did not guess how increasingly relevant they would become. Their exhortations in 2017 to "ignore *Roe*" and other established law, and to rally the locals against supposed tyranny, became more important and mainstream than I could at that time see.

I *Victims*

1 *Protecting Women from Abortion around the World*

What Is a Woman, or Who Are Women?

When I heard that Joe Walsh was coming to campus, featured in a program titled "What Is a Woman?" I thought, "Cool. He's a good guitarist." I was psyched for a new Eagles album about rock and roll women. Then I learned I had the name wrong. It wasn't Joe Walsh. It was somebody else named Walsh. And students were not happy he was coming to campus.

Word was he was a rabid homophobe and anti-trans troll. Students had reason to be fearful or outraged. Violence against LGBTQ people was up. Students were talking about how a fan of this man had killed a woman for displaying a rainbow flag earlier, in August. I shared the students' sense of unease, but I decided to attend the event with the curiosity of a female Columbo, the seemingly hapless TV detective. So, while our smart associate dean arranged for counter-programming for LGBTQ students and their allies scheduled at the same time, creating a positive community space for them, I put on my best rumpled Talbots blazer to hear what this Walsh guy had to say.

I was impressed by the setup. The theatrics of the scene were production-company level. There were two policemen with dogs sniffing around the perimeter of the event venue. The dogs were alert and doing their jobs, but the police looked nonplussed, like suburban dads taking the family pet out for a walk around the neighborhood. One of them was looking at his phone while the pooch pulled him along. It seemed to me that these were bomb-sniffing canine units, but the human counterparts did not look the least bit concerned.

Lining up to enter the auditorium, I was asked to empty my pockets. I had my phone. And my wallet. And a small date book. And a pen. And a little scratch pad to take notes on. All were crammed into the pockets of my jacket, so I fumbled a bit to get them all out. One of three people with metal-detecting wands became impatient with me and told me to just hold everything out in my hands. He wanded my cupped hands and then went up and down my legs. What his metal-detecting wand didn't detect were the car keys in my pants pocket. Apparently, the security screening of audience members for weapons was only for show.

I went through another pre-entry screening point where I received a wristband for some reason. As far as I could tell, the reason for all these concentric circles of showmanship security—from the lazy canine perimeter sweep to the bogus metal detecting of every audience member to the encircling of each wrist—was to heighten the audience's expectation of danger and excitement, and to ensure that everyone knew how important the speaker supposedly was, someone worthy of armed security and surveillance.

In the auditorium they had cordoned off the side sections so everyone would sit in the center, providing the illusion of a full house for the cameras. After a foreboding welcome from a Young Americans for Freedom host who admonished audience members ahead of time for opposing the speaker, he came on and proceeded to talk for less than thirty minutes. I dutifully took notes. Most of it struck me as pretty funny, including the title of his talk, for instance: "What Is a Woman?"

According to this guy, a woman is a *what*, not a *who*.

And what makes a woman a woman is her reproductive capacity.

And what makes him, not women themselves, an expert on what a woman is is that he's a Catholic who believes in the truth.

"Well," I thought, "bless his little sacred heart."

The speaker proceeded to discount supposed arguments from trans activists, none of whom were there, so far as I could tell. Especially when he kept directly addressing "you trans activists," I felt like I was coming in in the middle of a conversation that this fellow was having with some imagined people. After about twenty-five minutes of this weird monologue, it was time for the Q and A.

Here's where it got really Jerry Springer. Back in the day, Jerry Springer had a television talk show on which angry guests frequently ended up throwing punches at one another. According to rumors (which Springer denied), the guests were paid actors who aimed to escalate yelling to physical altercations that were conveniently timed to happen right before commercial breaks. Walsh had started out in talk radio, and the practice of this kind of setup seemed to have carried over from talk media into his live events. People lined up to ask questions, and as they did so I saw they were all looking intently at their phones, apparently reading. I suspected they were reading the question they were assigned to ask.

I also noticed there was a cadence to the questions. After an especially heady and contentious question—about abortion, say— there was a question that provided comic relief. It ended with a lighthearted exchange in which the speaker appeared personable and relatable. The last question was from a guy who wanted to know what to tell his girlfriend who didn't like his beard. I thought at the time someone could have joked, "Your girlfriend is your beard," but I didn't. I was audibly yawning at this point in the evening, bored with the play-pretend debates. The speaker, who also had facial hair, laughed and told his questioner in a bro-code kind of way, "Tell her to let you enjoy your masculinity." Remarkably, I had just read an article that examines how men involved in the men's rights movements in India grow moustaches in antifeminist solidarity, protesting what they see as unfair alimony or custody laws that men endure.[1] Men's facial hair, like all hair, can be political stuff. But here in the campus auditorium, the lighthearted question about facial hair between dudes sounded innocent. The levity relaxed the players, applause ensued, and the event ended.

As I exited, I watched the audience. Some people were as old as I was. If had thought I would get an earnest answer, I would have asked the audience how many came with a church group, and did the church promise them dinner or money in exchange for their attendance. Instead, almost out the door, I took a step back and addressed one of the policemen flanking the entrance to the auditorium. I asked, "I have one more question. Who paid for all this security?" His answer was "I don't know."

Despite my detective best, then, I didn't learn a lot about women at this event. It was all about men. And what they were saying was, "I know more than you do about women, even if you're a woman." The speaker's message also seemed to be "My superior knowledge entitles me to protect women from dangerous people and ideas. And, thirdly, "As a man, I am also under attack." These messages have been around for eons. This time around, superior guys are couching the messages in fears about "gender ideology," an umbrella term they use to group together anyone who does not conform to their worldview that defines women primarily in terms of their biological capacity for bearing children.

Clearly, some people who spuriously ask "what is a woman?" are antagonizing transgender people and haggling over definitions of biology and cultural expression of gender to exalt women as baby makers. The goal seems to be to diametrically oppose reproductive women with transgender people, pitting them against each other as if those groups don't or can't overlap. In protesting the "what is a woman" enterprise, students see through this false dichotomy. They know it is possible and good to uphold rights for transgender people as well as for reproducers because, of course, transgender parents abound and cisgender and transgender people are not enemies. For example, on the campus of Kent State University, the question "what is a woman" was painted on a rock in yellow and black as an advertisement for a speaking engagement by Walsh.[2] Students repainted it to assert "trans rights" and adorned their message with hearts and the women's symbol.[3] In doing so, the students overwrote and overrode what they saw as a hateful message of asking what a woman is, as if women are *whats,* objects to be discussed and juxtaposed against transgender people who are equally dehumanized in the process. Moreover, in dehumanizing transgender people to exalt reproductive women, the "what is a woman" enterprise ignores and detracts from the actual lived experiences of reproducers who seek to have healthy babies as much as those who seek to terminate pregnancies.

In the United States it is Black women who most struggle to deliver healthy babies. The maternal and infant mortality rates for African Americans is staggeringly high, well above those of any other racial or ethnic category.[4] Historically and today, all people of color, but especially Black women, have had to demand that their womanhood counts in a society that deems them animalistic, sexually depraved, and not worthy of reproducing. At the "What Is a Woman" event I did not notice any people of color. Perhaps nobody on the event's team recruited at Black churches, or maybe people of color avoided the speaker knowing that, as a 2022 headline announced, "Murders of trans people nearly doubled over [the] past 4 years, and Black trans women are most at risk."[5] Or it might be that when conservatives start talking about women, everybody knows they mean white women.

The right-wing attention on women, who are nearly always imagined and understood to be white, is important to consider because it is not new. Long before conservatives profited off telling you *what* a woman is in opposition to "gender ideology" and transgender people, they were focusing on women to feed their antiabortion empire. And I do mean empire. The way the United States has exported its antiabortion rhetoric, funds, tactics, and personnel to other countries is worthy of the word.

As with other right-wing movements worldwide and historically, U.S. antiabortion rhetoric redeploys colonial and civilizational narratives about white women as victims. As supposed victims of abortion as a medical procedure, white women purportedly suffer postabortion mental illness or physical disease allegedly caused by terminating pregnancies. As presumed victims of an abortion "industry," white women purportedly suffer sexual abuse and financial exploitation at the hands of doctors and clinic personnel. Such narratives depicting white women as dupes of a sordid, satanic system of abortion provision ignore the fact that most people report feeling relief—not grief, regret, or trauma—after terminating an unwanted pregnancy.[6]

To get a sense of the political and cultural influence that right-wing movements gain when they play the woman card, we can trace the transnational traffic among antiabortion personnel, funds, and tactics. In what follows I consider how the U.S. right exports its antiabortion ideas and strategies to Ireland and Russia, two other countries whose national identity is profoundly bound up with whiteness. The case of Ireland shows us how motherhood and national belonging make abortion a crisis of identity and worthiness for white women especially. In addition to showing Ireland and Russia how to "protect" women from abortion, the United States exports a sense of time running out. Arguing that outlawing abortion is necessary to avoid losing political and cultural dominance, some Russian antiabortionists reveal how their devotion to women is undergirded by white supremacist fears and imperial ambitions to expand their political power across national boundaries. These ideas come from the United States, but opposing abortion serves rightwing populism around the world.

Promoting National Mothers in Ireland

In 1983, Ireland passed a constitutional amendment (the Eighth Amendment, or Article 40.3.3) that quintessentially asserted a right-to-life argument: "The State acknowledges the right to life of the unborn and with due regard to the equal right to life of the mother, guarantees in its laws to respect, and, as far as practicable, by its laws to defend and vindicate that right."[7] Opposition ensued over the years, and by 1992 the Irish Supreme Court recognized women's health as an important factor to consider. That decision was further condoned and codified in 2013 with the Protection of Life during Pregnancy Act, which kept abortion a crime unless the pregnant person's life was at risk. In 2017, a Joint Committee on the Eighth Amendment continued this line of argument and recommended that Article 40.3.3 be repealed in a referendum planned for 2018. As the right-to-life argument swung in favor of the right of people to terminate pregnancies that might kill them if continued, abortion opposition began to focus, too, on women's health, a tactic that never lost sight of the rationalist approach of swaying lawmakers and voters.

In May 2018, Ireland overturned the Eighth Amendment in a historic victory for abortion rights advocates. Consequently, Ireland became aligned more than ever with the liberal-secular consensus of Western countries, even as "elsewhere that consensus is under sudden strain and threat."[8] There is no doubt that international activists from both sides of the debate supported competing Irish campaigns through 2017 and 2018. With help from the United States and its U.K. neighbors, the pro-choice forces won. Especially compelling for the pro-choice side was the tragedy of Savita Halappanavar, a thirty-one-year-old woman who was denied an induced abortion after her pregnancy had failed and a hospital team recognized that miscarriage was inevitable. But they heard a fetal heartbeat. Irish law forbade their inducing abortion. Without intervention, Halappanavar died of septic shock. Because of the anti-choice law, a woman who very much wanted to be a mother lost her life.[9] The story mobilized millions. Pro-choice efforts focused on the compelling tragedy. Antiabortion forces at the same time turned to manipulating social media. Key influencers were from U.S. political groups. Reports about the 2018 referendum on the Eighth Amendment illuminate how U.S. antiabortionists sought to influence Irish voters in ways similar to how they had deployed social media during the presidential election of 2016.

According to the *New York Times*, U.S. youth funded by antiabortion organizations and professional pro-life advocates traveled overseas to sway people in public and in person. The arguments deployed avoided religious sentiment and instead turned "to arguments that abortion harms women's health. They are also turning to social media tools."[10] There were online campaigns that strived to subvert Ireland's rules against political advertising on television and radio. A Washington, DC–based "firm that has developed apps for the Trump campaign, the National Rifle Association, the Republican National Committee and Vote Leave," which encouraged the British to exit the European Union, was also retained by Ireland's antiabortion campaigns. Those who tracked the ads recognized that the opportunity to influence voters through unregulated social media represented a "serious vulnerability in our democratic system."[11] The result was an onslaught of Facebook ads in favor of retaining the Eighth Amendment. Most of the advertisers were from the United States. The names of these U.S. organizations and their slogans attest to the focus on opposing abortion to protect women and mothers. For example, "one of the American groups is called Expectant Mother Care." Another American antiabortion organization, Live Action, created the hashtag #WomenBetrayed to campaign against the repeal.[12] This level of influence by U.S. antiabortionists deploying pro-woman rhetoric in Ireland was a digitalized acceleration of decades of importing American antiabortion personnel who increasingly played the woman card.

As the Protection of Life during Pregnancy Act was being debated in Ireland, abortion foes hosted the 2012 International Symposium on Maternal Health, thereby emphasizing women's well-being instead of emphasizing saving fetuses.[13] One result was the creation of the Dublin Declaration on Maternal Healthcare, which argues that there is *never* any medical reason that justifies abortion. Based on junk science, this declaration contradicts the established worldwide data that demonstrate how maternal mortality rates go up when abortion is criminalized. Moreover, the Dublin Declaration has been a boon to the "global expansion and consolidation of Catholic health care facilities" and has proven effective in Latin America, especially in El Salvador and Chile.[14]

Another result of the 2012 international symposium was the importation of U.S. speakers, one of whom, Priscilla Coleman, writes academic studies perpetuating the idea that abortion psychologically harms women. Like the Dublin Declaration on Maternal Healthcare, Coleman's studies are not reliable. The journal in which she published her initial study on that subject in 2012 subsequently agreed that there were fundamental analytical errors in her methodology.[15] Another article that she published in 2022 was also retracted.[16] Coleman returned to Ireland in 2017 to speak at a conference hosted by Human Life International. In addition to Coleman, the conference featured Abby Johnson, the former director of a Texas Planned Parenthood clinic who decided that she was pro-life and who joined Trump at his rally before the attack on Congress and the riot at the Capitol on January 6, 2021. (We will hear more about Abby Johnson in chapter 3.) Throughout the process, U.S. women were at the forefront of fending off efforts to repeal the amendment criminalizing abortion in Ireland.

On the one hand, these U.S. speakers were following a well-trodden path made by American abortion foes to Ireland and back. Americans United for Life (AUL) boasts about their impact on Ireland beginning decades ago: "In 1979, AUL played a pivotal role in amending the Irish Constitution to protect life by precluding abortion." Later, when Ireland's "pro-life constitution was challenged before the European Court of Human Rights," AUL again "served as a consultant" and continued to do so throughout the efforts to rescind the Eighth Amendment.[17] In addition, Joe Scheidler of Pro-Life Action League has long been influential in exporting militant tactics to Ireland. Specifically, Scheidler mentored Youth Defence—Ireland's major antiabortion organization, which has been linked to far-right movements in Europe—by speaking at its conferences and bringing its speakers to the United States.[18] Scheidler's tactics promote the kind of aggressive behavior that ushered in the "direct action" militancy that emerged in the United States in the 1980s and 1990s. His book *Closed: 99 Ways to Stop Abortion* (1985) remains a how-to manual for militants who want to drive reproductive health care workers out of business through harassment and deter women seeking abortions through scare tactics and shaming.[19]

On the other hand, Coleman and Johnson, as women, diminished the reputation the pro-life movement has for such shaming and misogyny. Their claim to oppose abortion for the sake of women's protection and well-being represents the way today's right-to-life argument portrays women as victims of an abortion industry. This rhetorical strategy of opposing abortion to protect women goes back to the 1970s, as Karissa Haugeberg's book, *Women against Abortion,* attests.[20] But it was *systematized* in the 1990s.

The 2016 book *The Changing Voice of the Anti-Abortion Movement: The Rise of "Pro-Woman" Rhetoric in Canada and the United States* traces the proliferation of pro-woman rhetoric to the mid-1990s. Legal scholar Mary Ziegler also chronicles the shifts in official argumentation by key policy and lobbying organizations of the antiabortion movement. But in such accounts an important source is largely overlooked. In 1992, Life Dynamics founder Mark

Crutcher promoted the idea of appearing to work on behalf of women while opposing abortion in an influential underground manual called *Firestorm: A Guerrilla Strategy for a Pro-Life America*. He writes that abortion rights advocates "are evidently so accustomed to our arguments being focused only on the unborn baby, for us to voluntarily talk about the woman catches them totally off-guard."[21] Consequently he recommended that "legislation should be sold as 'pro-women' and/or 'consumer protection' legislation."[22] Furthermore, *Firestorm*, which lays out a legislative plan for all fifty states and a decentralized infrastructure to ensure its implementation, insists that "in all cases make sure the person delivering the message [in court] is female."[23]

Firestorm, a playbook that was meant to stay underground, makes it clear how the militant mindset of leaderless resistance was shaping pro-life legal strategy and was blatantly cynical about helping women. Moreover, *Firestorm* was a "guerrilla strategy" meant to go undetected. Looking at it shows us how callous and calculating some pro-life groups were and how much they believed abortion was a wholesale demonic enterprise. *Firestorm* makes clear that legislative efforts were meant to capitalize on the antiabortion violence that was emerging in the 1990s. Crutcher wanted to "coordinate our efforts [with those] of other organizations (like Operation Rescue)" for cumulative impact.[24] While more established pro-life organizations repeatedly claimed that their movement did not condone violence, *Firestorm* is one artifact that suggests otherwise.

We can see a legacy of *Firestorm*'s argumentative approach to opposing abortion. In December 2017 Abby Johnson used the same tactic of supposedly protecting women against deceptive exploiters when arguing against the Irish campaign to decriminalize abortion.[25] At a conference meant to bolster support for retaining the

Eighth Amendment, she said, "Abortion can never be safe," either for the "unborn children" or "their mothers." In this way she reinforced the message that Priscilla Coleman had voiced just months earlier at a Human Life International conference in Dublin on the supposedly deleterious effects of abortion on women.[26] The messages exported by Catholic Americans Abby Johnson and Priscilla Coleman function to expand the antiabortion rights-based rhetoric from the unborn to women.

In the face of unprecedented support for repealing the Eighth Amendment, this appeal to women as health care consumers blended easily with the traditional conception of women as mothers of the nation. Throughout the twentieth and twenty-first centuries, according to historians such as Cara Delay, Irish women have experienced a loss of national belonging when they have crossed the border to obtain an abortion. As we explored briefly in the introduction, nationalism is historically intertwined with motherhood. Being a good citizen typically means reproducing for the nation. Being a good mother is typically seen as synonymous with loving one's country. Consequently, people are made to feel that terminating a pregnancy is tantamount to betraying their country. The continuity of women's experience in Irish history is exploited by the purportedly pro-woman approach delivered by Coleman and Johnson on behalf of Human Life International. Their approach could only exacerbate women feeling alienated from their country "because they chose abortion over the national ideal of motherhood."[27] This international traffic in gender-based antiabortion work preserves and promotes Irish nationalism, embracing the state and lawmakers at the expense of women, despite their ostensibly pro-woman rhetoric that has been systematically deployed since the 1990s.

Compared to Ireland, Russia has a very different history of the legality of and access to abortion. Nevertheless, U.S. antiabortionists have a history with Russian activists that goes back to the 1990s.

Running Out of Time in Russia

Russia has a complicated past regarding abortion. The Soviet Union led the world in decriminalizing abortion in 1920. A little more than a decade later, however, the Soviet government banned it. By 1955 it was decriminalized again, but the conditions under which women terminated pregnancy in the mid-twentieth-century U.S.S.R. were awful. "Considering abortion an undesirable social practice, state officials gave no thought to women's comfort during the procedure," which sometimes was done without anesthesia, without privacy, and with the attitude that women need to suffer for relinquishing motherhood.[28] Unlike the American decriminalization of abortion in 1973 with the Supreme Court decision of *Roe v. Wade,* Nikita Khrushchev's relegalization of it in 1955 was not so clearly a win for Soviet women. This is especially true because abortion was the primary method of fertility control, as barrier methods of contraception were not produced or encouraged. Consequently, unlike abortion in the United States, abortion in Russia was nearly a universal experience for women, a necessity rather than the choice of self-determined women.[29]

Much of the discourse determining these changes focused on demographics. Anthropologist Michele Rivkin-Fish has traced the subtleties in language and argument regarding birth rates to provide a genealogy of the "demographic crisis" in Russia.[30] Throughout the twentieth century, "fertility analysis [was] used in national political struggles in Russia," and anxiety over a diminishing birth rate returned with a vengeance in the 1990s, when attempts to curtail access to abortion resumed with new determination as a "postsocialist panic."[31] Especially since the Soviet collapse and the ascendance of the Russian Orthodox Church, imports of U.S. antiabortion tactics and rhetoric have aided Russian attempts to thwart abortion as a supposed cause of demographic demise. "From the beginning of the 1990s, Russian nationalists seized on abortion and contraceptives as insidious practices contributing to the nation's low fertility and rapidly decreasing population."[32]

The global antiabortion movement, led by the United States, provided ongoing support to Russians opposing abortion since the 1990s. In 1995 the World Congress of Families (WCF) was founded in Moscow as a collaboration between U.S. Christian conservatives and Russians. The WCF enables right-wing U.S. evangelicals to persuade Russians to adopt particular antiabortion tactics. The U.S. antiabortion strategists helped Russia to implement mandatory waiting periods, ranging from forty-eight hours to a week, and counseling sessions that include ultrasounds.[33] These mandates entail familiar scare tactics such as falsely claiming that abortion causes infertility or breast cancer. There was also an increase in "American-style pickets of abortion clinics" in Russia, as well as "graphic web sites, posters and leaflets [that] are supplemented with sweeping references to Russian history."[34] The most insidious innovation has been the Russian adoption of what we in the United States call crisis pregnancy centers. These centers are also known as fake clinics because they deceive people by posing as a place that offers or supports abortion. They have emerged in Russia as places to support women by providing counseling, temporary housing, and sometimes job training.[35] But, like the offerings of their U.S.

counterparts, the offers of aid, comfort, training, or donations come with scare tactics designed to sway the client not to terminate their pregnancy. Information at these fake clinics is designed to look like scientific evidence when it is actually biased information, often delivered by psychologists paid for with antiabortion money.[36] These tactics reflect other supposedly pro-woman anti-abortion campaigns around the world. But who is paying for them?

The financial and institutional links among American and Russian antiabortionists demonstrate a transnational web of net-working. It is difficult to tell who is profiting from the political power or money transfers that circulate through churches, nongovern-mental organizations, and nonprofit antiabortion organizations.

Especially through the WCF, some of the "most powerful organizations in America's religious right, including Concerned Women for America, Focus on the Family, and Americans United for Life," have brought their homophobic and antiabortion influ-ence to Russia.[37] Yearly WCF demographic conferences helped shape late twentieth- and early twenty-first-century Russian atti-tudes and policies that opposed abortion under the guise of pro-tecting women. In the first decade of the twenty-first century, two initiatives emphasized the purported harms of abortion to Russian women: 1) the "maternity capital program" that provided "finan-cial bonuses to women giving birth to two children or more" and 2) guidelines on how mandated preabortion counseling was to be administered.[38]

Maternity capital hearkened back to "socialist ideals that the state should bear some of the burden of raising children,"[39] but it paradoxically provided material support only if the woman increased her family's material need by having another baby. Groups such as the Sanctity of Motherhood Program and the

Patriarchal Commission on the Family and Protection of Motherhood and Childhood carried forward the idea that fighting abortion should be seen as a matter of protecting women from the abortion "industry," supposedly run by exploitive, corrupt, unclean, evil, or even satanic people. But these state-run programs did not provide funds for preabortion counseling. The maternity centers that were mandated to offer such counseling consequently relied on outside money tied to "deeper collaboration" with antiabortion groups, some from the United States.[40]

In the second decade of the twenty-first century, those collaborations increased. In 2010, the managing director of the WCF, Larry Jacobs, "held dozens of meetings with Russian policymakers and leaders."[41] One of these leaders was a Russian antiabortionist who the following year visited Dallas, Texas, as a guest of an oilman with ties both to Russia and to Koch Industries, the influential U.S. oil and gas company.[42] After these meetings, "a package of anti-abortion laws—the first new anti-choice laws in Russia since the fall of the Soviet Union," followed in 2011. Accompanying these antiabortion laws was companion legislation outlawing gay "propaganda."[43] Policymakers responsible for this legislation met multiple times with Jacobs. One of them served on the planning committee for the eighth WCF conference. This conference was rebranded after Russia annexed Crimea and the United States imposed "economic sanctions against many Russian leaders, including two major backers of WCF" in 2014.[44] By 2015 symposia focusing on fetal pain and maternal trauma featured American scientists such as Maureen Condic, an associate professor of neurobiology whom LifeSiteNews referred to as a "professor of obstetrics and gynecology" in their reporting of the event. Condic's claim during the symposium that there is "universal" agreement among doctors about how and when fetuses experience pain has been disputed among experts of fetal development.[45] Nevertheless, the symposia attracted attendees from twelve different countries and a hundred cities.[46] A year later, in 2016, antiabortionists convened a "For Life festival, an annual gathering of Russian activists and international guests involved in the global fight against abortion."[47] As a result of this convention, For Life became an umbrella organization for more than four hundred antiabortion entities, consolidating power to push for a ban on abortion and to persuade women to reject the practice of abortion until it is banned.[48] Russia's pronatalist nationalism relies on a transnational movement of U.S. funds, personnel, and tactics.

In light of the investigations into Russian interference in the U.S. presidential election of 2016, we should ask how much antiabortion organizations in Russia and the United States are part of the transnational finances that shape oligarchies, right-wing movements, and the Trump-Pence administration. Three years before Donald Trump shocked the American public by consistently praising Vladimir Putin while campaigning, WCF managing director Larry Jacobs was complimenting Russia for its conservatism. He explained that "for 70 years we fought the communists, and some conservatives still associate Russia with a far left communist country, when the reality is, among the more powerful nations, Russia is one of the most conservative countries in the world."[49] Well before Trump, antiabortion conservatives were making friends with Russians who had for a long time been seen as America's enemy throughout the Cold War.

WCF leaders claimed, "Russia could be a great ally for conservatives, on issues like defending the family, abortions, even strengthening marriage and promoting more children."[50] Jacobs and WCF founder Allan Carlson have "built strong relationships" with influential Russian oligarchs and policymakers. One of these operated in Italy as a representative of the WCF, rubbing elbows with prominent far-right members of the Netherlands' Party for Freedom, France's National Front, and Italy's Northern League.[51] In Italy, politician Luca Volontè, who received the "Family and Truth" award from Americans United for Life, was charged with laundering bribes through various organizations. One of these organizations was an antiabortion organization that supported Trump strategist Steve Bannon's "video address inside the Vatican."[52] Volontè had a variety of roles: European People's Party president, founder of Novae Terrae Foundation, and president of the pro-life Dignitatis Humanae Institute. In these roles Volontè "channeled 2.39 million [Euros] to [these groups] in return for undermining reports on Azerbaijan's record of human rights abuses at the Council of Europe."[53] The charges against Volontè yielded a conviction in 2021; he was sentenced to four years in prison for corruption and banned for life from the Council of Europe.[54] The pronatalist messaging shared by far-right populists and transnational antiabortionists such as Volontè consistently strikes an apocalyptic tone and fuels the white supremacism of the global right.

In Russia, partners of WFC such as Archpriest Dimitri Smirnov, the top Orthodox official and chairman of the Patriarchal Commission on Family Matters and the Protection of Motherhood and Childhood, has sounded an alarm of apocalyptic proportions. "There is very little time left until the death of the entire Christian Civilization," he claimed. How much time was left? "Several decades," he predicted, "perhaps 30 years, well, maybe in Russia it will last 50, no longer."[55] Structuring the political and moral dilemma of abortion in this way is a means of manufacturing a sense of time running out, of creating a sense of urgency to act lest the nation be lost.

But lost to what or to whom? Because atheism was state policy in the Soviet Union, the scare tactic of saving the soul of the nation before the return of Jesus Christ was unlikely to work as it has among evangelicals in the United States. But since the 1990s, that atheism has come under fire as President Vladimir Putin has overseen a "clericalization of Russia" in which speaking out against religion or religiosity has been outlawed.[56] The exact content of the apocalyptic, nearly-no-time-left narrative that structures much of U.S. pro-life politics is unlikely to influence Russian people, but the *urgency* generated by that no-time-left, we-must-act-now rhetoric is a deployment of apocalyptic temporality that appears to be highly effective. The narrative in Russia is therefore not that God will lift his veil of protection if citizens do not stop the "national sin" of abortion, as it has been among U.S. evangelicals.

Instead, the contemporary Russian antiabortion narrative is about losing the nation to those who may outbreed the Russians. The Russian version of the apocalyptic narrative asserts that demographic decline brought about by abortion will usher in a larger Muslim population and the end of white civilization. During pro-life conferences sponsored by the WCF in Moscow, "the high birth rate among Muslims in Russia was spoken of with some awe, both as a threat and as something to emulate."[57] The fact that the WCF was founded by a couple of professors whose academic interest is demographics suggests that the fear of losing cultural and political dominance has been an issue from the very beginning of Russian-U.S. antiabortion collaboration. In 1995, Anatoly Antonov, a Russian sociologist, and his colleagues were eager to discuss "Allan Carlson's work on demographic changes in the United States—

work that claims feminism and homosexuality have led to population decline, precipitating a crisis of the American family. Antonov and Medkov saw the same thing happening in postcommunist Russia and felt they had much to learn."[58] What they learned, and taught to others, was how to shift a whole country from leftist to right-wing perspectives on abortion.

This was the beginning of what now operates as a transnational network of organizations. According to Siân Norris, the network consists of these organizations and more: Agenda Europe, CitizenGO, Political Network for Values, Alliance Defending Freedom, the American Center for Law and Justice, the European Center for Law and Justice, and Council for National Policy as well as the WCF.[59] It was the antiabortion groups who initiated this multinational network, according to the European Parliamentary Forum. "The first attempts" to create geopolitical push for "alt- and far-right political parties" were facilitated by "the establishment of Christian micro-parties by leaders of national anti-abortion movements which then infiltrated the mainstream centre-right parties."[60] WCF's antiabortion collaborations in Russia were among the earliest such creations.

Ethnographic studies illuminate what this targeting of abortion means for Russian women. Women are depicted as victims of abortion as well as sinners. Antiabortion activists claim that women experience a debilitating postabortion syndrome, which underscores the notion that women have suffered exploitation by the state as well as having perpetrated state violence against the unborn.[61] But in this formulation, opposition to abortion is not argued in terms of murdering babies because historically the unborn in Russia have not been imbued with individual, inherent rights, as the more (classically liberal) right-to-life arguments insist in America.[62] Because "the unborn foetus as a rights-bearing person did not enter Soviet discourse," the unborn in Russia are more comparable to the unborn of pro-life conservative nationalism; they represent the collective future of a nation.[63] Russian women's experiences of expiating abortions reveal that "anxieties about demographic development turn unborn children into symbols of a desired future."[64] And, based on how male Russian antiabortionists talk about it, the collective Russian unborn can also symbolize an *undesired* future, one that is too Muslim.

Constructing a pronatalist, pro-woman nationalism that argues against abortion in the name of women's rights, U.S.-Russian collaborators have created an antiabortion force that is also anti-Islamic. Saving the so-called unborn becomes tantamount to saving women becomes tantamount to saving the nation from Muslims lest "Russians . . . become an ethnic minority in their own vast country."[65]

In the Russian context, the so-called unborn signifies the Russian people in a new narrative of post-Soviet populism. This new narrative rewrites the very meaning of *proletariat*. According to Stoeckl and Uzlaner, post-Soviet antiabortion strategy is tantamount to a "cult of the Russian nation." They focus on a particular group led by Vladimir Potikha, who promotes the prohibition of abortion as a means to restore Russia as a great empire. Potikha "created an emblem based on the state emblem of the Soviet Union, replacing the hammer and sickle in the center with a baby inside a uterus, his organization's symbol."[66] This updating of an iconic Soviet symbol also came with a reinterpretation of the slogan "Proletarians of the World Unite." He explained that this call for worker solidarity and uprising "had a hidden meaning, because the Latin term *proles* originally meant 'offspring.' Potikha glossed over the paradox that abortion in the Soviet Union had been legal; as a matter of fact, he blamed the legalization of abortion in the Soviet Union on Jewish doctors and hailed the Stalinist period of criminalization of abortion as a successful project and a response to eugenics in Nazi Germany."[67] This revisionist definition of *proletariat* is remarkable in its adherence to the antisemitism that underlies much of U.S. opposition to abortion. It is yet another way Russians are opposing abortion by imagining future offspring to muster Christian nationalist populism.

How Opposing Abortion Serves Right-Wing Populism in the United States

The defeat of Donald Trump by Joseph Biden in the 2020 U.S. presidential election provided little comfort to those attuned to right-wing movements and the potential for authoritarian populism. Examining recent anti-gender campaigns and antiabortion efforts in Europe and the United States tells us that the age of populism is still on the rise.

To be sure, the man who came to my campus to ask "What Is a Woman" is only one cog in the transnational machinery of "anti-gender" campaigns designed to rally support for Christian nationalism and/or authoritarian populism. In their examination of anti-gender campaigns currently sweeping Europe and the Americas, Agnieszka Graff and Elzbieta Korolczuk declare "anti-genderism is best seen as a brand of populist discourse." Their notion of anti-genderism includes the fight for reproductive rights and access to abortion. Their book details the transnational political and financial connections that have developed and escalated anti-gender tactics as part of a larger right-wing populism sweeping the globe.

Anti-genderism is best understood in populist terms, they argue, because it taps "into the anti-political resentment observed on both sides of the Atlantic, which in turn fuels electoral victories of right-wing populist actors and political successes of extreme right-wing parties."[68] As a subset of today's anti-genderism, antiabortion efforts can be seen in the same populist light.

Indeed, it is important to consider how opposing abortion has politically achieved in the past what anti-gender campaigns are now attempting to achieve. Opposing abortion played an important role in the American conservative resurgence known as the Reagan Revolution of 1980. It also had a major impact in the 2016 election that elected populist Donald Trump. Let's compare these two turning points.

In the late 1970s, New Right architects, including Richard Viguerie, convinced influential leaders, such as Phyllis Schlafly and Jerry Falwell, to mobilize Christian evangelicals as never before. Previously apolitical and averse to worldly politics, Christian evangelicals were rallied at this historical juncture via infrastructures created or supported by Washington, DC, conservatives. Some of these infrastructures were Schlafly's mother's movement, Falwell's Moral Majority, and the Heritage Foundation's parents' rights movement, articulated by New Right strategist Connie Marshner in *Blackboard Tyranny*.[69] In particular, the Moral Majority was charged with making abortion a matter of single-issue voting; they told congregations that if a candidate wasn't against abortion, evangelicals should not vote for him or her. Schlafly also is recognized as ushering in an antiabortion imperative along with the drive to quash the campaign for an Equal Rights Amendment.[70] These coinciding efforts registered a newly politically awakened critical mass to vote, culminating in the election of America's first self-described pro-life president, Ronald Reagan.

In 2016, Donald Trump again relied on abortion to appeal to Christian evangelicals.[71] He promised to secure for them the appointment of Supreme Court justices who could overturn *Roe v. Wade*, the 1973 decision that legalized abortion with nationally standardized regulations. The evangelicals got what they wanted, in spades: Trump appointed three justices and *Roe v. Wade* was successfully overturned in 2022.

In both turning points of U.S. politics, 1980 and 2016, opposing abortion fueled the electoral victories of right-wing actors, even though statistically the American public overwhelmingly and historically approves of abortion rights. While Reagan was no populist, Trump is. In both cases, courting the Christian vote was key. The relationship between religious conservatives and right-wing populists is therefore important to consider.

Javier Corrales and Jacob Kiryk consider this as they examine the anti-gender campaigns currently spreading throughout Europe and the Americas. They address the recent uptick in anti-gender campaigns as "homophobic populism," although what they document certainly isn't limited to homosexuals and most vociferously targets transgender people. Their study recognizes the links, both ideological and organizational, among religious conservatives and right-wing populist movements. Corrales and Kiryk begin with the established observations (by Cas Mudde) that populism is structured with a "thin" core of beliefs, namely the idea of the people in conflict with a corrupt elite. This thin ideology, they say, can combine with a variety of ideologies in an effort to amass a broader following. They demonstrate how the religious right serves as a "populist helper" without identifying as populist or having membership in any populist party. They spell out key affinities among conservative Christianity and populists. Both groups perceive "followers to be the 'real people' in conflict with a corrupt 'other.'" Both groups perceive society in terms of fundamental bifurcations and binaries: "the righteous and the sinful; the pure and the corrupt"; the save and the damned. And both groups present themselves as the "morally deserving people."[72]

I take from Corrales and Kiryk their idea of the populist helper: campaigns that support and propel populism regardless of whether those who conceive of or carry out the campaigns are themselves populists. As with anti-genderism, opposing abortion has functioned as a populist helper in the United States. The people who are opposing abortion and/or what they call gender ideology are therefore not necessarily populists themselves, but what they are doing is enhancing populist sentiment and giving people a taste of populism.

I like the idea of populism helper because it reminds me of a food product that I grew up with: Hamburger Helper. An innovation in response to high meat prices in the 1970s, Hamburger Helper is a box of seasonings and macaroni or rice that you mix with ground beef to create a skillet dinner. It extends the meat and gives it a different flavor, supposedly fooling your family into believing they have a nice new meal instead of the same old tired ground beef. Like Hamburger Helper, populism helper extends the life and adds a seemingly novel flavor to whatever is being served by conservatives or the far right.

When I listen to some of today's fears about gender, I see a repackaging of some old right-wing arguments. For instance, I don't believe there are multitudes of men cunningly transitioning into women so they can win trophies in women's sports—like I never believed teens were getting abortions just so they can fit into prom dresses and claim homecoming queen crowns. I don't believe there is a rapid onset of gender dysphoria affecting children that will result in whole generations of mentally ill, bodily mutilated, and sexually dysfunctional tragedies—like I never believed that a crack epidemic was going to result in whole generations of mentally ill, underdeveloped, and bodily addicted people who will rely on welfare, creating a permanent underclass of Americans. I don't believe there is a transgender craze promoted by the medical profession so doctors can profit off hawking hormone treatments and surgeries—like I never believed abortion is an unclean industry run by greedy, exploitive doctors who are the bottom-feeders of society. I didn't and don't believe these claims. The parallels in argumentation are clear. The anti-trans, anti-gender panic is repackaging old, baseless fears in new bodies. And the gory emphasis on picturing mutilated bodies carries over from antiabortion to anti-gender arguments. They are dishing up old red meat with the aid of populism helper.

While my decades-old research suggests that antiabortion rhetoric and tactics in the United States have always promoted elements of populist thinking and tactics, it is important to consider what is happening now. While some may chuckle at the ridiculous and repackaged assertions right-wingers make, others are all too aware that the laws they are passing have enormous and painful consequences. Queer, transgender, and nonbinary people, in particular, are maligned and murdered. Anti-trans bills have been introduced at a dizzying rate, with many becoming laws. This state repression of transgender people echoes the state repression of homosexuals during McCarthyism. In such a political climate, violence ensues. People are emboldened by state-sanctioned suspicion and contempt, fueled by misinformation and fear, and sometimes compelled to take action on the interpersonal level, goading vulnerable kids into suicide or committing deadly violence themselves.[73] Anti-trans laws, like antiabortion legislation, deny people dignity, put people in life-threatening situations, and defy democracy. These antidemocratic laws also push the populist sentiment that *the people* need to oppose the experts, the lawmakers, and governing officials and take matters into their own hands.

In 2020, Texas legislators proposed Senate Bill 8.[74] SB8 inaugurated a new approach to not only restricting abortion but also potentially criminalizing all involved in terminating a pregnancy. SB8 achieved this by effectively deputizing citizens to surveil and sue "anyone—from an Uber driver to a doctor—who knowingly 'aids and abets' a woman getting an abortion after the sixth week of pregnancy."[75] The bill went so far as to reward successful lawsuits with more than ten thousand dollars plus legal fees.

This new frontier in abortion politics codified and legalized what has been for decades the mindset of vigilante antiabortionists— the idea that defenders of the unborn must take matters into their own hands in opposition to a tyrannical federal government lest the whole nation or race or Western civilization end. Such an apocalyptic narrative has operated for decades, producing political subjects and historical actors who see themselves as warriors in a zero-sum game.[76]

In the age of Trump, this once "extremist" idea of antiabortion citizens taking matters of law into their own hands for racist or religious reasons became legitimized by the state. Although the federal government and individual states had for decades often turned a blind eye to antiabortion extremism, the government never actively supported those extremists who felt they could be judge, jury, and executioner of abortion providers. In the 1990s seven people were murdered by antiabortion snipers and bombers. In 2009 pro-life assassination returned when Dr. George Tiller was killed. In each of these cases, the government worked to punish those who took the legal issue of abortion access into their own hands. SB8 actually sharpened the edge of dissent among local abortion opponents and emboldened them so they not only *feel* entitled but *are* entitled to take matters of the law into their own hands.

We should see the Texas law in the context not of the right-to-life sentiment, which was indebted to liberal notions of rights for yet-to-be future generations, or even of the pro-life movement, which sees the state as a potential ally to woo to their side. Rather, the Texas law is more aligned with an "abolitionist" antiabortion sentiment that criticizes pro-lifers for being "incrementalist" in their legislative approach to repeal *Roe* and that often sees the federal government as the enemy.[77] (We will learn more about abolitionism in chapter 4.) With SB8, Texas put the law in the hands of the people, granting regular citizens the power to discern for themselves who is acting in a criminal manner. This do-it-yourself policing threatens to turn family members against family members and to perpetuate stochastic terrorism like the massacres by white supremacists and the murders of abortion providers.

It also advances the thinking that people educated and trained to do professional jobs can and should be doubted, checked, or surpassed by regular people, amateurs with no training or formal education. This thinking infuses many current right-wing campaigns, including the granular approach of installing first-time polling place workers who, believing the "big lie" of supposed voter fraud, plan to challenge their superior election officials. Moreover, once the decision of *Roe v. Wade* was effectively repealed in 2022, initiatives like SB8 proliferated.

After the 2022 *Dobbs* decision, in which the Supreme Court rejected the precedent of *Roe v. Wade*, opponents of abortion were not satisfied with shifting to the states the power to regulate abortion. Some pushed for a federal ban. Others proceeded along the lines of SB8, effectively criminalizing anyone who sought to obtain an abortion—or anyone who helped them. In 2023 Texas proposed not only outlawing medical abortions by prohibiting mifepristone, a drug that was deemed safe more than twenty years ago by the FDA. Texas also proposed surveilling highways and roadways that pregnant people would use to leave the state to get an abortion in another state. Again, the state encouraged private citizens—the people—to police these areas and to effectively enforce this authoritarian measure. This situation, in which citizens—not only law enforcement—are encouraged to spy on and capture people leaving the state if they intend to terminate a pregnancy may seem like a dystopic brave new world.

But according to historian Heather Cox Richardson, these travel bans and the people invited to enforce them echo the laws and practices of the slavery era. Richardson recognizes how citizens policing interstate travel during slavery was codified by a series of legal measures, including the 1850 Fugitive Slave Act. Comparing then and today, she writes, "It is impossible to miss the parallels between these ordinances and the various laws that circumscribe the lives of Black Americans before the Civil War here in the United States. In that era, free Black Americans had to carry identification papers, known as 'free papers,' to prove they should be allowed to travel. White Americans had no such requirement. Enslaved Americans could not travel at all, of course, unless they accompanied their enslavers; they were confined to the states in which they were enslaved. . . . Those turning in Black refugees were paid a fee and the costs of their effort."[78] Likewise, ordinances like SB8 provide a bounty; in Idaho the promise is "$20,000 to family members who sue, including 'a sibling of the preborn child.'"[79]

Indeed, as of September 3, 2023, "at least 51 jurisdictions in Texas have passed ordinances to make it illegal to transport anyone on roads within city or county limits to get an abortion. Their hope is to target interstates and the roads around airports to block off routes out of Texas and keep pregnant women trapped in the anti-abortion state."[80] Any private citizen is legally allowed to "sue any person or organization they think is violating the ordinances." What remains certain in the present, therefore, is that under the guise of opposing abortion, the state is legitimizing behavior that once was seen as extremist: having family members, neighbors, and even strangers intercept pregnant people's actions because they supposedly know better. In this situation, bodily autonomy and the freedom to travel are stripped from Texas citizens who become pregnant.

Also, under the guise of opposing abortion, the people are encouraged and legally entitled to take the law into their own hands precisely because they are the local power. What emerges is a practice of empowering the local people as the moral standard-bearers in need of no official status to serve as deputies of the authoritarian state. You'll recall from my earlier discussion of Matthew Trewhella and the *Doctrine of the Lesser Magistrates* that the antiabortion movement has provided a precise rationale for this populist approach of relying on the people or on lower-ranking officials who are aligned with, or part of, the people. We need to see these antiabortion tactics as right-wing populist efforts on the local level to thwart federal laws and democratic procedures in the United States. The recent laws being enacted, such as the Texas law I've focused on here, tell us that this populist sentiment spread through antiabortion discourse is a tool of authoritarianism that welcomes an uprising from "the people" in order to criminalize its opponents and seize antidemocratic power.

Indeed, such a strategy is working in Poland, where people who terminate a pregnancy are not yet considered to have committed a crime, although that is what the far-right government was aiming for.[81] However, "anyone who provides or helps a woman to get an abortion outside [limited legal] grounds, is liable to prosecution and the penalty is imprisonment."[82] In Poland, as in the United States, pregnant people have been forced to leave the country or their state to access abortion in other European countries or other American states. Americans are migrating in this way to avoid the increased criminalization evident in the United States. According to a recent Pregnancy Justice report, "1,396 criminal arrests [of pregnant people] took place over the 16.5 years between January 1, 2006, and June 23, 2022, the day before the Dobbs ruling. This represents a startling increase compared to the findings of [an earlier] study [published in 2013], which reported 413 cases during a 33-year period: over three times as many cases in half as many years."[83] Will American citizens march in the streets in protest of these criminalizing antiabortion laws, as they have in Poland? Or will "the people" arise in concert with authoritarian laws said to protect women?

That is my fear. I worry that the decades of opposing abortion ostensibly to protect women—here in the United States, in Ireland, in Russia, and around the world—has prepared people to accept old lies in new packaging. I worry that people will feel entitled to take matters of law into their own hands, with no regard for the rights of people who don't share their religious beliefs or political views. And I worry that the secretly desired answer to the question of "What Is a Woman" is . . . property. At least I started to worry about that more when another group came to campus.

2 *Vulnerable Guise and Racial Demise*

Women Are Property, Men Are Created Equal

A man amid a sea of students held aloft a large vertical banner that read "Women Are Property." Lest anyone miss that message, another dude held a banner that offered a list: "Types of Property: WOMEN SLAVES ANIMALS CARS LAND ETC" (figure 4). "Swell," I thought as I approached the crowd.

I had been walking to my car, ready to head home, but I decided this hogwash was worth ten minutes. Over the years I had seen a lot of horrible demonstrators occupy the so-called free speech zone on campus: hate preachers who goaded students with homophobic slurs dressed up in Bible verses, Turning Point USA hucksters peddling the so-clever message "Big Government Sucks," and, of course, semiannual antiabortion displays that never failed to result in a student running to my office or emailing me: "Dr. Mason, have you seen what's on the quad?!" As at those times, this time the faces of students were contorted with disgust and confusion as they engaged these demonstrators.

The demonstrators told women in the crowd that their attire made them "rape bait." One young collegian approached a police

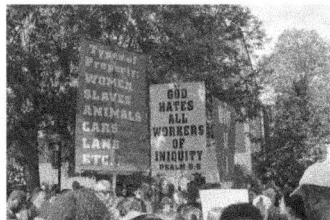

FIGURE 4. Demonstrators claim that women are property in Lexington and Louisville, 2023. Photo of Louisville demonstration by Allison Jewell, used with permission.

officer and asked him why these people were allowed to be here. She looked completely distraught as the officer explained that it is not considered hate speech until someone issues a particular threat to an individual. "But they have," she protested. She asked for clarification about the difference between free speech and hate speech and received no satisfying answer. She looked hurt and scared.

The demonstrators were big beefy white dudes, except for a younger and taller white man who refused to talk, even when I asked him what church he went to. He was there with a camera phone, recording every verbal interaction between demonstrators and students, every exchange between officer and demonstrator. I tried to engage one man in a discussion of eschatology because he held a "Repent" sign, but he told me to ask the guy holding the "Types of Property" banner what his views were.

Students were engaging the "Types of Property" guy, asking sharp questions that he spit back answers to—until he didn't. All of the sudden, just at a point in the exchange when several young challengers were getting really mad, the demonstrator ducked behind his big banner. The banner was now a shield. Instantly I thought I saw what he wanted, which was to have a student bat the banner out of the way. It was clear to me that he was egging on this group of students. But the students, to their credit, showed restraint. One said something like, "Oh, you're hiding your face now? Now you can't face us?" For hours these verbal matches went on between students and the demonstrators while the University of Kentucky police appeared only to look on.

News accounts of the demonstrators revealed that this group had been on the University of Louisville campus in the days following their visit to my campus in Lexington. Professional news outlets—such as the local Fox TV channel and the city paper, the *Lexington Herald-Leader*—published official statements from university lawyers and leaders.[1] The *Louisville Cardinal* reported that "these same organizers held a demonstration on campus in 2019," four years earlier.[2] A student journalist from nearby Transylvania College reported:

> I asked a UofL student about her feelings on the protests. "The whole situation made me feel very disturbed and anxious. As a Christian and a woman it was very upsetting . . ." The UK student I interviewed had a different thought. "I believe they [the protestors] are scam artists attempting to sue the school when a student assaults them." Both students I interviewed had heard rumors that these protestors were purposefully attempting to incite violence, but these rumors could not be confirmed.[3]

Give that young Transy journalist a prize. The students knew that this was not a matter of protest or proselytizing. The students recognized it wasn't free expression of religious belief. This was a kind of fight club.

Actual fight clubs have proliferated in right-wing circles worldwide. Gyms that train in mixed martial arts (MMA) especially attract white supremacists and other militants.[4] What I saw on my campus wasn't exactly that kind of fight club, but I suspect that it was part of the same right-wing ecosystem. I suspect that these men wanted to fight but didn't want to throw the first blow. I suggest that they wanted to be seen as fighting as an act of defense. My guess is that they wanted to be seen as being under attack. Why? Yes, so they could sue the individual or the university, but also so they could show on social media how victimized they are. White Christian men under attack: that's the image they want to capture and project, I suspect.

Why do I think this? Because it is a strategy that antiabortionists have been perfecting for more than a decade.

As the previous chapter attests, opposing abortion as a matter of protecting women has been the norm, a transnational strategy since the 1990s. In such pro-woman rhetoric, women are depicted in much the same way as are unborn babies: as victims of a depraved abortion "industry." Scholars have long ago demonstrated that the "view that abortion is murder is a relatively recent belief in American history."[5] The transition of seeing abortion as a medical rather than an ambiguously moral issue occurred from the nineteenth to the twentieth centuries according to Kristin Luker in her seminal book *Abortion and the Politics of Motherhood*. In this transition the embryo became synonymous with the fetus, a medical term that gave way to the more sentimental term "unborn child," which was further popularized as "the unborn." All of these names for prenatal life connoted a vulnerability and a humanity that antiabortionists politicized as having a moral value equal to a person and sometimes greater than the mother.

Moreover, scholars have more recently recognized that the antiabortion movement often racializes the unborn to collectively symbolize an imperiled white future and the end of Christian civilization.[6] This symbolic depiction of the white minority in the making has encouraged white men to see themselves as Christian warriors who are fending off a presumed apocalyptic future in which they are demographically and culturally subordinated. What comes into focus now, at a time of heightened right-wing militancy across the globe, is an escalation in the use of the unborn to fuel racist, populist beliefs that white *men* as well as women are facing not only a precarious future but also an embattled present. Representations of the unborn are currently used as an occasion in real time and space to invite conflict and to provoke actual physical altercations in which white men do not prevail but are shown, instead, as victimized. I have seen this happen in the work of the Ohio-based antiabortion group Created Equal.

The Lead-Up to Created Equal

An important context for Created Equal is the men's movement called the Promise Keepers. The Promise Keepers formed in 1991 "to disciple men through vibrant men's ministries to become godly influences in their world."[7] Promise Keepers encouraged revival and spiritual awakening because "men across the country had abdicated their responsibilities to their families and their church."[8] Men were encouraged to compassionately but firmly retake their rightful place as head of family and society, where women had been given too much responsibility and too many decisions to make. The Promise Keepers emerged, therefore, as part of what Susan Faludi then labeled a cultural backlash against feminist gains in policy and the popular imagination.[9] The premise of the Promise Keepers complemented sentiments by contemporary antiabortionists such as Michael Bray, who laid out a rationale for stopping abortion with lethal force and in 1994 argued that men were suffering from a "testosterone deficiency."[10]

Around the same time—the mid-1990s—Klansmen contributed to this idea of men being oppressed by women by picketing a Florida abortion clinic with signs protesting "Big Sister Federal Tyranny."[11] This phrase encapsulated an anti-government sentiment that was suffusing paramilitary culture with both patriot and antiabortion iterations. Riffing on the Orwellian idea of Big Brother, such militants felt threatened by a purported omnipresent "big sister" of federal overreach, surveillance, and subjection, a tyrannical power that worked on behalf of women to the detriment of men. Militants such as Bray and the antiabortion Ku Klux Klan argued in the 1990s that men needed to take measures—including killing physicians to stop abortions—to end such emasculation. With this mindset, antiabortion militants of the 1990s saw the Supreme Court decision of *Roe v. Wade* as an assault on men's right to make decisions about their own families. Prominent female public figures and cabinet members, such as Hillary Clinton and Attorney General Janet Reno, became symbols to these anti-statist men who felt under siege by a female-controlled federal government.

This siege mentality blended well with two movements of the 1990s: the bourgeoning militia movement and church-based efforts to convince youth that they are "survivors" of abortion. The militia movement dovetailed with both the white power movement and the antiabortion movement, which became more militant in practice and more apocalyptic in tone, resulting in domestic terrorism in the form of clinic bombings, sniper shootings, and threats of chemical warfare targeting physicians and clinic personnel.[12] Seven physicians and clinic workers were murdered in the 1990s: Leanne Nichols, Shannon Lowney, James Barrett, Robert

Sanderson, John Bayard Britton, Michael Griffin, and Barnett Slepian. Perpetrators justified the homicide of physicians and clinic workers by claiming abortion was a holocaust. Around the same time, in the 1990s, thousands of American youth who attended certain Protestant churches were being taught the same lesson: abortion is a holocaust and they, as living people, should consider themselves "survivors" of that holocaust.[13] In this way, the siege mentality that motivated militia groups, antiabortion killers, and paramilitary white supremacists was also systemically introduced to the youngest members of the American right: kids of Christian conservatives. These youths were taught to believe they were targets of state-sanctioned genocidal efforts. The false equivalency of 1) individual women choosing to terminate individual pregnancies with 2) state officials planning and executing mass murder of imprisoned citizens or slaves was perpetuated by homicidal abortion foes *and* churchgoers at Sunday schools. It was also the basis of the Genocide Awareness Project, which was founded in 1997.

The Genocide Awareness Project illustrated this false equivalency by juxtaposing magnified images of stillbirths and extracted fetal and uterine flesh with historical pictures of the lynching of Blacks in the U.S. South and the genocide of Jews in Nazi Germany. As I explain in my book *Killing for Life,* the analogy of abortion as slavery and the Holocaust is not merely a comparison. It purports a timeline of human atrocities in which abortion appears as the most heinous culmination of end-times evil.[14] It effectively relegates racial and religious persecutions against people of color and Jews to times gone by. The human atrocities of enslaving Africans in America or gassing Jews in Nazi death camps are in the past, but the plight of the unborn is the present-day concern. In this way, racism and antisemitism "read as manifestations of historical prejudice that have been resolved."[15]

Moreover, the Genocide Awareness Project images promote an urgent sense of horror, deploying gothic themes of gore, injury, and dismemberment displayed as supersized vinyl banners. Individual fetuses are innocent victims in this rendering, imbued with the same collective identities and societal connections that characterize entire cultures. Existing scholarship examines such representations as matters of racial appropriation, historical cooptation, visual misrepresentation, and medical misinformation.[16] More to my current point, in claiming fetuses as victims of violence perpetrated amid a so-called testosterone deficiency, the Genocide Awareness Project reflected the particularly male supremacist siege mentality of the antiabortion, militia, and men's movements in the 1990s. Indeed, the Genocide Awareness Project debuted at the 1997 Promise Keepers assembly in Washington, DC; its acronym was intended to correspond with the assembly's biblical theme of "stand in the gap."[17]

The Genocide Awareness Project was a program run by the Center for Bioethical Reform (CBR), a pseudoscientific pro-life organization devoted to arguing that abortion is categorically genocide.[18] In 2003 the Midwest director of the CBR, Mark Harrington, left the group to found Created Equal, where he continued the racial and religious assumptions of the Genocide Awareness Project while overtly appropriating civil rights rhetoric.

The Racial and Religious Assumptions of Created Equal Media

A pamphlet I obtained from Created Equal when they came to campus exemplifies the group's appropriation of African American

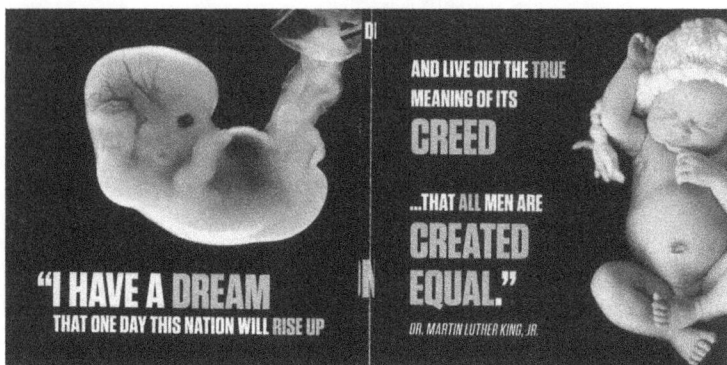

FIGURE 5. Interior of antiabortion brochure distributed on campuses appropriates African American history. Photo by author.

history, specifically that of Martin Luther King Jr. and the civil rights movement (CRM). Showcasing the quotation from which the group apparently took its name, the pamphlet reads, "I have a dream that one day this nation will rise up and live out the true meaning of its creed . . . that all men are created equal" (figure 5). Who are the "all men" depicted by the accompanying images? An embryo backlit to appear as a shining white biological specimen of humanity and a white-appearing infant who is naked except for a white knit hat. These racialized images represent the "all men" who are "created equal." Moreover, as one sharp-eyed audience member pointed out to me once when I showed this at a conference, the infant has a raised fist that resembles the Black power salute made famous in the 1960s and 1970s. The pamphlet juxtaposes very white images with unmistakably African American references.

According to Michelle Kelsey Kearl, Created Equal taps into the "American public memory" of Martin Luther King Jr. and the twentieth-century CRM while projecting "their own connotative meaning" onto them. "This appropriation or coopting of the rhetorical legacy of MLK and CRM," argues Kearl, "allows Created Equal to repurpose the past towards contemporary political ends incongruous with King and the movement."[19] Coopting the framing of African American campaigns for civil rights was an explicit and conscious decision by Harrington: "Needing a model to give direction to the vision," according to the Created Equal website, "Mark turned to stories from the Freedom Rides of the 1960s," which challenged Jim Crow prohibitions on interstate travel by racially integrated parties.[20] Kearl carefully delineates how Created Equal's Justice Rides "appropriate a specific anti-racist strategy and repurpose it in form only."[21] The result is a jarring juxtaposition of civil rights activists who withstood ambush, arson, beatings, murders, and state-sanctioned violence with "white teenagers braving public conversations about abortion."[22] Created Equal personnel participating in antiabortion Justice Rides "are not putting their lives in danger and are rarely, if ever, harmed in any way." Moreover, as Kearl avers, Created Equal manages to "stake out an anti-racist position without being anti-racist."[23] Under Harrington's leadership, Created Equal has continued to depict opposing abortion as activism on par with fighting against segregation and for equality, even while opposing anti-racist organizations and appearing antagonistic to people of color.

Examples of comparing abortion foes to civil rights activists abound in videos documenting Created Equal in the public sphere. Says one Created Equal spokesperson, "I think back on the civil rights movement, and I think, you know, if I were living in that time I would have been on those marches, I would have been breaking segregation laws with people and just challenging that."[24] The spokesperson goes on to say that people will look back on this time and ask why others didn't fight abortion. Evident here is not only an appropriation of Black history but also a usurpation of the moral high ground that the civil rights movement represents in national memory. As Daniel Martinez HoSang and Joseph E. Lowndes explain, some white right-wing actors who appropriate the African American struggle for themselves create "a redemptive subjectivity, in which Blackness becomes represented as the ethical embodiment of a distinctly American national identity and exceptionalism."[25] Created Equal's embrace of Martin Luther King Jr. exemplifies how "longstanding narratives of Black uplift" and "the moral perseverance of the civil rights movement are repurposed to defend and naturalize" structural inequalities and neoliberal policies that keep the majority of Black people down.[26] Created Equal personnel who challenge passersby with an admonishing claim of righteousness by comparing their antiabortion stance with civil rights are perversely redefining reproductive control as a pursuit of American equality.

Students of conservatism know that such perverse redefinitions are hardly new. In particular, redefining what it means to be created equal can be traced back to Barry Goldwater's 1960 *The Conscience of a Conservative*. This immensely popular book elucidated a logic in which conservatives recognize that all men are created equal by their creator, as the Declaration of Independence claims. Of course, the exclusivity of the phrase "all men" already limits the purview of the declaration to males. But Goldwater—or, more precisely his ghostwriter, L. Brent Bozell—made explicit additional limitations implicit in that Declaration. Americans are, according to the conservative conscience, "all equal in the eyes of God but we are equal *in no other respect*."[27] Understanding this statement as an underlying logic helps illuminate why, without a sense of hypocrisy, conservatives can uphold the idea of being created equal while assiduously opposing the goal of an egalitarian society, which, according to Goldwater, "does violence both to the charter of the Republic and to the Laws of Nature."[28] Harrington's adoption of the phrase "Created Equal" as a name for the group was likely not a conscious reference to *Conscience of a Conservative,* but rather was taken from a quotation by Martin Luther King Jr., whose recorded speech on the National Mall in Washington is used as a voice-over in several of Created Equal's videos. Nevertheless, the same Christian conservative logic articulated in 1960 helps explain why Created Equal does not consider it hypocritical to appropriate Black history while denying racial equality. We are, according to this logic, all equally loved by God because we are all created by him—but any sexual, gender, class, or racial divisions remain as his laws of nature.

We see this logic operating in podcasts of *Radio Activist: The Mark Harrington Show.* On his 2020 New Year's Eve broadcast, one of Harrington's guests cites this concept in discussing the "racial tensions" on campuses that teach critical theory.[29] "Whereas we believe that all people have a common shared humanity and that we're all image bearers of God," the guest contends, critical theory ostensibly prescribes—rather than describes—different classes in society and analyzes the power relations among them. As Harrington and his guest go on to discuss the Black Lives Matter movement, they say that blaming "social ills" instead of taking "personal responsibility" is not commensurate with the Christian worldview. The Black Lives Matter (BLM) movement is therefore anti-Christian, they say. The emphasis on personal responsibility redefines "neoliberalism as a form of antiracist freedom,"[30] while the idea that we are all image bearers of God underscores the religious foundation of being created equal. Both views allow for a complete and disdainful dismissal of the movement for Black lives.

In a different episode that delineates why Christians should not participate in or sympathize with the Black Lives Matter movement, the concept of "created equal" emerges again.[31] Harrington's guest for the November 2020 show was Ryan Bomberger, an employee of the Atlanta-based Radiance Foundation, which in 2010 launched a mass media campaign that purported abortion is Black genocide on large billboards.[32] The campaign was, according to some analysts, an attempt to sow division among African American voters during the midterm elections of Barack Obama's first term.[33] Building on this established history of channeling resentment over the oppression of Black people into the antiabortion cause, Bomberger directly relies on the religious idea of being created equal to situate the issue of Black lives in a Christian conservative view. He opines, "Of course we believe that Black lives matter. Why? Because we are all created in the image of God. And we're all loved equally by God." Then Bomberger, an African American man, delineates objections to BLM, including the oft-repeated ideas that there is more Black-on-Black violence than interracial violence and that police kill more white people than Black in any given year. He ignores the fact "that police kill Black men and women at disproportionate rates, ranging from 2.5–3 times more often than white Americans, according to reports" and academic studies.[34] Despite the existence of such studies and reports, which are not very difficult to find, Bomberger claims that "the abortion industry" has killed more Black people than cops have and blames an "epidemic of fatherlessness" for all violence.

The "epidemic of fatherlessness" he cites is a familiar conservative narrative used to explain Black poverty as the result of a lack of male leadership in families and communities,[35] and it reinforces the overall presumption that men are dispossessed of their rightful role in society. The podcast implies that to protect men from continued dispossession and degradation, they need to oppose abortion as a means of restoring the natural order of life according to a Christian belief that we all—men, women, unborn, Black, white, Jew, gentile, young, and old—are equally created by God.[36]

But, as these broadcast conversations illustrate, this belief in being created equal by God demands recognizing one's place in this supposed natural order. Created Equal's patriarchal traditionalism sees that natural order as men serving as leaders and women serving as reproducers. Abortion, in their view, offends this natural order, so opposing abortion protects men's rightful place. Moreover, Created Equal consistently depicts opposing abortion as a matter of national and racial pride. It does so by co-opting the heritage of the civil rights movement and the valorized figure of Martin Luther King Jr. as an exemplar of personal responsibility, American exceptionalism, and moral perseverance. Created Equal's videos defend this highly religious and racialized stance against interlocutors who recognize that the racial pride that Created Equal promotes is not synonymous with racial justice or equality for people of color.

Videos of Created Equal in the Public Sphere

Created Equal's videos exemplify how conservatives make art that they market as documentary film. The Created Equal website contains an archive of videos that show how they use public spaces to proselytize an antiabortion faith even as they eschew religious rhetoric. The videos are designed to show an apparent dialogue in which antiabortionists, whose faces viewers often don't see because the camera is attached to their bodies, convince passersby that abortion is wrong. Each video aims to present an evenhanded dialogue in which the antiabortionist appears to win fair and square, intellectually and dispassionately. Opponents of the antiabortionists are presented as hostile, irrational, or feeble. Documentary filmmaking has always appealed to objective truth telling, despite the fact that it is an art form with formal aspects that are intentionally designed. Especially in their capacity to document what appears to be a political debate, the videos produced by Created Equal follow filmmaking techniques and adopt a rhetorical style that characterizes other conservative documentaries.

In particular, the Created Equal videos are similar to recent documentary films produced by conservatives in which the "formal appearance of political debate" is deployed "for a contradictory end: to deny outright an encounter with political difference and thereby to refuse any serious consideration of the issues, ideas, or arguments expressed by a political opponent."[37] These videos simulate dialogue "in a manner that maintains a fundamental barrier against any significant exchange between self and (an antagonistic) other."[38] This is especially clear when onlookers raise the question of the conditions under which people become pregnant as something that Created Equal personnel are not taking into account. In several videos, onlookers try to steer the conversation toward the socioeconomic situations that may contextualize an unwanted pregnancy. They raise questions about structural inequalities that shape people's ability to meet the needs of a pregnancy or parenthood. The conscientious weighing of their own capacity to take on such responsibilities is inverted into a lack of morality. If conception is a life, then ending conception is killing.

As explored more fully below, this bottom-line thinking is a "simplification of complex subject matter into moralistic binaries [which] is an all too common feature of contemporary political discourse."[39]

One video in particular demonstrates how Created Equal avoids analyses of structural inequalities and provides a "simulacrum of debate intent on the denial of political difference."[40] When a young Black woman approaches Created Equal personnel, she points out that the person seeking to terminate a pregnancy may have been raped. Rape is an issue of male dominance that is historically intertwined with gendered and racialized violence. At the word "rape," the white male Created Equal representative responds with a fluid and measured contention that the resultant baby may be unloved, but that does not justify killing because it is not right to kill the unloved or the unlovable, using teenage girls and the homeless as examples of others who are unloved but not killed.[41] Moreover, as Kearl notes, "the visual representation of white men, who [as Created Equal personnel] believe themselves to be part of an oppressed group, engaged in prescribing behaviors and beliefs to black women about abortion and/or their reproductive objections should cause some alarm."[42] This particular video does not include the Black woman's response. Instead, at the close of the specious chain of equivalences delivered by the Created Equal representative, a white woman approaches to shake his hand and says, "We need people like you." In this way, the Black woman's reasonable intervention is overwhelmed by a steady stream of paternalistic condescension, which a white woman then compliments in a de facto act of racial solidarity.

The exchanges in this Created Equal video exemplify the tendency of conservative films to "revel in the accumulation of facts, details, and qualifications that distract from, but do not fundamentally respond to, material appearances of political difference."[43] The "material appearances" of race appear inconsequential in this video. Any racial differences are absolutely ignored on the scene and in the discussion. Created Equal personnel do not respond to the larger implications of the Black woman's point, to the fact of her race, to her perspective as a woman of color, or to any lived experience she brings to bear on this issue. She is shut down. But the filmmaking—the formal aspects of the video—suggests that this has been an equitable exchange of opinions in which the apparent victor has played fairly and honorably.

These videos put the viewer in the shoes of the Created Equal representative. The camera often situates the video viewer as the antiabortionist, whose voice emerges as the individual spectator's. The voice also functions as the seemingly omnipotent speech effect known as the "voice of God" in documentary filmmaking, which is fitting because the actual argument made is essentially a religious appeal to the idea of conception as a "life" and as "human." This religious argument assumes life is created by God and therefore cannot be tampered with without spurning the gift of God. This religious argument sidesteps the fact that since 1965 the American College of Obstetricians and Gynecologists has defined pregnancy as a fertilized egg implanted in the uterine lining.[44] We never see anyone acknowledge that not all fertilized eggs latch onto the uterine lining; some fertilized eggs get washed away during menstruation. According to the videos, once you concede conception is life you must also say that ending conception is killing, and that therefore anyone who ends conception is a killer. The basis of this equation goes back to the religious belief that life is God's dominion and you are a sinner if you spurn his gift of life.

Created Equal personnel avoid stating any such underlying religious assumption in favor of humanistic inferences. The belief in pregnancy as God's sacred gift is delivered in a secular frame of human rights and equal rights that obscures this fundamental religious ideology.

Doctrine of Demons

Devoted to Christian views, Created Equal uses films to translate that religious perspective into secular frameworks. The gothic genre is instrumental in this regard. *Abortion: A Doctrine of Demons* is a Created Equal production that uses generic conventions of gothic horror to convince viewers that abortion is fundamentally a demonic enterprise rather than one of the most common and safest medical procedures done in the United States and around the world.[45] Moreover, the film has an apocalyptic tone and argumentative structure that reduce the issues down to a diametrical opposition between good and evil. The good people are Christians who oppose abortion: no surprise there. The bad people "have a religious dogmatism of their own" but in an inverse way: they are "religiously secularist" in their quest for "autonomy," and "the greatest representative of pursuing autonomy is Satan." A voice-over provides a caveat, claiming that "mocking Christianity does not prove a doctrinal connection between killing preborn babies and satanism, but those who love death are quick to embrace its tenets." This manufactured moral divide is the bedrock of the apocalyptic narrative that reads abortion in the United States as a sign of the end times of American decency, white civilization, and the Christian nation.[46] The film goes on to interview Zachary King, a "satanic high wizard" who claims to have used blood obtained by abortions for demonic worship. The film includes many references to Satan, apparently gleaned from heated exchanges when facing off with counterprotesters and from more elaborate street theater and performance art. In their original presentations and venues these references to Satan likely were meant to indict and ridicule the use of gore, depravity, and demons by abortion foes. In *Doctrine of Demons,* any such ironic images are stripped of their original context and re-presented as sober evidence of mocking Christ and supporting the supposed satanic blood sacrifice that is, they claim, abortion.

The idea that abortion is an anti-Christian and even a satanic practice is a very old idea rooted in the ancient antisemitic myth of blood libel.[47] Antiabortion materials have, since the 1970s, purported to uncover the hidden truth that physicians performing abortions are Jews who kill children as a sacrificial rite.[48] They imply and sometimes outright claim that abortion providers constitute a satanic Jewish-run cabal. This portrayal blends with the related antisemitic myth that asserts that a Jewish cabal is conspiratorially and secretly controlling the government and the media. Most recently, we can see this kind of conspiracism reflected in Trump supporters who followed Q, the supposed government insider who ostensibly provided clues about how Democrats and the Hollywood elite would be exposed for their sex trafficking of very young children, some of whom were sacrificed in weird rituals.[49] For example, the Pizzagate conspiracy theory purported that Hillary Clinton was operating such child sacrifice out of the basement of a pizza parlor in Washington, DC. It wasn't true. The pizza parlor in question did not even have a basement. But such horror stories (or depravity narratives) helped to demonize Clinton during her 2016 presidential campaign. Like Pizzagate and QAnon conspiracists, abortion foes pit a satanic cabal craving baby flesh against humble heroes who supposedly can see what less enlightened people cannot.

Journalist Siân Norris has detailed how followers of QAnon have deployed rumors about satanic, pedophilic politicians who purportedly abduct children for ritualistic sacrifices online and in the public sphere. "The links," she notes, "between anti-abortion and the #SaveTheChildren QAnon conspiracy theory are not hard to find: at the time of the 2020 U.S. presidential election, a brief search for the Twitter hashtag generated numerous references to Democrat elites, satanic ritual abuse, and abortion rites."[50] Norris recognizes how easily the rumors spread and merge with white fears of genocide caused by being "outbred" by Muslims and other people of color (as we saw with the case of Russia discussed in the previous chapter). Norris sees this so-called great replacement of Christian white populations working so closely with the satanic panic about child sacrifice that she dubs them "twin conspiracy theories."[51] Her astute analysis is bolstered by recognizing how much and how long the antiabortion movement has been deploying these ideas. In its regular depiction of clinic workers and reproductive health care professionals as depraved and bloodthirsty, abortion foes primed the American imagination for QAnon conspiracism.

In addition to the old accusation of abortion as blood libel and the newer misnaming of abortion as child sacrifice, there is an even more commonplace depiction that situates the lie that abortion is intrinsically bloody, injurious, demonic, and depraved firmly in the secular register. The gothic is used to create the more secular, less overtly antisemitic version of abortion as a satanic practice. Haunted houses are quintessential examples of American gothic.

Since the 1990s, evangelicals have organized haunted houses for the Halloween season designed to teach youth not to sin, with abortion being the most bloody and demonic sin depicted. Organizers' handbook for such "hell houses" list props, including medical garb, a surgical table and instruments, a small vacuum for sound effects, vats of theatrical blood refreshed nightly, and raw meat in a glass bowl of blood meant to represent the products of abortion. The cast of characters include a nurse, a sadistic doctor, and a "demon" who chides "Chrissy," a young woman who is supposed to scream and writhe in pain before reaching for the bowl of bloody meat in remorse for supposedly killing her baby. One such haunted house, which cost twelve dollars for entry, was the subject of a 2002 documentary film that "featured such horrific scenes as a girl spewing vats of blood from her vagina area after an abortion." This over-the-top gore traumatizes kids and completely misrepresents abortion procedures (over 90 percent of which are done in the first twelve weeks of pregnancy, and most of which are performed using pills) and patients (about 60 percent of Americans terminating a pregnancy are already a parent). But the gory satanic depiction matches a long history of abortion as a gothic scene.[52]

As literary scholar Karyn Valerius has shown, the gothic genre has been deployed to vilify abortion for more than a century. Since the 1800s, gothic conventions have served to portray "abortionists as depraved villains who prey on female victims in vice-ridden urban space."[53] One twentieth-century example is *The Silent Scream,* a highly controversial 1984 film featuring antiabortion physician Bernard Nathanson. Valerius analyzes the film as a disingenuous depiction of abortion built on conventions of the gothic. She writes, "*The Silent Scream* falsely claims to present empirical evidence that abortion causes fetuses to suffer, but the video's moral authority depends on this faulty evidence and on the emotional force of Nathanson's decidedly gothic narration. This gothic narrative transforms a routine medical procedure into a violent spectacle as it encourages audiences to identify with a fetal protagonist said to experience emotions and physical sensations."[54] Similarly, the gothic narrative of *Doctrine of Demons* is also transformative. It renders abortion a depraved spectacle and invites spectators to immerse themselves in the generic pleasures and powers of horror.

Doctrine of Demons sets up an apocalyptic pairing between Christian religion and "religious secularists" aligned with Satan. In addition, the film is marketed as a forbidden and "banned video" with graphic depictions and exposés of debaucherous scenes and criminal activities. Ominous music, slow motion, dark hues, and other editing features add to the foreboding tone. It is a creepy film used to disgust and delight those already predisposed to see abortion as an evil enterprise instead of a safe and common medical procedure. Like *The Silent Scream*, it "resembles gothic fiction in both form and content: it promises to frighten and appall readers; it uncovers the 'hideous truth' about secret crimes; it uses lurid description to simultaneously express moral outrage and excite fascination with the illicit activity it depicts; and it refuses to name the unmentionable topic it nonetheless discusses in colorful detail."[55] In *Doctrine of Demons,* the unmentionable topic is the presumption that Jews, acting in concert with or as satanists, are responsible for abortion. *Doctrine of Demons* approaches this unspeakable topic when it examines "child sacrifice" that goes back to "antiquity." It then asserts that this ancient practice is as current as 2016 Jewish presidential candidate and Vermont senator Bernie Sanders, whose pro-choice answer to a debate question is evidence that, as the voice-over claims, "many still call for child sacrifice." *Doctrine of Demons* never explicitly equates Jews with satanists; it only implies this supposedly most horrific of secrets and thereby conforms to all of the generic conventions of the gothic. These gothic conventions enact the powers of horror that make abortion a lurid and forbidden practice and its proponents a spectacularly depraved bunch. Putting abortion in a gothic light secularizes the more religiously based narrative that abortion is a sign of the end-times, evidence of culminating events that are part of a cataclysmic conflict between satanic and Christian forces. Created Equal straddles and merges both narratives of abortion: abortion becomes a sign of impending apocalypse and abortion becomes a matter of gothic horror. We can see this merger reflected in their campus activities as well.

Antiabortion Protest on Campus

Created Equal sometimes comes to the University of Kentucky twice a year. Signs on the campus lawn alert students that they are about to encounter something upsetting. Further along the path, they see gory signs and, finally, a large digital screen in the center of the quad, roped off but visible and visually dominating the space. The digital centerpiece is a Jumbotron, usually used as a score-board at sporting events. This technology has been borrowed from the highly masculinist rituals of sports entertainment to create another sphere of masculinist ritual: scaring and enraging pas-sersby on college campuses. Although the jumbotron is said to show footage of "a baby being dismembered," the moving images are moving only because they are animated by probing instru-ments and fingers.[56] The digital screen shows video of rubber-gloved fingers fondling bloody fetal parts. One particularly cringe-inducing moment occurs when a gloved hand rolls what appears to be a fetal eyeball.

Often students readily recognize that the images are not accurate depictions of terminating a pregnancy. They know fetuses are not that big, for one thing, and most of my students are incensed that Created Equal is putting abortion—an elective medical procedure that people choose to have—in the same category as slavery, an entire economy of the American South in which whole communities of people forcibly removed from Africa were legally robbed of any free will. As scholars have noted, comparing abortion to lynching and slavery tends to "trivialize the historical enslavement of black people, their experience of neo-slavery in the post-emancipation south, and successive regimes of subordination that extend to the current era of colorblind racism and mass incarceration."[57] My students understand that these rhetorical and visual comparisons—such as a picture of a bloody fetus displayed side by side with an image of a victim of lynching hanging from a tree—are generally bogus. But the validity of the images is not the issue. Instead, it's the volatility of emotions they provoke that seems more important. Students want to know why these guys get to provoke them on their way to classes. What right do they have?

For those who are against abortion, what they see on the Jumbotron can be enraging because it represents to them dismemberment. And those who are not against abortion might also be enraged because the images might represent the need for abortion as a consequence of unwanted sexual activity that resulted in pregnancy. The issue of consent is literally at hand. Whose flesh is the Jumbotron exposing, and who has the right to look at it and touch it? Who has given consent to obtain and film the uterine flesh?

Whose flesh is it? Who owns it? Who owns the person it came from? Who gets to see, who gets to show, who gets to touch—and who is being victimized—are issues that override questions of whether or not the projected images are true.

In the midst of the Me Too movement and debates about how Title IX should be implemented to combat sexual assault on campus, Created Equal redirects big questions about unwanted touching away from what women say to what Created Equal's opponents do. *Implicit* questions of ownership and consent become *explicit* questions of ownership and consent when passersby are provoked into action and knock down or flip over any of the organization's signs or equipment. The opponents of Created Equal are then accused of destruction of private property, theft, or vandalism. It is not, therefore, only a politics of abjection or gothic horror operating in the spectacle of the enlarged, medically misleading, gory images. It is also a politics of touching, consent, and property. Created Equal's politics of touching successfully decenter and deflect women's experiences of nonconsensual touching and sexual assault that may lead to unwanted pregnancy.

A 2017 video produced by the *Kentucky Kernel,* a student newspaper at the University of Kentucky, demonstrates this confluence of issues during a visit by Created Equal.[58] In October of that year Created Equal met spirited opposition from students on the Lexington campus. In one scene of the video, a student, Adrienne Rogers, is shown to have been angered by Created Equal's display, which she considered hate speech rather than free speech. She flipped over one of the large lawn signs sporting a gory image. Campus police then pursued her. The video shows police following Rogers through the crowd, grabbing at her shoulder and her backpack. When she stops, University of Kentucky police captain Bill

Webb confronts her, calmly admonishing her for knocking over one sign. He explains that Created Equal has permission to be on campus: "It's their right to be here." Rogers responds, "It's also my right to push that over. I didn't touch anybody. This is a public space." As she continues to detail her rights, Webb cuts her off: "I'm not going to argue with you. Please don't touch the property." Immediately another female student interjects, "Please don't touch *her*." Rogers repeats, "Yeah, please don't touch *me*." Before Webb can think about what to say, the other student emphasizes, "Don't touch my girlfriend." At this point, Webb seems confused. He stammers. He closes his eyes. Webb is momentarily rendered speechless.

The women have not only made a demand; they also have made a comparative inquiry. Why does his entitlement to pursue and touch her without consent trump her right to topple an inanimate object, even if that object belongs to someone else? Why is she less protected than a lawn sign? Why does she have fewer rights than a piece of plastic and board? Rogers was not charged with any criminal misconduct. In this instance, the woman's right not to be touched commanded the center of attention. And the declaration that one woman was the other's girlfriend nodded to a whole different economy of consent and touching, in the face of which patriarchal law appeared momentarily dumbfounded.

Created Equal may suggest that their occupation of the public sphere is a level playing field on which, Harrington says, you should "bring your point of view in the marketplace."[59] But the "marketplace" is neither a neutral space nor a level playing field. To rebel against the disparity of access and financial means that Created Equal represents to individuals is to risk being sued, which could add to the organization's revenue and fuel the fire of Created Equal's male persecution complex.[60] Antiabortionists' attempts to propagandize a siege mentality and to profit from it have proliferated. This proliferation is an expansion of the tactic that Mark Crutcher of Life Dynamics started in the 1990s when he launched a campaign called ABMAL, short for "abortion malpractice." Like ambulance chasers from law firms hoping to profit from accidents, the ABMAL campaign sought to convince people that they may be "victims" of abortion. Life Dynamics offered legal advice and support for anyone who would come forward. ABMAL was part of Crutcher's "guerrilla strategy for a pro-life America" that also systematized cynical pro-woman rhetoric, as we saw in the previous chapter. The ABMAL campaign came under scrutiny when it was discovered that Crutcher had paid an "eyewitness" to testify with lies about the "abortion industry" in 2000.[61] Since then, the tactic of weaponizing lawsuits against abortion providers or advocates has shifted from clinics to campuses.

The Genocide Awareness Project, Created Equal, and anti-abortion student groups began in the 2010s to make legal claims regarding their right to free speech on campus. Various lawsuits emerged, capitalizing on the offended and outraged opposition that the Genocide Awareness Project provoked in onlookers. In 2013, for example, a pro-life student organization sued Oklahoma State University, citing First Amendment rights, when they were denied space on campus.[62] In 2014 a University of California, Santa Barbara professor was sued for assault after taking a sign from a teenage antiabortion demonstrator.[63] In 2015, Boise State University paid a pro-life student group twenty thousand dollars to settle a free speech lawsuit, only a hundred dollars of which went to the group; the remainder covered fees for legal services by the Alliance Defending Freedom, a right-wing organization.[64] In 2017, students aided by the Alliance Defending Freedom sued Miami

University in Ohio.[65] That same year, Cal State University San Marcos was sued by Students for Life represented by Alliance Defending Freedom; eventually, the university paid $240,000.[66]

In each of these examples, the issue of free speech emerged in the same way that it did for the alt-right. In 2017, the free speech issue erupted as the "Battle of Berkeley" pitted the alt-right against the University of California. When university officials denied conservative celebrity speakers Milo Yiannopoulos and Ann Coulter the right to speak on campus, the alt-right staged protests that resulted in street fighting between progressive and far-right demonstrators.[67] Far-right strategist Richard Spencer saw the conflict on Berkeley's campus as a good indication that more campus demonstrations could unleash street fighting and force people to pick sides, so he with other organizers set out to reproduce the melee several months later on the University of Virginia campus in a campaign to Unite the Right in Charlottesville.[68] What the alt-right did on campuses in 2017 on a large scale was what antiabortionists had been doing for decades on campuses nationwide. The tactic of provocation deployed by both has particular objectives. It seeks to make opponents appear as the hostile, irrational, and reckless instigators of physical altercations. Documented or live streamed, the fight can ostensibly accomplish at least two goals: one, to create a basis for a profitable lawsuit and, two, to prove that white Christian men are under attack.

Caught on Cam

Created Equal produces and distributes short video clips to news media to promote and popularize the idea that men are victims of violence perpetrated by women. Inverting understandings of domestic violence and sexual assault as crimes of power exerted by men over women, this idea that women attack men is as old as the caricature of the henpecked or cuckolded husband. The particular news clip I analyze below corresponds, intentionally or not, with how online communities known as the manosphere characterize women as exerting too much power over men. Men who are disgruntled with women's sexual power, including incels (who claim to be involuntarily celibate because women ignore them as potential sexual partners) and pickup artists (whose disdain for women leads them to serial fornication as a matter of subjection), populate the manosphere. Their fear and loathing of women's presumed sexual power is the flip side of the fear and loathing of women's power to terminate a pregnancy that results from sexual activity and that abortion opponents try to stop. In both cases, men are seeing in women a sexuality and power that men cannot control, which they see as the problem. It is a problem because men, according to this view, are the victims of out-of-control women who attack them.

As if to prove this idea, Created Equal distributes media clips that can end up as features on local television, as was the case with the news spot "Caught on Cam: Pro-Life Activists Confronted, Attacked by Woman," which aired on a local Columbus, Ohio, channel before being posted by pro-life websites and featured on the nationally syndicated program *Fox & Friends*.[69] In this clip, a young woman is shown profanely yelling at an apparently younger man who is identified as a teenage summer intern. We hear nothing about what he may have said prior to the news clip, but she is heard contesting the validity of the images depicting products of an aborted pregnancy.

The clip mirrors the basic assumption that women must be stopped from dominating men. In particular, it resembles scenarios from the manosphere. In the manosphere, a particular type of victim, the nerd or geek, is subject to attacks from "normies" and "basic bitches" (read: unintelligent women) who infiltrate their digital space. The news clip resembles this scenario by interspersing points of view from a handheld camera and a body cam. The result is comical or cringeworthy, depending on your sense of the politics of the situation. The view from the body cam provides a sense of being aggressively pushed by the woman's larger, bulkier body, and the angle of the camera provides a full view of her chest. The view from the handheld camera shows an aggressive face-off with the woman yelling profanity at the teenager, often with her index finger pointing at him as he stands his ground silently. These actions appear to be uncalled-for, and the woman comes off as not reacting to the arguments or materials in particular but as a volatile, irrational bully who is out of control with unwarranted anger. The cameras focus on and exacerbate her corpulence, presenting a cartoonish caricature of an out-of-control woman. One need not condone her actions to recognize that the editing of the encounter results in a clip that provides us with the stereotype of the angry feminist. The cultural work that this clip performs is to encourage viewers not only to laugh at or disdain her but also to feel sorry for and defensive on behalf of *him*. He is depicted as the victim. Created Equal's creation and distribution of this depiction fits precisely in its overall view that men are under attack and that opposing abortion is an honorable way for men to stand their ground against the onslaught of women's rights and abusive feminists.

A reporter later follows up with the woman to get her point of view. By asserting that she "assaulted" the Created Equal crew, the reporter puts the woman on the defensive. She defends herself by questioning whether knocking down signage and shoving a cameraman who had no consent to film her constitutes assault. Ultimately, a judge ordered the woman to pay eighty dollars for the two signs she knocked down, and the prosecutor dropped charges of assault and criminal damage.[70]

In interviews about the situation, Harrington predictably invoked the legacy of Martin Luther King Jr. and expressed pride in his staff and Christian concern for the woman. As we saw in the video from the University of Kentucky, the contest of consent over touching property overrode the issue of whether or not the images in the signs she knocked down were medically accurate and truthful depictions of abortion. Moreover, on *Fox & Friends* the Created Equal director of summer programs, Seth Drayer, reports that their goal is to de-escalate violence; he also indicates that recording action to be used in court is the ultimate goal. "When people respond that way we don't try to win the debate or challenge their claims; we just want to try to diffuse the anger while still again documenting so that later our rights and the law will be upheld," resulting in a public opinion or legal win.[71] This quotation suggests that going to court is the goal of these encounters in the public sphere. Not fighting back and not engaging in honest debate to address political differences are part of the plan.

Caught on Cam is a clear example of how Created Equal visualizes opposing abortion as a call for protections for men as well as for women and the unborn. Opposing abortion helps protect white men from purported federal tyranny orchestrated to dismantle men's privileges and exalt women's sexual and political dominance. Opposing abortion helps protect white men from accusations of rape by delegitimizing and decentering women's experiential knowledge in campus contests of consent. Opposing abortion helps protect white men from succumbing to a demographic decline, the supposed end of the white race. Opposing abortion helps protect Christian men from accusations of antisemitism because if abortion is a holocaust, they are fighting the premier signifier of antisemitism. Perhaps most clearly, opposing abortion helps protect white men from accusations of racism by wresting the moral high ground from the civil rights movement and the movement for Black lives.

What Created Equal Teaches Us about Right-Wing Victimhood

All these representations of Created Equal—the films and videos they produce as well as those made about them—bear witness to a broader trend among right-wing movements to vilify women and position men as underdogs. It is important to note this trend because it is one of the unifying aspects of right-wing movements and ideologies worldwide. Opposing abortion by positioning men as victims to be protected fits and fuels larger populist campaigns. This is especially true for far-right populists who depict white people as under siege by people of color who threaten to overpower them demographically with high birth rates. This fear of demographic and cultural demise has for years manifested as opposition to abortion for white people. The fear of being a minority has been promoted alongside the satanic panic purporting that anti-Christian demons are ritualizing abortion as part of an ongoing (or in a lead-up to) apocalyptic battle. Created Equal's materials and practices reflect all these fears, apparently stoking them for profit. As such, they exemplify how some scholars of right-wing studies are theorizing victimhood.

According to such scholars, in many far-right and conservative communities the idea of being a victim is not about who has sustained injury or endured suffering but is instead about who occupies the lowest stratification of the social hierarchy.[72] In this way victimhood is imagined to be both reversible and reciprocal. In other words, white people who have occupied the privileged position atop the social hierarchy imagine that any change to that status will surely result in total and violent subjugation.

I believe that the antiabortion movement has supplied images of injury and violence that have contributed to these fears of white Christians being victimized. The antiabortion movement has visualized, and encouraged others to visualize, the dissolution of the white race with gothic fetal imagery. Christian white people have been taught to see themselves as survivors of abortion and to identify with the unborn, bloody images of which signify the dismemberment, torture, and debasement that would befall them if what they perceive as the natural order erodes. For some white Christian men, abortion signifies no longer an impending apocalyptic battle between Christian and anti-Christian forces but an apocalypse that is already in progress. Images of white men as victims of women's abuse confirm their sense of this conflict. Therefore, it should come as no surprise that groups such as Created Equal are investing in visual narratives of men withstanding verbal and physical attacks. The fact that they create spaces and opportunities in which such altercations are bound to occur indicates not only a profitable weaponizing of lawsuits but also a psychological wage of confirming their dystopic worldview that the "natural order"—patriarchal traditionalism—is imperiled and that men must be protected.

II *Warriors*

3   Radicalization and Race in Women's Pro-Life Writing

In "Reconsidering the Sexual Politics of Fascism," Robyn Marasco reminds us that the insurrection of January 6, 2021, entailed the death of two women. Rosanne Boyland was waving the snake-on-a-field-of-yellow Gadsden flag, the message of which is "Don't Tread on Me," when she was—ironically enough—trampled by a crowd of Trump supporters storming the Capitol. We don't hear much about her. There has not been a lot of media investigation into why she was there or what her background was. She seems to have faded into obscurity, just one of the women who were compelled to participate in an unprecedented and illegal protest of the peaceful transfer of power from one president to another. It was a group called Women for America First that organized the morning Save America Rally on the Ellipse that gathered thousands of protesters that day, so you would think that all the women in the Make America Great Again movement would be well scrutinized. But much more attention has been paid to the other woman who died during the insurrection. Her name was Ashli Babbitt. The video of her being shot as she was hoisted through a broken glass window in a locked door of the Capitol building is horrifying and heartbreaking.[1]

We know a lot about Babbitt.[2] She was a divorcée whose pool supply business in Southern California wasn't doing very well. She had voted for Barack Obama long before becoming an avid Trump supporter and QAnon follower. In embracing the QAnon myths she was swept up in believing, living by, and recirculating conspiracy theories that have no merit, which is known as conspiracism. She was a military veteran who was conventionally attractive: blond, slender, and sporty. She had a feisty personality. Her social media posts indicated an increased concern about America and enthusiasm for attending the Save America Rally on January 6. It was initially reported that she was unarmed when the officer shot her as she was breaking into the Capitol. Later it was discovered that she was carrying a weapon. She had been carrying a ParaForce folding knife in her pocket.

Multiple journalists and scholars have documented how Babbitt has become a martyr for the right. Some investigators, such as Jeff Sharlet, note that her being white and the police officer being Black triggered an old Southern narrative of vigilante violence being justified to protect white womanhood.[3] Trump supporters appropriated from the Movement for Black Lives the tagline "Say Her Name" in remembrance of Babbitt. The politics of race and gender are inextricable in how Babbitt is remembered and held up as a reason to continue to fight for the reinstatement of Donald Trump as president (even though he lost the election) in 2020.

"The martyrdom of Ashli Babbitt," according to Marasco, "raises two separate but related questions—what the Right says *about* women and what the Right says *to* women."[4] Given that Women for America First organized the rally preceding the riotous violence at the Capitol, we might refine that pair of questions: What do women on the right say to each other and about themselves? And, given my focus on how abortion foes have primed the American imagination for white nationalism and authoritarian populism, I'll refine it even further. What do antiabortion women say to their peers about their mission and about themselves?

Women's antiabortion memoirs and movement literature have reflected political currents that took the American right from Cold War conspiracism and apocalyptic fundamentalism to anti-statist terrorism and Tea Party populism. Reading the writings of women helps us understand the racialization and radicalization of the anti-abortion movement from the 1970s onward. Knowing what they have written shows how we got to a point where people are willing to wage actual war against the United States government.

Mildred Jefferson and Cold War Conspiracism

Mildred Jefferson was a triple threat to those seeking to decriminalize abortion in the 1970s. As the first Black woman to graduate from Harvard medical school, she was a powerful pioneer and defiant crusader. Archives of her life are full of examples of the sexism and racism she faced in the medical profession. She devoted her energies to the right-to-life movement when professional opportunities to practice as a surgeon were withheld from her.

Based in Boston, Jefferson was in 1970 a founding member of Massachusetts Citizens for Life, joined the Value of Life Committee, and became a conservative star when she participated in a televised panel on the impending decision in the *Roe* case on a PBS station. Jefferson claimed she was "hardly qualified to testify" in the case of *Commonwealth v. Kenneth Edelin*.[5] But she did. This case from 1973 was the first time in U.S. history a physician was charged with manslaughter of a fetus. Prosecutors claimed he killed babies presumed to have lived after abortion procedures, including per-forming a hysterotomy. Edelin, a Black doctor, was initially con-victed by an "all-white 12-member jury, which included nine men and 10 Roman Catholics."[6] This conviction was subsequently over-turned, but the case was significant for initiating fetal imagery in lawsuits and legislation. It also solidified Jefferson as a national fig-ure who could deliver compelling testimony. A year later she became the president of the National Right to Life Committee. As a Methodist, Jefferson helped dispel criticism that the Catholic church controlled the antiabortion movement. As a woman, she thwarted the idea that only men were in charge of the movement. As an African American, she delivered race-based arguments against abortion with an authenticity that the then predominantly white Catholic organizations against abortion could not.[7]

A prolific writer and orator, Jefferson was well loved by conserv-ative politicians and mostly embraced their rationales for opposing abortion. She routinely argued against abortion rights as a matter of individual responsibility. In *Ebony*, she opined, "You can't give the individual the private right to kill, no matter what kind of justifica-tion they can come up with."[8] "The ethic of personal responsibility was paramount, and it was a central reason that she opposed abortion."[9] Jefferson thought legal abortion was granting a single individual the right to decide who lives and who dies. This focus on individual rights exemplified the contemporary framing of abortion in classically liberal terms, by which I mean in terms of individual liberties. Whose individual freedoms were more important? The woman's or the fetus's? Of course, this line of argument necessi-tated convincing people that the fetus is an individual person, and much of the writing of the right-to-life movement in the 1970s was about proving the fetus's personhood in moral, legal, and biological terms. For example, in 1975 the first volume of the journal *Human Life Review* recognized that there is a significant difference between abortion and "the murder of a full member of society, whose life intermeshes with the lives of many others."[10] That recognition faded from antiabortion arguments, but the emphasis on rights and individual responsibility was predominant in the 1970s. Jefferson maintained the focus on individual rights and responsibility.

The focus on individual responsibility helped counter the contemporary radical feminist arguments that women *as a class* were *collectively* oppressed by curtailing reproductive freedom. By centering attention on the individual, right-to-lifers helped structure an abortion debate of only two camps—for or against abortion, which left out a string of other reproductive issues such as sterilization. White liberal feminists who also focused exclusively on the individual right to abortion aided this formulation of an abortion "debate" that framed a myriad of reproductive issues in the narrowest of bifurcated terms. Jefferson's emphasis on the individual's right, then, perpetuated a certain kind of discussion that foreclosed larger, more intersectional discussions about how abortion and other reproductive issues affected different women differently. She opposed all abortions and callously found fault with the women who terminated pregnancies.

When she did venture into race-based arguments, she had opportunity to politically align with progressive women of color. Jefferson wrote that abortion was a new Civil War.[11] Other times she said that legal abortion constituted genocide.[12] Such arguments suggest that she would be sympathetic to Latina and Black women who were debating whether the contraceptive pill, sterilization practices, and abortion were indeed genocidal tactics targeting communities of color in the 1970s. Jefferson also drafted an essay demonizing Margaret Sanger, founder of the American Birth Control League (the precursor to Planned Parenthood), arguing that abortion is an extension of eugenics. Jefferson's photo and quotation appear in a Massachusetts Blacks for Life pamphlet, although she is not listed among its board members. Sometimes, therefore, her arguments lined up with those of Black and brown feminists and nationalists who were sincerely investigating new technologies, like the pill, and new revelations, such as the 1973 sterilization of Minnie Lee and Mary Alice Relf, two Alabama teens whose fertility was destroyed because they were deemed mentally inferior. The history of such investigations into fertility control, sterilization abuse, and reproductive injustice in general spans activist and academic literature, comprising a profound body of scholarship that has been written since the 1970s. Jefferson did not collaborate with progressive women of color on these issues, though. She did not share their aims or ideologies.

Jefferson did not consider herself a feminist or a womanist. She didn't think organizing exclusively with other women or other Black people was effective or desirable. Despite the rancorous sexism and racism she faced in the medical profession, she rarely expressed racial solidarity. Indeed, she opposed identity politics and rejected political mobilizing as Black people. For instance, she repeatedly rebuffed outreach from members of the NAACP to join them.[13] She adamantly opposed the formation of a "minority alumni society" at Harvard, writing a formal letter that berated it as a "Jim Crow" organization, a return to "segregation," a radical "separatist" group, and a "policy of socio-academic apartheid in America."[14] She was also, despite being a "Nixon loyalist," unyielding in her opposition to affirmative action, about which she said, "Indentured slavery might have been kinder; they may have resisted it."[15] Her uses of history, therefore, were never aligned with progressive or radical women who were working at the time to secure equal rights for women and for people of color. Instead, she aligned herself and her arguments with the most religiously conservative players in the Republican party and in antiabortion circles.

Jefferson's understanding that abortion was a genocidal tactic was not, therefore, a matter of race consciousness. Rather, it was part of an apocalyptic narrative spun by Paul Marx. "If our efforts to defend life succeed and our civilization survives, historians will one day name Father Paul Marx as the 'Saver of the Modern World,'" wrote Jefferson.[16] As mentioned in chapter 1, Marx, the founder of Human Life International, promoted the idea that abortion providers were mostly Jewish and were orchestrating abortion as part of a clandestine plan that would wipe out Christianity. He worked to spread this antisemitic framing of the abortion issue throughout the world in person and in print. He wrote two books, beginning with *The Death Peddlers* (1971), in which he explicitly argues that the medical establishment behind reforming abortion laws was composed primarily of Jews who were secretly meeting to orchestrate systematic abortion. Marx bragged about how he registered for a 1971 meeting in Los Angeles organized by and for medical professionals, "Therapeutic Abortion: A Symposium on Implementation." In this way he suggested that his cunning was necessary to thwart those who were meeting in secret, which was false, to make nefarious plans (also false). *The Death Peddlers* argues that physicians were plotting to circumvent laws because they had lost their moral compass, they had jettisoned the Hippocratic oath, and they had become something less than doctors, something more sinister. This line of thinking made a deep impression on Mildred Jefferson. She wrote,

"Without his book *The Death Peddlers,* many doctors and I would not have recognized the extinction-peril of converting physician-healers into social-executioners."[17] Marx's and Jefferson's idea that physicians were being converted into "social-executioners" went beyond a mere claim that abortion kills.

The idea that doctors were "executioners" suggests that abortions were political acts comprising an actual war waged with intended and unintended consequences. *The Death Peddlers* and subsequent writings by Marx were Catholic iterations of far-right Cold War anticommunist conspiracism. Such conspiracism circulated in the form of depravity narratives that described horrifying scenes of lewd and barbaric behavior promoted by "ungodly" communists to undermine American culture and wholesomeness.[18] Marx's opposition to abortion incorporated diatribes against sex, popular culture, and news and entertainment media. "Rock [music] and Hollywood have homogenized the culture, and the media are largely in the hands of the antilife/anti-family devil," Marx wrote.[19] Then, as now, antisemites used the terms "the media" and "Hollywood elites" as coded language for Jews. Marx said he wanted to end abortion everywhere and for everyone, regardless of race, but he also pointed out the consequences of family planning in racialized terms, reflecting and feeding fears of whites' demographic demise—what in the nineteenth century was called "race suicide" and in the twenty-first century is called "the Great Replacement." (We'll look at this more in chapter 4.) In various print sources Marx sounded the alarm that "Moslems are taking over Western Europe," feeding the fear that whites are being overrun by brown and Black people. As another example, regarding South Africa, he wrote, "Contraceptive whites are no longer replacing themselves, having barely two children per completed family; the blacks average five, the 'Coloreds' 3.29, and the Asiatics 2.7. For the whites, the handwriting is on the wall!"[20] Jefferson likewise deployed the abortion-as-extinction argument in terms of demographic decline; she opined, "The people who are fewer will disappear faster."[21]

Jefferson's claim that abortion was "extinction-peril" was thus derived from Paul Marx, a white Catholic Cold War conspiracist who consistently blamed the Jews for abortion. She deployed his idea in speeches and interviews, even if it meant taking aim at fellow doctors: "I am not willing that my profession should exchange the role of healer for that of social executioner."[22] So, while people championed Mildred Jefferson as representing a non-Catholic view and a Black woman's perspective, they did not know about or downplayed how her perspective reflected the thinking of conspiracy theories in general and, more specifically, the thinking of a zealous Catholic priest who blamed Jews for abortion. Moreover, in promoting such thinking as a physician, Jefferson gave the impression that she was a practicing medical doctor. This was false. Her commitment to antiabortion politicking meant letting go of her long-held dream of serving as a doctor. By 1973, "save the occasional consultation, she practiced no medicine. Opposing abortion was now both her life and her living."[23]

Moreover, as Josh Prager shows in his narrative history of Jefferson's rise and fall, the antiabortion movement never knew much about her. She kept secret her white husband and the fact that he stopped living with her because she became a pathological hoarder. Jefferson downplayed that she was childless. She hypocritically insisted that being a mother would fulfill any woman and shamed those who sought to terminate a pregnancy. When she was excused from the National Right to Life Committee (NRLC) because she was not a fiscally responsible leader of the organization, it could have been that racist scapegoating was at work. But, given her personal finances, which archives show were a mess, that might be a charitable interpretation. Indeed, as Mary Ziegler notes, the NRLC had spent a lot of money on pushing the Hyde Amendment, which ensured that abortions would not be paid for with federal funding. "NRLC members believed that the spending habits of Mildred Jefferson, the organization's charismatic president, had put the organization in a bigger hole. During NRLC's 1978 internal election, Jefferson lost both her seat on the board of directors and the presidency. Her divorce from NRLC was messy."[24] As her personal life spiraled out of control throughout the late 1970s, 1980s, and 1990s, Jefferson consistently seemed to gravitate toward the most zealous abortion foes.

In addition to containing Marx's *The Death Peddlers,* one of her most cherished books, her library came to include a copy of *Accessory to Murder: The Enemies, Allies, and Accomplices to the Death of Our Culture,* a 1990 book that explained how the antiabortion movement was becoming more militant.[25] It contained a personal inscription and was signed by the author, Randall Terry, who founded the direct action antiabortion group Operation Rescue. As I mentioned in the introduction, Operation Rescue infiltrated or blockaded clinics to prevent them from doing business. In doing so, the blockaders and saboteurs believed they were "rescuing babies." "Rescues," however, did not begin with Randall Terry, the leader who made them famous. They began with John O'Keefe, a Catholic who linked opposing abortion with opposing the war in Vietnam.[26] They also became a widespread—though decentralized—strategy for one of Mildred Jefferson's contemporaries, Joan Andrews.

Joan Andrews, Rescue, and Race

As Mildred Jefferson was doing her best to thwart the idea that opposing abortion was not limited solely to white Catholic men, white Catholic women were also making contributions to the right-to-life movement. Historian Karissa Haugeberg has detailed such contributions by Joan Andrews in *Women against Abortion*. From Haugeberg's research we know that Andrews's Catholic upbringing during the 1960s influenced how she saw the war in Vietnam and the 1973 decriminalization of abortion via *Roe v. Wade*. Andrews claimed that the country was becoming more like Hitler's Germany. Horrified at what she saw as citizens' complacency in the face of war and legalized abortion, Andrews became a "reluctant" activist. She was compelled to sabotage clinics instead of working in policy or proselytizing. She believed the United States is a Christian nation and should not wage war against Indochina or the unborn.

Beginning in the late 1970s and throughout the 1980s, Andrews was at the heart of the so-called rescue movement. She was part of a core of maybe twenty activists who organized as many as two thousand people in various attacks and orchestrated infiltrations of reproductive health care clinics. Once inside a clinic, people would destroy equipment, harass clinic workers, shame clients, and blockade doors so that a clinic could not operate that day. These efforts at "rescue" were widespread and effective. The federal government repeatedly refused to categorize such terrifying activity as terrorism. Prosecutors routinely declined to charge the white, religious offenders with anything worse than disorderly conduct or trespassing.

Haugeberg notes that race played a role in why "rescuers" got off so easily. Sociological accounts of prosecutions at the time reveal that a person who was Black was more likely to be charged than a white person for the same crime. The white rescuers inspired by Andrews experienced few legal ramifications for their illegal activity. The rescuers were allowed to commit repeat offenses because of their white privilege. According to Haugeberg, this "nebulous group spent their days in a cycle that consisted of invading clinics, posting bond, and violating the terms of their bonds by returning to clinics. The small band of pro-life activists who deployed overtly violent strategies for ending abortion unleashed a reign of terror."

Consequently, the attacks on clinics continued unabated. "By the mid-1980s, prolife activists had deployed coercive, intimidating, or violent tactics at nearly every abortion clinic in the United States. In 1984 alone, antiabortion activists bombed or set fire to twenty-four clinics, destroying six of them. The cost to providers was staggering."[27] Mainstream organizations like National Right to Life Committee distanced itself from violent tactics, but activists recognized that the work of the mainstream policy- and education-oriented organizations could benefit from the terrorism of "rescue" attempts. They understood that "pro-life physicians and nurses who contested hospital policies, politicians who offered antiabortion legislation, and attorneys who challenged laws that permitted abortion complemented the efforts of direct action groups."[28] Mainstream organizations could say they were condemning these extralegal tactics so they would not be held legally liable and so that they would not cede the moral high ground, but the destruction and terrorism at clinics complemented the more palatable antiabortion work, and vice versa.

Andrews's personal writings and experiences as an activist show how she embraced becoming a mother figure for the "rescue movement." Her specialty was destroying clinic property and equipment, actions for which she was arrested more than 150 times. In 1985 she was sentenced to five years in prison on charges of burglary and she was imprisoned from 1986 to 1988. Andrews's imprisonment was seen as drastic because so few of the white activists had suffered any prosecution appropriate to the campaign of terror they were orchestrating in the 1980s. While Catholic leaders supported her conviction, she gained devotees among evangelicals.

Reports about her noncompliance in prison inspired evangelicals. Andrews is said to have learned noncompliance tactics from peace activists, Quakers in Pennsylvania. When apprehended by the police at a clinic or by a guard in prison, Andrews went limp so that they would have to carry her. Going limp was a signature tactic of activists protesting racial segregation throughout the 1950s and 1960s as well as that of antiwar and antinuclear activists. Andrews's rationale for this common tactic was skewed toward her cause. She went limp in solidarity with the fetus, the baby that she was supposedly rescuing. She literally took the fetal position, curling up and going limp to emulate the individual fetus she intended to rescue.

This sentimental approach to resisting arrest matched the kind of rhetoric that the right-to-lifers preferred—the idea that the fetus was an individual with a right to live. Andrews was the surrogate for the fetus in a sense. She was not a surrogate mother who carried someone else's baby but a surrogate of the fetus, a stand-in in what Andrews saw as a war. In equating her body with the fetus's, Joan Andrews embodied the idea of the right to life even as she was discounted by mainstream right-to-life organizations. She was a "rescuer" through the 1970s and early 1980s, reflecting a kind of sentimental attachment to the fetus. Andrews exemplified a motherly protectionism despite the fact that, like her contemporary Mildred Jefferson, she never was a mother.

Maternal protection is often expressed in racialized as well as sentimental terms. Andrews's work as a rescuer had an implicitly racialized rationale. When we look closely at her own writings instead of at historians' interpretations of them, we see that Andrews's relationship to the peace movement and to civil rights was quite limited. Moreover, she viewed privilege and discrimination in ways that accommodate racist thinking. In letters sent from her time in prison, published in a book titled *You Reject Them, You Reject Me,* we see that Andrews's concern with race had little to do with establishing an egalitarian society for which political movements of the time were striving. Andrews discusses the trajectory of her political awakening, beginning with a notable childhood fantasy of wanting to be Native American.

When I was a preschooler, I wanted to be an Indian, and lamented that our family wasn't a little redder in skin-tone.

More and more as I got near my pre-teens I began to develop a strong interest via revulsion in the Nazi holocaust. And I developed a deep desire to know how one should respond to any given situation morally—as God would want one to. So I read and watched TV programs with these questions in mind.

During high school, [I had only] a little civil rights involvement, though I became very involved in opposing the Vietnam war. Not in demonstrations, as there were none around my environment in Nashville during those years, from 1962 to 1966. It rather took the form of debate and prayer. At college, there was some civil rights involvement on a minor scale, though in the spring 1966 semester I became very involved in anti-war protests, fasts, and prayer. But I became disenchanted with the anti-war group on campus and left it and school after that one semester. I also left because I was emotionally distraught because my brother John was drafted during that semester.[29]

According to this first-person account, Andrews's involvement with the civil rights movement was "little" and "minor." She spent one semester involved in antiwar efforts but dropped out. She was "disenchanted" with collegiate antiwar efforts and, presumably, the analyses that undergirded their protest. Most college-based antiwar work entailed a criticism of how the United States was not simply fighting communism but also engaging in an imperialist endeavor in Vietnam. Andrews's take on fighting war never echoed that critique. Her own colonialist fantasy of wanting "to be an Indian," however juvenile and naive, remains intact in this rendition of her political awakening. Andrews's writing reflects no consciousness of how the American war in Vietnam was, broadly speaking, an extension of white America's imperial subjugation, elimination, and dispossession of indigenous people. Her devotion to civil rights and, by extension, racial equality, was "minor," "little." Her repulsion by World War II atrocities—the Holocaust—as well as at the war in Vietnam never acknowledged the white supremacist elements of each. Her antiwar activism was colorblind.

Without attending to the racial, political, and historical aspects of the peace movement, Joan Andrews saw injustice as a matter of dualistic hierarchy. One was either "discriminated" against or "privileged." In her words quoted by her editor:

"The closer we are to the preborn children," she wrote at that time, "the more faithful we are, then the *more identically aligned* we become with them. This is our aim, and goal, to wipe out the line of distinction between the preborn and their born friends, becoming ourselves *discriminated* against. . . . The rougher it gets for us," she continued, "the more we can rejoice that we are succeeding; no longer are we being treated so much as the *privileged* born, but as the *discriminated* against preborn. We must become aligned with them completely and totally or else the double standard separating the preborn from the rest of humanity will never be eliminated."[30]

In this explanation of antiabortion rescue, to "align" oneself is to become discriminated against. For Andrews, "becoming discriminated against" can be achieved by identifying with the preborn. In her white imagination, being discriminated against is, oxymoronically, a tool for achieving equality. For Andrews, being held accountable for breaking laws is being discriminated against. She claims for herself the status of being discriminated against while choosing not to fight for those who are discriminated against on colonialist and racist grounds. We can concede that Andrews's activism may have been an expression of Catholic martyrdom. If so, such martyrdom was certainly imbued with a colorblind reluctance to recognize the political, racial, and historical particulars that comprise structural inequalities.

As Joan Andrews was hailed as a martyr and served her sentence, the tactic of rescue came under the purview of evangelicals.[31] They retained Andrews's idea that opposing abortion was about war. But instead of opposing abortion based on the principle that one should be opposed *to* war, the rescue movement that emerged in 1986 opposed abortion as an engagement *in* war. The aforementioned leader of Operation Rescue, Randall Terry, explained noncompliance at clinic protests very differently than Joan Andrews did. "Why do rescuers go limp?" he asked. The explanation: "It's simple. We cannot willingly walk away from the scene of a murder. If I was standing between an assailant and his victim, and the assailant ordered me to move, I could not in good conscience comply."[32] As a matter of noncompliance, going limp for the evangelical Randall Terry is a matter not of American protest heritage or principled opposition to war. Instead, Terry explains, it is a matter of engaging in an apocalyptic battle with anti-Christian forces. In *Accessory to Murder* he explains, "Rescues are neither demonstrations nor acts of civil disobedience in which we hope to get arrested in order make a point."[33] No; rather, the point is fear of God's wrath, which Terry admits is a "righteously selfish motivation. *We're acting on behalf of our own children and their futures.* We understand the imminent danger we face as a nation. God could at any time severely chasten us because of the blood that cries from the ground for vengeance."[34] There are two important assertions in this statement by Randall Terry.

It is important to note that Randall Terry claims to fear God's wrath. God, he says, will chasten us if abortion is not stopped. This idea and the accompanying gothic imagery of blood crying from the ground were becoming dominant among "rescuers" whose vigilantism wreaked havoc on the reproductive health care community throughout the 1980s. Clinic attackers embraced the apocalyptic urgency and the gothic imagery. Convicted clinic bomber John Brockhoeft attested that to gear up for such illegal work he would spend time imagining in great detail what abortion would be like if it were happening to him. He imagined being in the place of the fetus during an abortion procedure. He spoke about being dismembered, torn limb from limb.[35] This gory depiction is a significant departure from how Joan Andrews showed solidarity with the fetus. To take up the fetal position is to represent the individual baby she wanted to "rescue." In serving as the surrogate for the fetus, Andrews put herself in harm's way. But this sentimental idea of *showing solidarity with* the fetus, as Andrews did when she went limp, became more a matter of *identifying with* or even *as* the fetus, as Brockhoeft reveals. The fetus became a proxy for these men rather than the other way around. The men of the rescue movement were decidedly more committed to waging war than opposing it. Moreover, if we are to take Randall Terry at his word, the war they felt they were waging was an apocalyptic one in which God's wrath was a key motivation.

Further, Randall Terry's rhetoric about "*acting on behalf of our own children and their futures*" mirrors the language used by militant groups on the far right. Terry chose to emphasize the message of protecting the future. The message is very similar to another famous rationale that was penned around the same time. In the mid-1980s antiabortionists were becoming more militant in opposing abortion, and so were other members of the far right. White supremacists were on a parallel path, increasing their violent tactics throughout the late 1970s and 1980s.

As we will explore further in the next chapter, a variety of white supremacists and anti-government militants struggled with membership and focus during the post–World War II years. They consolidated in the 1970s and became more active in the 1980s. Like Joan Andrews and some of her colleagues, some of these racists and radicals emerged from the domestic antiwar scene or from the war in Vietnam itself to embrace a new cause. By the late 1970s, various factions of the far right put aside their differences and joined umbrella organizations such as the Aryan Nations. They began to train in paramilitary fashion. Patriot militia groups, which were simultaneously emerging, did the same. Why? What compelled these white people to become militant?

One general line of thinking foregrounds the issue of race, specifically of how the state began to see and treat white people differently from how it had before. Scholars have described the farm crisis of the 1970s and 1980s, when "three federal policies operating two decades in advance helped create the crash"—an economic catastrophe for farm and ranch owners in the United States.[36] "The results were hundreds of farm foreclosures and economic depressions throughout American farming communities, many of which have not recovered. It is in this wreckage—generated by financial ruin and deep frustration at ineffectual government policies—that extremist rhetoric took hold in some pockets of the farming West and Midwest."[37] That rhetoric led to the militancy of the U.S. farming population, which had gradually whitened over the past fifty years.

We can see the farm crisis in the context of a general shift in policies and attitudes regarding white poverty. In the 1960s, the War on Poverty portrayed white indigency as an exceptional and awful thing that could be corrected through social programs. By the 1990s the federal government had begun to treat "poor whites" more like they had "urban Blacks": as degenerates whose lifestyle choices, drug use, and family structures perpetuated a "culture of poverty."[38] Some white men resented being condemned for poverty that was not of their making and struggled to make sense of their white manhood in changing times of greater equality for women, people of color, and members of the LGBTQ community. Motivated in part by such resentment, these militant racists, so-called "rural radicals," and anti-statist patriots began using guns and bombs to attack their enemies.

In the early 1980s there was further consolidation in ranks and goals. By 1984 George Dietz had launched the first electronic bulletin board posts, precursors to the internet, to facilitate fast, clandestine communication nationwide.[39] According to Kathleen Belew, 1983–84 was the year that Aryan Nations adherents adopted an anti-state attitude, that is, a desire to thwart federal governance, to wage a war against what they believed was a "Zionist occupied government," a conspiracy theory that was built on centuries of antisemitism.[40] The culmination of these activities was the Oklahoma City bombing of 1995, the largest domestic terrorist attack to date. Prior attacks led to charges of murder and sedition in the early 1980s. A Jewish radio host, Alan Berg, was murdered in 1984. Among those charged for the murder was David Lane. Around 1985, Lane penned a credo in fourteen words that would motivate white supremacists for decades. It sounded very much like Randall Terry's italicized emphasis on "our own children and their futures." Lane's famous fourteen words are "We must secure the existence of our people and a future for White children."

Operation Rescue's Randall Terry chose words that are clearly reflective of pro-life rhetoric. But are they also reflective of the white supremacist concern over white children, their futures, and the so-called white race? How parallel were the movements against abortion and for white power in the 1980s and beyond? When and where did these parallel movements intersect? Some might point to the fact that Joan Andrews teamed up with a former Ku Klux Klan member, John Burt, after she was released from prison in 1986. Andrews taught her rescue tactics to evangelicals, indicating a commingling of the white supremacist world and the antiabortion militants.[41] Burt was known to display a Confederate flag and has been identified as the man who goaded Michael Griffin into killing an abortion provider, Dr. David Gunn, in 1993.

Indeed, the 1990s ushered in unprecedented antiabortion violence. Seven reproductive health care workers, including medical personnel, office workers, and security, died at the hands of antiabortion murderers. Existing scholarship details these murders and the cultural logic that allowed a movement championing "life" to remain intact and credible after their constituents began, ironically enough, killing for life. How did the movement deflect these murders and the increased violence throughout the 1990s?

Among other points of deflection, women's writing helped to divert attention from the violence. The following two examples, Norma McCorvey's and Abby Johnson's pro-life memoirs, were similar narratives in slightly different contexts with the same political result. They both steered the headlines away from truly horrifying homicides by abortion foes.

Norma McCorvey's Apocalyptic Fundamentalism

McCorvey, the Texas plaintiff in the 1973 case *Roe v. Wade,* has been heralded as a pro-choice hero and then mythologized as a pro-life hero. Her first autobiography, *I Am Roe,* was published in 1994 to document her participation in the landmark case, providing a personal look at how she came to terms with being a historical figure. Two years after that book was published McCorvey changed her tune. Operation Rescue leader Flip Benham led her in a very public conversion to Christianity via a swimming pool baptism in 1996, which was a public relations coup for the antiabortion movement. Her 1997 memoir, *Won by Love,* details how she became aligned with Operation Rescue. Later McCorvey admitted that the baptism publicity stunt and her supposed conversion itself were a matter of money; Operation Rescue paid her a salary and expenses.

Won by Love perpetuates the idea that women must be protected from the supposedly evil cabal of greedy, unclean, money-grubbing doctors who provide abortions. *Won by Love* also perpetuates the antisemitism of Paul Marx and Mildred Jefferson's contention that doctors are corrupt and nefarious "executioners." Moreover, *Won by Love* depicts McCorvey's conversion away from the pro-choice movement and to the pro-life movement with gothic tales of haunted clinics and ghostly children representing the babies supposedly murdered.

In *Won by Love,* as I detail elsewhere, readers witness how McCorvey contends with many spooky incidents.[42] She hears auditory hallucinations of children running and laughing when none are around. She thinks she sees a head floating by in a clinic storage room where, purportedly, "babies were stacked like cordwood." She experiences guilt-ridden fantasies about attending church, fearing she will be subject to the wrath of God in a spectacular way that she imagines as an avid fan of Stephen King novels. In this way *Won by Love* self-consciously traffics in the horror genre.

This gothic sensibility that infuses the book is the backdrop to xenophobic, antisemitic, and racist depictions of so-called enemies of life. The doctor, a foreigner who speaks in broken English, is portrayed as unhygienic, unhealthy, and exploitive of workers and clients. The attorney Gloria Allred is referred to as a "Yiddish mamma" and a "media junkie," perpetuating stereotypes of Jews as manipulators of mass media. Minor players in the plot, such as the clinic guards, convey racist stereotypes of would-be Black rapists preying on white women. Moreover, given that McCorvey's conversion to pro-life Christianity meant a conversion away from a lesbian lifestyle, *Won by Love* also reinforced homophobia. As a book, then, *Won by Love* reflected the antiabortion movement's apocalyptic story of a "conspiracy against life," articulating in gothic terms how "enemies of life"—lesbians, foreigners, Jews, and Black people—were conspiring to kill babies.

Published in 1997, *Won by Love* served to deflect the fact that seven abortion providers had been gunned down in the 1990s up to that point. The movement had devolved into domestic terrorism. *Won by Love* steered attention away from the violence. McCorvey was celebrated as someone who had seen the light and who had joined the fight to "save babies."

Won by Love only implicitly suggests *whose* babies are imperiled. A year after its publication, Norma McCorvey was a featured speaker at a Jubilation event, where Christian Identity adherents gathered. The May 1998 event was advertised in the *Jubilee Newspaper,* which used the at-the-time "usual conspiracy theories about 'Clintonistas,' 'globalism,' and 'Zionism'—not to mention frequent reference to abortion, multiculturalism, immigration, and homosexuality—to call for the establishment of a theocracy."[43] These white supremacists' embrace of Norma McCorvey after her conversion proved how salient her book—and the apocalyptic story of antiabortion work—was to those who understand "killing babies" to mean taking "our" white children.

Thirteen years after McCorvey's *Won by Love* appeared, Abby Johnson's memoir told practically the same story for a twenty-first-century audience. Johnson's book, *Unplanned,* featured another woman who was committed to abortion rights and worked at a clinic before she was born again into the pro-life fold. Johnson's story repeats most of *Won by Love*'s characterization of the abortion "industry" as a profiteering racket that exploits women who need to be protected.

Abby Johnson's Tea Party Populism

Indeed, the financial aspect of the exploitation supposedly committed by the abortion "industry" is paramount in Johnson's story. Although *Unplanned* is very similar to *Won by Love* as a conversion story, Johnson's memoir demonstrates a dynamic that is particularly attuned to the Tea Party populism of its time. The Tea Party emerged as a response to the election of the first African American president of the United States, Barack Obama. In 2010, the year Johnson published her memoir, antiabortion activity was ramped up because of the midterm elections. Johnson's story highlights a key antiabortion development of that time, a project called 40 Days for Life. Presented as an innovation in prayer service, the forty days of prayer involved stationing at least two antiabortionists outside the clinic where Johnson worked every hour of the day for over a month. For clinic workers this sustained antiabortion presence was an established tactic of surveillance and intimidation.[44] The relentlessness was especially intimidating because just four months earlier, on May 31, 2009, Kansas physician George Tiller was murdered—the first homicide of an abortion provider since before 9/11. Johnson's conversion came in the midst of the news of Tiller's death and amid the forty days of constant clinic harassment.

According to *Unplanned,* Johnson was asked to help a physician in her clinic with an ultrasound-guided abortion. Viewing this abortion was a revelation and the catalyst for her conversion, Johnson maintains, which seems incredible given her position as the director of the clinic and given that ultrasounds prior to abortions are standard procedure.[45] This dramatic response to the ultrasound echoes the gothic description offered in *The Silent Scream,* a 1984 film that used the then novel technology of ultrasound to show the "truth" about abortion.[46] Moreover, Johnson's self-consciously gradual conversion culminates in church—just as McCorvey's does. Johnson's story even uses some of the same affective descriptions of supernatural spirituality that McCorvey's features. But it was Johnson's supposed gradual "discovery of Planned Parenthood's revenue agenda" and its "money-first attitude toward abortion, especially late-term abortions," that led to her claim that women are "victims" of proabortion profiteers who seek to exploit them for financial and political gain.[47]

This focus on money supplants the focus in McCorvey's memoir on the unsavory people in the abortion "industry." While *Won by Love* demonizes McCorvey's depraved coworkers-turned-adversaries with racist, antisemitic, xenophobic, and homophobic depictions, the conflict in *Unplanned* is focused primarily on a supposed demand for increased abortion revenue. The financial exploitation is the depraved situation in *Unplanned*. Those who don't understand it are deemed stupid. This includes the book's protagonist, Abby. While this is a memoir, and the protagonist and the author are therefore the same person, I think it is helpful to refer to the protagonist of the book as Abby. Abby is a character in the memoir, and I distinguish her from Abby Johnson, the author, to maintain an awareness of how much creative license is at work in the narration of the plot of *Unplanned*. Johnson narrates Abby as someone who is at first dismissed as a naive idiot. For example, when Abby protests to her boss, she is cruelly belittled for not understanding a dubious distinction:

"But we are nonprofit!" I declared in a passionate plea.

"Abby," I was told pointedly, "nonprofit is a tax status, not a business status." I was ordered to get my priorities straight—which meant I had to get my revenue up. As the meeting continued, I sat there stunned.[48]

On several occasions Abby is dismissed when she raises questions or objections to the clinic's financial plan. This persistence is then met with disciplining by her boss. She is called to the headquarters in Houston and "formally reprimanded."[49] She is at first incredulous and then resents her superiors. The narrative becomes a classic worker's story of disbelief at management's behavior. "In my eight years with Planned Parenthood, I'd never received anything but praise. Never a single black mark, never a warning. I'd never received so much as a correction, much less a reprimand." After signing an acknowledgment of the reprimand, Abby reflected. "I felt like a whipped dog—and, I confess, a resentful one."[50] The incident therefore only strengthens Abby's convictions that the clinic is threatened by her probing questions about money.

After helping the doctor with an abortion, Johnson finally decides to leave the clinic. She also seeks help and solidarity from those who have been monitoring the clinic as part of the 40 Days for Life project. Subsequently, Planned Parenthood accuses her of tampering with the clinic's records. Abby's former employer then seeks an injunction against her on the grounds she had jeopardized patient records and privacy. A courtroom drama ensues. Aided by a pro-life lawyer, Abby ultimately prevails. She not only wins the case but is also presented as the moral victor. Her resentment at being made to feel stupid becomes contempt for those who she says victimized her. Her new pro-life friends that heretofore have been maligned and mocked by the clinic staff help Abby reverse the accusation that she was the dunce.

The antiabortionists are depicted as so humble, unassuming, humorous, and good-naturedly righteous that seeing any of them as any kind of danger or doofus is nonsensical. In the first part of the book, told from the point of view of a clinic administrator, the antiabortionists are depicted as dangerous and stupid. In the second part they are shown as calmly condescending toward those who had so obviously maligned and misjudged them. Abby expresses this when she describes their courtroom defeat:

> They moved quickly to pack everything away, and then they began shuffling out through a side door. Clearly they had no desire to speak to me or the media. In fact, they looked as if they were in shock. I didn't see an angry face among them. It was more as if they couldn't fathom what had just happened. I thought about how much I'd loved this organization, how I'd wanted to serve and please them. Now they looked like a sad and sorry lot to me.[51]

Unplanned thus narrates an important transition: individuals who resent feeling put down move from a sense of victimhood to a sense of being on top, in the know, and morally superior to those who demeaned them. This important transition has historical roots that tie it to both Christian fundamentalism and right-wing populism.

According to Lawrence Rosenthal, the tendency to malign fundamentalists as stupid or backward goes back to the news portrayal of anti-evolutionists of the 1920s. The Scopes trial, often known as the "monkey trial," occasioned a level of derision of fundamentalist religion and its populist practitioners that has remained current for a century. There is a straight line between H. L. Mencken's characterization of the "yokels" and the "booboisie" of the anti-evolution movement and, say, Bill Maher's relentless characterization of American right populists as ignorant and superstitious on his cable TV program and in his film, *Religulous*.[52]

Abby faces accusations of being ignorant and imprudent from her coworkers and boss. Her internal monologues give voice to fears of being called superstitious or hysterical. As a character, Abby is someone who fits precisely the role of the virtuous one who faces the mean girls until she buddies up with those also demeaned and, together, they reign superior as their tormentors get their comeuppance. Because this narrative structure is commonplace in popular culture, it functions also in political terms. Again, I turn to Lawrence Rosenthal for explanation:

> One of the dynamics of a populist mobilization—when populism on the right becomes a political force or a political movement or when it has been roused by a demagogue—is that the populists' sense of resentment is transformed into contempt. The looked-down-upon now collectively feel themselves looking down. The populists together become contemptuous of the elite. This is the social psychological step, the flip-flop, that's needed to turn populist sentiment into a political mobilization. It is emotionally transformative at both the organizational and individual levels, empowering the movement to act, to cure the pervasive and festering one-down sensitivity [as opposed to one-upping someone] that is resentment's characteristic mood.[53]

In *Unplanned,* Abby cures that sense of being put down with the action of converting to the antiabortion side. Her success in court ends up making the losing side look elitist and yet also stupid because they do not win.

In the process, *Unplanned* assures those who participate in the 40 Days for Life campaign that their work is successful. Antiabortion harassment should continue unabated, according to the book. *Unplanned* functioned to deflect from the news of Tiller's murder, just as McCorvey's conversion steered media attention away from the pro-life murders of the 1990s. And, just like McCorvey, Johnson, it would appear, was also offered money to come to the other side. An investigation by journalist Nate Blakeslee turned up evidence—including Johnson's own Facebook post—saying that she had received a negative performance review, she feared she was going to be fired, she was considering bankruptcy, she was tired of harassment and death threats, and she had no support from her family, who were not pro-choice. According to a friend and coworker of Johnson's, the antiabortionists across the fence offered her at least three thousand dollars in speaking fees to convert to an antiabortion stance.[54]

Blakeslee's investigation also revealed that Johnson's account of the abortion she witnessed, which supposedly had been a catalyst for her conversion, was not supported by Planned Parenthood's records. She had stated that the abortion happened at thirteen weeks' gestation and the woman terminating her pregnancy was African American, but the records show that no abortion that day had been performed on a pregnancy more advanced than ten weeks. Moreover, the only Black patient who terminated a pregnancy that day was only six weeks along. Nor was her gory account of the abortion, including her claim to have seen "an unborn baby fighting back," supported by science since a fetus does not have the neurobiological capacity to feel pain at thirteen weeks.[55]

Johnson's memoir, and the film it inspired, are incredible. Johnson is an unreliable narrator. Nevertheless, her writing functions to replicate unsavory depictions of abortion providers that pro-life people seem to find irresistible. It also deflected the antiabortion violence that was grabbing headlines at the time. And it demonstrated the "social psychological step, the flip-flop, that's needed to turn populist sentiment into a political mobilization." The fact that she has lied is part of a tradition of justifiable dishonesty that another woman warrior wrote about. In *The Army of God* manual, Rachelle "Shelley" Shannon and her coauthors explain why antiabortionists are as justified in lying as they are in killing.

Shelley Shannon's Backyard-Buried Book

Shelley Shannon was part of the movement that began bombing buildings and shooting people. She took the violent aspects of Joan Andrews's rescue movement—blockading, sabotaging, and setting fire to clinics—to a new level. Shannon is (in)famous for shooting Dr. George Tiller, a physician who worked in Kansas. When Shannon reached for a gun in hopes of murdering Tiller in 1993, the doctor flung up his arm, bent at the elbow. He was giving Shannon the bird, so to speak, showing her his middle finger. This action blocked the bullets fired by Shannon. She succeeded in shooting his arms, which were unintentionally shielding his chest.[56] This murder attempt, if successful, would have been added to the seven homicides committed by pro-life terrorists in the 1990s—murders often claimed to be the work of the Army of God, a term that was first coined in 1982, when a perpetrator who kidnapped an abortion doctor and his wife reported the crime to the FBI.[57] More a mentality than a member organization, the Army of God was deemed responsible for violent criminal actions against abortion providers and facilities throughout the 1980s and 1990s, some of which were never solved.

This violence was justified in a document called *The Army of God Manual*, a copy of which was found in Shelley Shannon's backyard in 1993. Shannon coauthored the text while imprisoned with other extremists in 1988.[58] A careful reading of the manual shows how much the militant antiabortion movement had in common with the white power and militia movements that were simultaneously gathering steam toward anti-state terror.

Most readings of the text remark on the fact that it has a lot of instructions for making bombs and explosives and information on other ways to sabotage or destroy reproductive health care clinics.[59] In this way it is similar to Joseph Scheidler's *Closed: 99 Ways to Stop Abortion* and has been seen as the antiabortionists' rendition of *The Anarchist Cookbook*, a 1971 countercultural how-to manual for do-it-yourself manufacturing of explosives for opposing the Vietnam War. While most of *The Army of God Manual* is devoted to the making of incendiary materials, the manual contains key discussions that illuminate the ideological and tactical similarities with, and connections to, the bourgeoning white supremacist and militia movements. These key discussions have been overshadowed by the bomb-making aspects of the manual. Additionally, some parts of the manual are not available online or elsewhere. Archival copies of the manual reveal what is excised from the version of the manual available on the Army of God website.

I received a photocopy of *The Army of God Manual* in the 1990s from the archives of Political Research Associates. It reveals the

ideological similarities among antiabortionists, white supremacists, and militia groups. One key idea is that white, Western culture is disintegrating. In *The Army of God Manual* this idea resonates with the Christian eschatological awareness of the end-times,
a sense of a final conflict with anti-Christian forces, represented by
those orchestrating the "child-killing industry."[60] Throughout
most of the manual, comparisons between abortion and the
Holocaust situate the perceived conflict much as Joan Andrews
had seen it in her early years: abortion is equated with the state-
sanctioned mass murder epitomized by Nazi Germany. The comparison is faulty in that legal abortion provision is not mandated or
carried out by the state but is an option for individuals to consider,
yet it reflects the orientation that the past is not something we want
to return to. The manual oscillates between this fear of returning to
a particular horror of the past and the need to fend off the future
demise of the West.

> We are living during the rapid decline of western thought and cul-
> ture. It is almost impossible for us to think logically and then act
> based on that logic. All of our education teaches us non-reason. All
> of our experience (in this dying culture) teaches us to sense and
> experience what is happening around us, but not to act based on
> that experience.

The Christian right circulated these fears throughout the last quar-
ter of the twentieth century as a fear of the end-times; most scholars point to the 1970 publication of *The Late Great Planet Earth* as
popularizing such apocalypticism. The Christian right channeled
this apocalyptic fear to mobilize evangelical voters and shape electoral politics in their favor. Additionally, white supremacists in the

1970s and onward framed this same apocalyptic fear of the decline of Western civilization as the dying out of the white race and a justification for a holy race war. Similarly, *The Army of God Manual* asserts this fear of the "dying culture" of the West as a justification "to act" that was not merely political and was something beyond protest.

What kind of action does *The Army of God Manual* call for?

Most of the manual appears to be promoting bombings and arson. As a prologue to the catalog of such "covert ways to stop abortion," the manual includes a six-page discussion titled "Rahab's Justifiable Lie." This discussion is left out of the version of the manual on the Army of God website. It is, basically, an appeal to good Christians to relinquish the idea that lying and deception are morally bad. The authors walk the reader through various real-world scenarios in which telling lies is acceptable: posting a "Beware of the Dog" sign on your property, for instance, to scare off would-be burglars when you really don't own a dog.

Turning to the Bible, the discussion features the Old Testament character of Rahab, who lied about her neighbor at Jericho to save others. She is used as "an early example of pious subterfuge." After an examination of the ninth commandment, "Thou shalt not bear false witness against thy neighbor," her example of Christian "falsehood" is then contrasted with "situation ethics," a supposedly corrupt secular concept that purportedly leads to unprincipled moral relativism. The upshot is this: "The Christian has no obligation to speak truthfully to those who have forfeited the right to hear the truth." One answer to the question of "in what contexts may the justifiable lie be rightly used" is, finally, that "he may speak falsehoods to totalitarian authorities when life itself is imperiled."

This robust defense of deceit precedes sections detailing ways of blocking entrances to clinics and sabotaging their operations by obtaining a "non-explosive demolition agent," "compromising alarm systems," creating "improvised explosives," mixing a "poor man's plastic explosive," and "making your own detonators for explosives." These explicit instructions indicate that the action needed amid the supposed demise of Western civilization is criminal deceit leading to destruction of property.

If the "enterprising" antiabortionist who is willing to undertake these unlawful acts needs further information and solidarity, the manual suggests looking at resources compiled by militia groups. The reader is told to go to a bookstore or newsstand and seek out "survivalist magazines such as *Soldier of Fortune, Survivalist,* and others of the genre. If you can't afford to pay the cover price (they can be steep), go through them and write down the names and addresses of the publishers of survivalist books and literature. Go home and call them or write to them and request a catalog."[61] *The Army of God Manual* proceeds to list the contact information and addresses for such outfits in Colorado, Washington, Texas, and Arizona. This instruction and the detailed list demonstrate that antiabortion militants were aware of the militia movement in the 1990s and were, moreover, seeking out connections with these antigovernment patriot and white supremacist "survivalist" groups.

Indeed, Shannon was familiar "with local militia men and white supremacists."[62] According to Karissa Haugeberg, some antiabortion activists responded to Shannon's shooting of Dr. George Tiller by disavowing any connection to her, perpetuating the strategy of leaderless resistance by declaring, "This woman is totally responsible for her actions. This woman acted as a lone ranger vigilante."[63] Others, especially antiabortionist colleagues from Oregon—including Advocates for Life Ministries employees Cathy Ramey, Andrew Burnett, and Paul deParrie (about whom we'll learn in the next chapter)—issued responses of support for her near-fatal attack of the physician.[64] Shelley Shannon's protégé, Scott Roeder, is the best-known example of a crossover member belonging to both militia and antiabortion groups. In the 1990s he was involved with the Freemen Militia, Operation Rescue, and the Army of God. Shannon and Roeder corresponded while she was in prison, where he also visited her repeatedly. He finished the job that Shannon first attempted; he shot and killed Dr. Tiller in 2009.[65]

Why didn't the FBI simply round up the group as a criminal organization when they unearthed the manual in Shannon's back-yard? This is another key similarity between antiabortion militants and the white power and militia movements. The organization of their criminal activity is purposefully designed to avoid criminal culpability. Here is how *The Army of God Manual* puts it:

> Fortunately the A.O.G. (Army of God) folks are not a real army, humanly speaking. It is a real Army, and God is the General and Commander-in-Chief. The soldiers, however, do not usually communicate with one another. Very few have ever met each other. And when they do, each is usually unaware of the other's soldier's status. That is why the Feds will never stop this Army. Never.[66]

The white power and militia movements describe this same idea as "leaderless resistance." Leaderless resistance is an alternative to the typical pyramid-style organization that features a leader at the top of a hierarchy with rank-and-file individuals below who do the leader's bidding. It is referred to as cell-like organization in which smaller groups carry out their own operations without direct instruction from any lead individual or overseeing council. As the quotation above attests, this kind of organizing does not require that people who share the same goal talk with each other about plans of destruction. They don't even know each other. Therefore, when criminal acts are committed, no one except the individual who did the deed can be held accountable. As early as 1982, the Army of God appears to have deployed the leaderless style of resistance that the militia and white power movements also embraced in the 1980s.[67]

This resistance to the federal government is the most significant similarity with organized white supremacists that the Army of God's manual articulates. The manual ends in a way that cements that similarity. After its pages instructing one how to blockade and sabotage clinic property, the manual in its last pages contains an epilogue that includes a "declaration" of decisive homicidal action and war against the government. This epilogue appears to have been added in 1992. Scholars who take note of it remark that it "introduced the justification for attacking human beings."[68] But it was more than marking a shift in rhetoric or the intention to commit what they saw as justifiable homicide. It was more than calling for an escalation in violence to the point of assassinations. It was a naming of the enemy as well. The epilogue named the United States government as the enemy and declared opposing abortion a matter of opposing the state, revealing an ideological intersection with white supremacism and patriot militias, all imbued with an apocalyptic urgency.

The epilogue's change in tactics, from focusing on property damage to an emphasis on murdering people, was couched in discussions that clearly aligned antiabortion militants with the militia and white power movements. In rather abruptly shifting the focus from the making of incendiary devices to taking up arms, the last pages of the manual argue that in response to the decline of the West and a federal government that made laws they saw as perpetuating "death camps," it was time to take up arms—not just bombs—and begin killing people. In the section titled "The Declaration," the coauthors write, "Beginning officially with the passage of the *Freedom of Choice Act*—we, the remnant of God-fearing men and women of the United States of Amerika, do officially declare war on the entire child killing industry." Presenting federal legislation as the last straw, this declaration continues to assert that efforts at "passive-resistance" to abortion provision were "mocked," and that the Army of God has no other choice but to wage war instead of limiting themselves to protest, sabotage, and harassment.

> No longer! All of the options have expired. Our most Dread Sovereign Lord God requires that whosoever sheds man's blood, by man shall his blood be shed. Not out of hatred of you, but out of love for the persons you exterminate, we are forced to take arms against you. Our life for yours—a simple equation. Dreadful. Sad. Reality, nonetheless. You shall not be tortured at our hands. Vengeance belongs to God only. However, execution is rarely gentle.

With this, the final paragraph of the manual's narrative, the coauthors walk back what had been a consideration earlier in the text. Prior to this declaration, the suggestion of assassinating physicians was dismissed. "Don't construe this to mean I recommend executing abortionists. I do not," reports the so-called Mad Gluer in a section of the manual titled "Interview." Instead, the Mad Gluer proposes to remove doctors' thumbs so that they cannot perform medical procedures. "For the rest, I think thumblessness a small price to pay. 'better to enter into life maimed . . .' (I finally found a present day application for those words)." In contrast to this aim of maiming physicians (and in this weird symmetry to John Brockhoeft imagining himself being dismembered), the concluding declaration resoundingly rejects the idea: "You shall not be tortured at our hands." Instead, the exhortation now is "to take arms against you" and take a physician's or clinic worker's life even if it means the shooter will, presumably through the death penalty, lose his or her own.

This proposed matter of "execution," then, signifies a commitment to homicide with "arms" as a way to oppose the "entire child killing industry" sanctioned through federal legislation. With the federal government as much in its sights as individual reproductive health care professionals, *The Army of God Manual* begins with convincing its readers to deploy "justifiable lies" and ends convincing them to commit what they saw as justifiable homicide. In so doing, the Army of God aligns more closely than ever with the militia and white supremacist movements that declared their racial holy war against a so-called Zionist Occupied Government.

With the emphasis on firearms as well as bombs, *The Army of God Manual* also announced its natural kinship with mainstream and militant Americans who saw owning any kind of gun as an American right. The National Rifle Association (NRA) had throughout the 1980s and 1990s become a powerful lobbying group whose aim was blocking any regulation of firearms. As a summer camp counselor, I had earned my sharpshooter medal in the late 1970s and was trained to be an NRA instructor at the camp's shooting range. I witnessed in my lifetime how the organization radically shifted away from primarily promoting skills, sportsmanship, and firearm safety to primarily fearmongering about the government's supposed intention to disarm the people by confiscating all guns and dismantling the Second Amendment.[69] The radicalization of the National Rifle Association emerged alongside the embrace of firearms by antiabortion militants, patriot militia groups, and organized white supremacists. These right-wing movements moved closer together, wielding guns as instruments of their shared strategy of leaderless resistance.

Where Are They Now?

When Shelley Shannon aimed at Dr. Tiller in 1993 she was fulfilling the vision spelled out in *The Army of God Manual* that she had cowritten and buried in her backyard. In 2009 she learned that her target had been gunned down by Scott Roeder, her friend since 1993 who visited her more than twenty-five times while she was in prison.[70] By 2018 she had served her sentence and left the carceral system.[71] She entered a world much changed. Taking up arms was now part of a gun culture in which mass shootings were an epidemic. White power and patriot groups now abounded. And a sizable number of white women helped elect a president who compensated for his own deeply misogynistic and sinful ways by promising the Supreme Court to antiabortion evangelicals.[72]

The apocalyptic fever of the 1990s that could have been explained away by fin de siècle hysteria was now ratcheted as high as ever. That apocalyptic fever was awash with gothic imagery that had prevailed in pro-life women's memoirs. That gothic imagery became repackaged in stories of Pizzagate and other tales of salacious, demonic sexual exploitation of women, girls, and infants. Pizzagate refers to a fictitious sex-slavery operation that Hillary Clinton was supposedly running in the back room of a Washington, DC, pizza parlor. The depravity narratives that were once the purview of the Cold War anticommunists and antisemites who inspired Mildred Jefferson's conviction that doctors were really "social executioners" were mutating faster and becoming more alarming in a world of social media. In 2018, in addition to tales of a satanic cabal running the abortion industry full of ghostly children and floating heads and operating in allegiance to a "doctrine of demons," depraved Democrats were, according to a supposed insider named Q, systematically stealing "our" children for blood rituals and sexual slavery.

Those Democrats, according to such conspiracism, were not only stealing children; they also stole an election. Abby Johnson was employed as a key speaker at two events that promoted the lie that the 2020 presidential election was stolen. On December 12, 2020, she spoke at the Jericho March, a demonstration that was officially dedicated to "election integrity" and that unofficially was a rehearsal for the later rally before the assault on the Capitol.[73] According to the Anti-Defamation League, "the Jericho March included many mainstream speakers including former White House Security Advisor Michael Flynn and My Pillow CEO Michael Lindell," as well as Abby Johnson.[74] Jericho March "also featured speeches by anti-government conspiracy theorist Alex Jones, as well as Stewart Rhodes, who founded the right-wing extremist group Oath Keepers. QAnon and Three Percenter flags and signage were in evidence at the Jericho March."[75] Following the Jericho March and prayer rally was a battle for the streets that journalists have recognized as a lead-up to January 6, 2021. On that day as well as on December 12, 2020, Abby Johnson was in the tent at the Save America Rally organized by Women for America First. This was the event for which militants had trained, the event that Trump had promised them "will be wild." In anticipation of that day, Johnson posted on social media her support of Trump and notified her followers, "Meet me at marchtosaveamerica.com. I'm speaking at the #WildProtest!!! Thank you to @ali and his amazing team. Let's do this!!!!"[76] In thanking "@ali," Johnson was acknowledging Ali Alexander, the chief organizer of several "stop the steal" rallies who not only believed and promoted the false claim that the election was fraudulent but also posted warnings that "America is demonically possessed" by "globalists" as evidenced by weather crises in the winter of 2021.[77]

Today's discussions of stolen children and stolen elections reflect a half century of antiabortion conspiracism, gothic depravity narratives, and apocalyptic urgency that pro-life women's writings from the 1970s to the 1990s (and beyond) exemplify. Mildred Jefferson was adept at both embodying and denying the history of Black women's reproductive control in America. She was able to both symbolize and deflect Black women's actual lived experience by adopting the conspiracism promoted by Paul Marx. Not only did that conspiracism prevail in subsequent pro-life women's writings; so, too, did the antisemitism, xenophobia, and racism. The memoir of Norma McCorvey coded these hateful ideologies in the demonization of her coworkers at the clinic in the same decade that Joan Andrews's antiwar opposition to abortion gave way to Shelley Shannon's war against abortion providers. The right-to-life movement based on individual rights for the fetus moved into a pro-life apocalyptic battle for Western culture that then entailed property damage in the name of "rescue" and, finally, homicide for God's sake. Each step along the way, antiabortionists were traveling a path parallel to—and sometimes intersecting with—white power and patriot militia members. The ideological and tactical similarities among all three right-wing movements—including the demise of Western culture, the leaderless resistance, the privileging of guns, and the declaration of the federal government as an enemy— are reflected in antiabortion women's writing.

4 *Lone Wolves, Abortion Abolitionists, and the Men Who Penned Them*

In anticipation of the thirtieth anniversary of a bombing that made "New World Order" a household phrase, I was invited to a podcast discussion about the man convicted of the bombing.[1] This wasn't, as one might think, about the Oklahoma City bombing and Timothy McVeigh. That event in 1995 was the most damaging act of domestic terrorism in the United States. McVeigh targeted the Alfred P. Murrah Federal Building and killed 168 people. He is often seen as the single perpetrator of these murders, a so-called lone wolf. His buddy, Terry Nichols, was also convicted on federal charges of co-conspiracy and manslaughter; the state of Oklahoma later convicted him of murder. But most people think it was primarily McVeigh's doing because he was the one who drove a truck filled with explosives and left it in the parking garage beneath the building. Never mind that he was connected to a variety of white power groups, attended militia meetings, and made phone calls to a neo-Nazi compound just prior to the bombing.[2] Likewise, the bombing I was asked to comment on is most often thought to have been the efforts of one man alone: Eric Rudolph.

In 1996, just about a year after McVeigh's murderous blast in Oklahoma, Eric Rudolph set off a bomb in Centennial Park, Atlanta, a busy spot where people were gathered for the summer Olympics. After the explosion a letter signed "the Army of God" circulated, taking responsibility for the detonation that injured more than one hundred people and caused one woman to die from a heart attack. The letter ended with "Death to the New World Order." These bombings—McVeigh's and Rudolph's—were only about fourteen months apart.

The messages they aimed to convey were similar. McVeigh was a proponent of white nationalism. According to Chip Berlet and Matthew Lyons, "All credible evidence suggests that Timothy McVeigh, convicted in the Oklahoma City Bombing, was a neo-Nazi trying to move the less militant and largely defensive militia movement into more aggressive insurrectionist action."[3] In today's parlance we might call him an accelerationist because he wanted to accelerate a race war. McVeigh's truck bomb was fashioned after one described in *The Turner Diaries,* an underground novel written by an influential neo-Nazi named William Pierce. Rudolph's bombing spree also appears to be as much provocation as protest. Rudolph named the enemy as the New World Order, a phrase used by far-right militants who believed the federal government was implementing a menacing new social order run by a secret Jewish cabal of corrupt and depraved elites. Today this paranoid belief is expressed as a fear of the "deep state" run by shady "globalists." These ideas derived from nineteenth-century antisemitism but were gaining traction among the far right when Rudolph bombed Centennial Park. Rudolph's choice of target, the Olympics, exemplified the multinational collaboration and cultural pluralism that purportedly characterized the so-called New World Order.

Rudolph subsequently bombed two women's health care facilities and a nightclub frequented by lesbians. Because he bombed the abortion clinics, his terrorist work is not seen as the same kind of terrorist work that McVeigh did. It is usually relegated to the history of antiabortion violence. The podcasters who invited me to talk with them about Rudolph had the same idea I do: these acts of domestic terrorism are not so different. Both men were aiming to provoke and accelerate militant action. Moreover, both bombers were probably not the single perpetrators—the lone wolves—they appeared to be.

Recognizing the similarities of various far-right militants and mindsets operating throughout the second half of the twentieth century and today is important. After supporters of Donald Trump attacked the United States Capitol on January 6, 2021, journalists recognized how a variety of far-right activists had come together during the riot. They readily recognized in the crowd white supremacists, patriot militia groups, Christian nationalists, and people who believed in conspiracy theories (such as QAnon) about a new social order secretly being planned by corrupt elites who target children for sexually depraved acts and demonic sacrifice. But only a relatively small number of reporters recognized the antiabortionists in the mix.[4] None of these right-wing groups is a hermetically sealed unit. Their members and adherents intermingle.

The harrowing incident at the Capitol raised questions of how connected various aspects of the far right were and are. My answer is that these movements, led mostly by white men, are parallel and sometimes intersecting. Flashpoints from the 1970s, '80s, and '90s demonstrate how these far-right movements evolved independently but also synergistically.

Parallel Movements: Antiabortion, Militia, White Power

The Stage-Setting Seventies

In the 1970s far-right movements were in disarray, but there were visionaries who were busy recruiting and writing. White suprema-cists produced two important works of fiction that helped various factions envision a revolution. William Pierce wrote *The Turner Diaries* in serial form, with new episodes appearing in issues of the tabloid publication *Attack!*[5] Another white supremacist novel that appeared in the early 1970s, *The Camp of the Saints,* was written by Jean Raspail in France.[6] These novels helped white supremacists picture their enemies and visualize revolutionary violence. In Raspail's book, the problem was decidedly immigrants from the Global South who were presumed to ruin Western civilization. In Pierce's case, it was "the system." Blaming "the system" was a bril-liant move. Pierce decided to use that term when there was much debate in racist circles. Who was holding back the white man the most? Some said Black people. Some said Jews. Pierce's term made this debate moot for all practical purposes. In *The Turner Diaries,* "the system" was simultaneously the Jews who were in charge of the federal government, the Black thugs who did their bidding, and the immigrants, mixed-race couples, and homosexuals who were considered race traitors and therefore accomplices to tyranny.

While white supremacists were explaining through fiction who their enemies were, rural radicals were staking claims to a citizen-ship that was not encumbered by federal definitions or laws, including income tax. Vigilante groups in the 1970s called Posse Comitatus sprung up in the Midwest. "Posse comitatus" is a Latin phrase that means "power of the county," indicating that local gov-ernment is paramount. These groups derived ideas from the nineteenth century, but in the 1970s Posse Comitatus groups became a political trend that articulated U.S. citizenship in racist terms. According to their members, Black people did not qualify as citizens and white citizens were not beholden to the federal government. They considered white men to be "state citizens" or "sovereign citizens"—true Americans, the real people of the United States. Black people, whose citizenship was based on their emancipation and the Fourteenth Amendment, did not count according to this mindset. The Posse Comitatus groups were precursors of the armed militia movement that emerged later and was comprised mostly of Christian patriots.[7]

As vigilantes of rural America were redefining citizenship to explicitly privilege white people, there were populist uprisings in the south and the northeast. Disputes over multiethnic curricula and busing to achieve racial integration in schools were opportunities for a bourgeoning New Right to foment right-wing populism.

A significant conflict happened in my hometown of Charleston, West Virginia, during which a curriculum dispute coalesced a wide swath of right-wing actors in 1974-75. As I discuss in *Reading Appalachia from Left to Right,* the Kanawha County textbook controversy showed a variety of right-wing factions how to shift protest culture from the left to the right. If, in the 1960s and early '70s, someone said "protest," you would likely imagine leftist and progressive causes and activists, such as antiwar student activism, Black nationalist activists protesting police brutality, or labor disputes with coal companies or other union activities. The Kanawha County textbook controversy helped shift that protest culture from the left to the right. The conflict revolved around a multiethnic language arts curriculum that was mandated by the state. Educators felt that the state of West Virginia could benefit from a language curriculum that represented a variety of different voices, including voices of people of color. That controversy brought together a variety of right-wing actors. They included moral crusaders from California, representatives from the Washington, DC–based Heritage Foundation, book-ban leaders from Texas, three KKK organizations from Ohio, Georgia, and Alabama, and internationally influential neo-Nazis. All these outside influencers agitated the conflict, which became violent on more than one occasion. Ideologically, this schoolbook conflict showed conservatives how to reframe their concerns without relying on race-based arguments. They stopped blatantly demanding the segregation of schools and ideas. Instead of playing the race card, they played the parents' rights card. The people who protested the books didn't win that fight in 1975, but it was a crucial time for right-wing influencers to figure out how to deploy populist sentiment in the form of a parents' crusade about maintaining their heritage and culture, understood to be white, Christian, and American.

Some of these protesters from West Virginia were wooed by the Populist Forum, which also fueled white animus via protesting school busing in Massachusetts. With attention from outside agitators, locals from the Charleston area, like locals in Boston, were stoked. According to Rick Perlstein, "Kanawha County, West Virginia, and Boston, Massachusetts: the same sort of politics of rage was coursing through both."[8] Conservative New Right strategists as well as self-described "populist militants" brought together these working-class white protesters. The New Right were invested in wooing the working class because they were desperate to change their image from blue blood to blue collar in order to appear as representatives of "the people" without owning up to wanting to represent white people exclusively.[9]

In the last months of the 1970s, Republicans were working to usher in Ronald Reagan as the first openly pro-life president. The far right was ushering in a new era, too, as evident by two key incidents at the end of the decade.

In the 1979 Greensboro massacre, a nine-car caravan drove into a group of North Carolinians who were protesting the Ku Klux Klan. Gunmen proceeded to kill five protesters. Some of these anti-racist protesters identified as communist in ideology if not party membership. This was a turning point for the far right: no more Klan hoods and secrecy; they were out of hiding and combat ready. Renaming white supremacist work as the work of patriot militias, Glenn Miller was at the forefront of the armed militia movement, which overlapped with the white power movement. It is important to note that not all militia groups were white supremacist, although recent scholarship argues that militias were "overtly paramilitary but covertly racist."[10] But Miller's attack in Greensboro was a bellwether moment that emboldened both movements because he was there to attack *communist* anti-racists. The anti-communism that had fueled the Vietnam War, which had ended just four years earlier, was reasserted on the home front in that fatal conflict in North Carolina in 1979.[11]

The second key event in 1979 for the far right was the first convening of the Aryan Nations. Richard Butler brought a variety of different white supremacist factions together to a compound he built in Coeur d'Alene, Idaho, which had a neo-Nazi church on the property. His plan was to establish a white bastion in the Pacific Northwest. He wanted to take over four or five states adjacent to Idaho and secede from the United States of America to begin a white ethnostate. Some scholars refer to Butler's first convening in Coeur d'Alene as the "nazification" of the Klan.[12] This, too, was a turning point for the far right because ideologically it was clear they had shifted their point of view about who they were fighting. They started to see the so-called international Jew rather than the African American as the white man's worst enemy—or they bypassed the argument altogether and vowed to overthrow "the system," as Pierce called it.

In the antiabortion movement, two key organizations emerged in the late 1970s. The first was the American Life League (ALL), which broke rank with the National Right to Life Committee (NRLC). Scholars recognize ALL as helping antiabortion rhetoric leave behind arguments based on human rights. Judie Brown left NRLC to form ALL "in 1979 with seed money from New Right leader Richard Viguerie." Brown represented an absolutist approach that aimed for the criminalization of abortion while also opposing sexual education in schools, gay rights, and contraception. Leaving behind right-to-life arguments, ALL was aligned with other antiabortionists who expressed disdain for the incremental legal strategies favored by the NRLC.[13]

The second key organization created in 1979 was the Moral Majority, founded by Jerry Falwell under the influence of New Right strategists such as Richard Viguerie and William Marshner. Like the American Life League, the Moral Majority helped shift the voting patterns of Protestant evangelicals in a way that resulted in a landslide victory for Ronald Reagan. His election is often referred to as the Reagan revolution because the New Right poured a lot of money into mobilizing Christian evangelicals for the first time. Historically, evangelicals had not been motivated to get involved in politics because they felt like electoral politics was too worldly. Republicans knew that good Christians felt they should have their eyes on heaven and not worry about the ballot box. When they saw that abortion could help win elections, they pumped a lot of money into organizations designed to woo evangelicals and demonize abortion. The Moral Majority was key in this effort, with a budget of more than three million dollars within the first few years of its existence.[14]

The Innovative Eighties

Among all the changes ushered in by the Reagan revolution, four phenomena made the 1980s a turning point. First, predominant antiabortion organizations such as the NRLC and Americans United for Life welcomed "many newly mobilized evangelicals" and "changed their movement's near-term goal" from creating a constitutional Human Life Amendment to overturning *Roe v. Wade*. According to legal scholar Mary Ziegler, "To achieve this objective, groups like NRLC and AUL fought to influence presidential elections and Supreme Court selections."[15] This new emphasis on electoral politics and the Supreme Court ultimately led to antiabortion groups' efforts to eliminate campaign finance restrictions, which Ziegler argues contributed to the "fall of the Republican establishment" in the twenty-first century.[16] Be that as it may, the early 1980s shift to overturning *Roe* coincided with militancy from antiabortion activists. Both the "mainstream" and the "extreme" factions of the antiabortion movement were amping up their efforts.

Indeed, and second, militant antiabortionists began bombing campaigns in ways that supplemented the so-called rescue movement without necessarily being connected to it. As we saw in the previous chapter, the rescue movement had been focused mostly on obstructing clinic entrances and sabotaging equipment, but in the 1980s arson, which aimed to destroy whole buildings, emerged as a tactic.

Third, white supremacists were stepping up their game. One telltale example of this was mentioned in chapter 3: the Order, a neo-Nazi group inspired by the writings of William Pierce, murdered Alan Berg, a Jewish talk radio personality, in 1984. Induction into the Order underscored the natural affinity neo-Nazis had with pro-life protection of their progeny. Inductees "stood in a circle around a white female infant, who symbolized the race they sought to protect," according to historian Kathleen Belew. They then swore "upon the children and the wombs of our wives," pledging to "deliver our people from the Jew."[17] Like members of the Order, another neo-Nazi, George Dietz, was inducting new recruits with his own innovations.

After popularizing rancor against the educators trying to implement multicultural language arts curriculum in West Virginia in his print magazine, *The Liberty Bell,* George Dietz started publishing the *White Power Report.* Letters to the editor of *White Power Report* attest to how white supremacists used the 1974 Kanawha County textbook controversy to meet, mingle, and recruit.[18] Dietz also inaugurated the Liberty Bell Network in 1984. The Liberty Bell Network was a telephone hotline before Dietz transformed it into the first electronic bulletin board devoted to communications among the far right. Although some scholars attribute the online flourishing of the white power movement to Louis Beam and Tom Metzger,[19] it is important to recognize that Dietz was the progenitor of it. Dietz, more than Beam or Metzger, exemplifies the crossover of "culture wars" campaigns and blatant white power organizing. His insistence on developing online communication to thwart the presumed Jewish-controlled media emerged from his investment in protesting multiethnic schoolbooks. Dietz's innovation allowed for a generation of far-right factions to talk with each other electronically very early in the age of such communication. But the Liberty Bell electronic bulletin board was not the only media innovation in 1984.[20]

Finally, a film titled *The Silent Scream,* narrated by Bernard Nathanson, was released in 1984. It portrayed the fight against abortion as Armageddon. This film was heralded as high-tech media that showed the "truth" of abortion by using ultrasound imaging. The film's power relied more on its narration of the images than on the images themselves.[21] Nevertheless, *The Silent Scream,* like the Liberty Bell network, signaled how both the white power and the antiabortion movements strived in the 1980s to reach more people through media innovations and to become more militant and violent.

The Explosive Nineties

The 1990s was the most murderous decade of the antiabortion movement. In 1991 the rescue movement descended on Wichita, Kansas, for what they called the Summer of Mercy. As mentioned in the introduction, this was a mass mobilization of thousands of people who effectively shut down clinics in the area. Somewhere among the antiabortion rescuers in Wichita, officers found the first copies of the underground writing called *The Army of God Manual.* The manual featured voices of militant antiabortionists, as we saw in the previous chapter's discussion of Shelley Shannon.

There were five main takeaways from that manual. First, the Christians who were fighting against non-Christians had a God-purposed license to lie about what they were doing. The second was that the manual advocated thinking not just about individual fetuses and their rights to life but also about saving Western civilization. In other words, the unborn were invoked as a *collectivity* representing the future of white Western civilization or the future of the nation. A third takeaway from *The Army of God Manual* was a recognition of the militia movement as something that antiabortionists could relate to in terms of tactical goals if not ideological similarity. The fourth is that the epilogue issues a "declaration" of war aimed not only at abortion providers or clinic workers—or even those who terminate their pregnancy—but the federal government itself. Moreover, the fifth and final takeaway is that the declaration of war against the state specifically emphasized taking up firearms to kill people. The manual documents the thought process that led from an antiabortion movement that was focused on the right to life of individual fetuses to a militant mindset that saw the unborn as symbolic of the future of white Western civilization and was prepared to wage war with guns to protect a white future.

In addition to *The Army of God Manual,* another key text was *Firestorm: A Guerrilla Strategy for a Pro-Life America,* which was published in 1992 by Life Dynamics and Mark Crutcher. This text was important because it noted the shift away from legislation protecting the fetus and toward legislation protecting the mother. Consequently, as discussed in chapter 1, the idea of opposing abortion to protect women became implemented as a strategy. Crutcher's *Firestorm* was a strategy playbook that was meant to influence quietly. Crutcher sought to influence established organizations like the NRLC and Americans United for Life, whose own lobbying and litigation arguments changed throughout the decades.[22] Just as importantly, he aimed to influence and employ nonprofessional antiabortionists as "guerrilla" "agents" who were not beholden to any mainstream organization. In this way, *Firestorm* reflected and promoted the decentralized style that became known as leaderless resistance.[23]

Just a year later, in 1994, antiabortionists published the first widely disseminated defense of antiabortion homicide. Michael Bray helped antiabortion assassin Paul Hill pen the Defensive Action Statement, and Michael Bray had been intellectually assisted by law professor Charles Rice. Rice drew from so-called natural law theory to argue that killing to protect the unborn would amount to retributive justice that supposedly restored the order of God. Rice argued that since pregnancy is a gift from God it is wrong to spurn that gift and that only God can give or take away life because life is God's dominion. Therefore, to kill those that Rice and other antiabortionists saw as taking life and spurning God's gift was tantamount to justifiable homicide.[24]

All this rationalization was marshaled as antiabortion gunmen started assassinating reproductive health care physicians and clinic workers. There were seven people in the 1990s who were murdered by pro-life gunmen and incendiary devices. In addition to guns, bombs were used not only to damage clinics but also to maim and kill people. In particular it was Eric Rudolph who initiated the bombing of clinics in a way that would ensure casualties. In my book *Killing for Life,* Eric Rudolph's story illustrates how the antiabortion movement, the militia movement, and the white supremacist movements could intersect, and in fact *had* intersected. But before I address Rudolph particularly, I want to continue with how the 1990s was a banner decade for the militant, murderous antiabortion movement.

As gunmen were shooting down clinic workers and physicians, activists were aiding that effort by doxing these people as targets.

Paul deParrie, who was operating in the Pacific Northwest, had been creating "wanted" posters that provided the personal information and sometimes photos of reproductive health care professionals. These wanted posters he gave to a man named Neal Horsley, who posted the information on a website called the Nuremberg Files. The name of the website alluded to their fervent hope that at some point, perhaps after abortion had been criminalized, there would be retroactive trials of reproductive health care workers as war criminals. It was an allusion to the 1945–46 Nuremberg trials after the fall of Adolf Hitler's army, when Nazis were judged on their collusion in the Holocaust that targeted Jews, homosexuals, disabled people, and Roma people. More to the point, the website disseminated all this personal, private information online and made it easier for any antiabortionists who felt homicide was justifiable to find their targets. Today we call these malicious disclosures of personal information on public platforms *doxing*. More information about deParrie's innovations will follow. Suffice it now to note that deParrie, like Rudolph and a number of pro-life assassins, contributed to the increase in violent rhetoric and violent actions in the name of opposing abortion.

In addition to this amping up of antiabortion rhetoric and violence, there was a new effort in the 1990s to export antiabortion tactics, rhetoric, and rationales abroad. As we saw in chapter 1, that effort was spearheaded by the World Congress of Families (WCF), which held their first conference in 1997, representing a new transnational effort between what had been Cold War enemies: the United States and Russia. The creation of the WCF was a turning point for the antiabortion movement because its founders were motivated by demographic changes. They were especially alarmed by low birth rates among white Western countries. With this particular worry, the transnational, cross-cultural antiabortion movement was tracking along some key developments in the far-right movements, the militia movement, and the white power movement.

The 1990s was a crucible for the far right as well as the anti-abortion movement. In 1992 in Ruby Ridge, Idaho, federal marshals had a fatal altercation with rural radicals who had created a white separatist community in the mountainous part of the state. The standoff that happened on the Weaver family homestead was a flash point for the patriot militia movement and organized white supremacists. The militia movement had emerged in the context of economic and military losses. As mentioned previously, the farm crisis of the late 1970s and 1980s entailed a record number of foreclosures of farms in the Midwest. The causes were economic and political. Farmers were encouraged to increase production during the Nixon years before Carter issued a grain embargo in response to the USSR's 1979 invasion of Afghanistan. Those farmers who had gone into debt to meet the needs of the 1970s couldn't emerge from that debt. A record number of farm foreclosures ensued. It seemed like a betrayal of white American farmers and heartland values, and some fell back on old antisemitic myths. They blamed a Jewish cabal of global financiers for their demise. Meanwhile, the withdrawal of troops from Vietnam also stoked anti-government ire. Militias emerged believing that the federal government had restrained the troops so much that they couldn't win in Vietnam, and that at home it was demanding too many taxes, curtailing farm subsidies, and regulating guns too much. Amid these deeply felt sentiments blaming financial ruin and moral abandonment by Washington bureaucrats, the shootout at Ruby Ridge was regarded as unwarranted assassination by the feds. Indeed, historians agree that "federal agents used excessive military force—and broke government rules of engagement."[25]

In the same year as the Ruby Ridge conflict, white supremacist Louis Beam published an essay about leaderless resistance against the federal government. This publication nearly coincided with the antiabortion call in *The Army of God Manual* to oppose abortion as individuals—lone wolves—whose crimes couldn't be traced back to any central leader. Militants on the far right—including militias, white supremacists, and antiabortionists—were declaring war against the federal government for slightly different reasons but with the same strategy of decentralized action, also known as leaderless resistance.

The federal agents' killing of members of the Weaver family was seen as evidence that the feds were out of control, as was the event in Waco, Texas, that happened a year afterward. In 1993 the federal government engaged in another standoff, this time with an apocalyptic religious cult led by David Koresh. The standoff ended in a devastating inferno that killed seventy-six.[26] Two years later, Timothy McVeigh retaliated by bombing the Alfred P. Murrah Federal Building in Oklahoma City. McVeigh not only learned how to build an incendiary device by reading far-right materials, including Pierce's novel, *The Turner Diaries*. He also frequented gun shows and paramilitary compounds, clearly espousing neo-Nazi and other white supremacist ideology. Although McVeigh was clearly part of the militia and white power movements, only he and Terry Nichols were held accountable for the bombing in Oklahoma. Only he was sentenced to death. The leaderless resistance strategy worked. According to Kathleen Belew, "Timothy McVeigh's execution cemented a perception of the bombing as unconnected to the events that came before, as an inexplicable act of violence carried out by one or a few actors. This idea threatened to occlude the white power movement altogether. Leaderless resistance had triumphed as a strategy to hide the broader movement."[27]

Because the white power movement and the militia movement were under increased scrutiny after the Oklahoma City bombing in 1995, the late 1990s saw less destruction from them than from antiabortionists. Before examining Eric Rudolph as a perpetrator of that '90s destruction whose writings exemplify the far-right mindset, let's continue with brief historical sketches that provide context for his words and actions.

The Nativist Aughts

The first decade of the twenty-first century—the '00s or aughts— was profoundly shaped by the attacks on U.S. soil by al-Qaeda that occurred on September 11, 2001. Terrorism was introduced to the American consciousness as something that could happen—and had happened here. The grand scale of the attacks, which included hijackers who took control of airplanes and used them as weapons by suicidally crashing them into key targets, was a shock to the American system. The military response was disingenuous because the American people were erroneously told that Saddam Hussein had weapons of mass destruction and that a new doctrine of preemptive war was the only way to prevent future terrorist attacks. The cultural response was a decisive turn to nativism, a mindset that spurred white people to attack immigrants and people of color and that spurred politicians to aim for stringent anti-immigration policies. Opposition to Barack Obama, the nation's first Black president, elected in 2008, took the form of objections that he wasn't born in the United States, a lie that relied on and reproduced nativist suspicion. Perhaps because the very tactics of terroristic attack deployed during 9/11 were some of the same tactics that antiabortion militants had been using to bomb clinics, antiabortion terrorism precipitously declined until the very last year of the decade. In 2009 physician George Tiller was assassinated, as discussed in the previous chapter. By this time, gun murders, mass shootings, and attacks on people of color were being revealed as ubiquitous, thanks to the introduction of the iPhone, which could record and broadcast images of violence instantaneously.

The Tea Party Teens

The Tea Party emerged as a right-wing populist response to the Obama administration. Unlike earlier iterations of populism in United States history that featured an inclusive redistribution of wealth to promote the American dream for more people, this iteration espoused exclusion. In opposing Obamacare, the national plan to provide health care for all Americans, the Tea Party was aligned with the Republican establishment as well as with free-market fundamentalists, according to Lawrence Rosenthal, but its focus shifted to immigration in 2015, which put the group's members out of step with those other conservatives who recognized that courting the Latina vote was important to winning elections.[28] Tea Party populists were adamantly nativist and shifted their allegiance to candidate Donald Trump, who got to the polls not only more working-class people but also more fringe elements such as online male supremacists in the "manosphere" and white supremacists. A 2015 white supremacist attack on Black church parishioners in South Carolina invigorated revolutionary racists, who "had had no role in national politics ... since the 1920s."[29] In addition to attracting white supremacists, Trump was wooing evangelicals, promising them he would install Supreme Court justices who would overturn *Roe v. Wade.* "In 2016, America's right-wing populists detached themselves from the extreme free-market agenda that had held sway in the Tea Party and reconnected to a different one—the America-First nationalism of Donald Trump."[30] Once in office, Trump double downed on anti-immigration politics, resulting in complaints of injustices such as caging babies and sterilizing women at the border. Anti-queer, antiabortion, and antisemitic shows of force during the 2010s proliferated. Perpetrators killed three people at a Colorado Springs Planned Parenthood, murdered eleven people at a Pittsburgh synagogue, and fatally shot forty-nine gay and trans people at a Florida bar. The deadly Unite the Right rally discussed in the introduction was a startling spectacle of racist hate. Also aforementioned is the 2015 anti-trans conference in Louisville that was followed by an onslaught of anti-trans legislation. The result was a demonization of gender, which began to operate as a "fearsome phantasm" because deploying the term came to mean something more nefarious than "both academic and ordinary usage" achieved.[31] Gender became the international hallmark of right-wing mobilizing; it was the "symbolic glue" connecting conservative and far-right entities worldwide.[32] Ending the decade was COVID-19, which required much federal oversight and regulation to curb the pandemic—efforts that spurred conspiracy theorists to spread lies about politicians, public health administrators, mask mandates, and vaccination programs.

The Riotous Twenties

The movement for Black lives, which had originated some years earlier in response to killings of African Americans by police officers, had international impact after George Floyd was murdered in 2020. Protests worldwide demonstrated the global desire for racial justice just about a year before white nationalists and other insurrectionists rioted in protest of the transfer of power from outgoing president Donald Trump to president-elect Joseph Biden. In that attack on the Capitol, a variety of right-wing actors came out of hiding with an unprecedented show of force that demonstrated shared ideology and sentiment. While the number of people in the riot was unprecedented, the fusion of Christian nationalism, antiabortion sentiment, antisemitic conspiracism, paramilitary prowess, and white power was not. The intersection of all these is exemplified by the aforementioned Eric Rudolph. His story takes us into the twenty-first century.

Eric Rudolph at the Intersection of Far-Right Factions

Eric Rudolph occupies the political intersection of patriot militia lifestyle, supremacist ideology, and antiabortion zealotry. Like members of Posse Comitatus and the militia movement, he eschewed taxes. He grew and sold marijuana for income. He was rumored to be a survivalist, presumed by all—including the FBI—to have adopted rustic and self-sufficient ways of living off the land. Indeed, this—aside from murderous blasts—is what he is most famous for.

Survivalist Lone Wolf

Once Rudolph was suspected of detonating the four bombs attributed to him, a manhunt ensued. He evaded the law for six years. He became a folk hero of sorts, supposedly hiding out in the

Appalachian terrain.[33] He was seen as a noble highlander, a rugged mountain man, a modern-day Davy Crockett whose skills and closeness to nature assured his evasion from the police. The way Rudolph was said to live on the lam in the thickly forested hills was celebrated by Appalachian residents, probably because it resembled tales of plain folk showing up the big-city elites. But in fact, as Appalachian scholar Douglas Reichert Powell notes, Rudolph "wasn't a native son of the mountains: his family moved around a shady network of white-supremacist communities before his mother moved to western North Carolina from Florida, precisely because of the reputation of the mountains as being hospitable to fringe white nationalist political beliefs."[34] I don't believe that everyone who delighted in the idea of Rudolph's hiding out in the mountains necessarily condoned the violence he perpetrated. In a similar way, people like movies about mobsters because they skillfully evade detection and apprehension, even though those moviegoers may not condone organized crime. The casual embrace of Rudolph while he was rumored to be in the mountain south is not a firm sign that the general public supported him or opposed abortion or shared Rudolph's conspiracist fear of a New World Order.

However, paramilitary Americans who claimed Rudolph to be "one of us" in public statements indicate a like-mindedness. One posted, "He is a soldier and an outdoorsman, an agrarian Christian and an Israelite."[35] This reference is to Christian Identity, a racist belief based in nineteenth-century British Israelism and spread widely throughout the Posse Comitatus groups; it "teaches that whites are the true descendants of the lost tribes of Israel and that Jews, blacks, and other minorities have sprung from Satan and are subhuman."[36] From prison, Rudolph explicitly denies subscribing to the ideology of Christian Identity.[37] Be that as it may, Rudolph was also hailed as "one of us" because "he has no bank account, no credit line, no social security #, no phone. He learned about avoiding a paper trail when he was 13."[38] Rudolph was also admired by convicted murderer Randy Duey, who was a member of the neo-Nazi group the Order, which robbed banks and killed the aforementioned Jewish radio personality, Alan Berg. Duey is reported to have said, "If a thousand Eric Rudolphs or twenty-five Orders arose, the system would really be in danger."[39] Such statements clearly condoned Rudolph's ruthless violence. The far right recognized his strategies and rationales. Rudolph was legible to militiamen, neo-Nazis, and others on the far right because his paramilitary tactics and supremacist ideologies resembled theirs.

Supremacist Extremism

Rudolph repeatedly has denied being a white supremacist or a racist. He writes, "I believe that Western Christian culture is superior to all other cultures. And I believe in cultural homogeneity— the keeping of one set of cultural values at the helm of society's social and political life. Here is wisdom: all history teaches that pursuing a policy of cultural diversity leads to division, oppression, violence, and eventually, to civil war. Thus, I reject all notions of 'multiculturalism.'"[40]

While he says he doesn't subscribe to such views based on race, he is motivated by the same claims of Christian superiority. He also exhibits the same alarm over racial demographic changes that he says portends the end of Christianity and of Western civilization, which is predominantly white. In an essay on "armed resistance to abortion," which he wrote in prison, Rudolph sounds an alarm of apocalyptic proportions. He writes, "The liberal regime behind abortion on demand has not only wiped out the equivalent of the populations of California and Texas, it fully intends to wipe Christian civilization off the face of the earth."[41] Who does Eric Rudolph imagine constitutes the "liberal regime" and how can he presume to know their "intentions"? While he is decidedly vocal on the issue of race and racism, which he repeatedly recasts as discrimination against white people, Rudolph in his prison writings avoids the issue of antisemitism.

In high school he wrote a paper that denied the Holocaust of the Jews. According to his sister-in-law, Rudolph referred to television as "the electronic Jew."[42] His brother, Daniel, also exhibited radical ways: he even sawed off his own hand in protest of the media and the FBI once Eric was under scrutiny. This self-mutilation stunt, which Daniel videotaped himself, was explained by one militant as a blood-for-blood affront to the "jewsmedia."[43] In addition to signaling a completely unhinged sense of vehemence, this gory exhibition also indicates a deep antisemitism. Eric Rudolph's other writings also exhibit conspiracist beliefs that accommodate if not emerge from racist religious ideas. After some of the bombings attributed to Rudolph, a letter signed "Army of God" was released. It not only tied him to antiabortion militants but also revealed a conspiracist notion that abortion was part of a global Jewish attempt to control the world. This antisemitic conspiracism presumes that by eliminating white babies and imposing a racially and sexually depraved multiculturalism, Jews would rule and subjugate Christians and white people.

The targets of Rudolph's bombs spoke to this conspiracist belief. Already noted was the 1996 bombing of Centennial Park in Atlanta during the summer Olympics, a celebration of global pluralism as well as a showcase of human ability. The bomb killed one person who suffered a heart attack when the explosion happened and injured more than one hundred people in the area. The following year, Rudolph bombed an abortion clinic and a lesbian bar on the outskirts of Atlanta. According to his former sister-in-law, the bombing of abortion clinics was all about race: "And you know why he bombed the abortion clinic? He believes that the white people are eventually going to be a minority instead of a majority. He believes that you should reproduce and be true to your race. He thought white women should marry white men and black people should marry black people."[44] All these bombings coincided with notes to the media accepting responsibility by the Army of God and promising "death to the New World Order."

In August 1996 Eric Rudolph visited the West, including Colorado, Idaho, and Montana.[45] Significantly, he traveled to Coeur d'Alene. This is where Richard Butler was attempting to start a racial holy war to eventually create the white homeland he dreamed about. Following Rudolph's visit, the Aryan Nations compound in Coeur d'Alene in 1997 was amping up their illegal antisemitic activities. According to one report, in addition to hosting racist groups at an annual convening, "the group's criminal activities escalated to include bombings, bank robberies, and even the firebombing attempted assassination of Bill Wassmuth, a prominent local Catholic priest and human rights activist."[46] For Rudolph to choose to travel to remote Coeur d'Alene at the height of its Aryan Nations activity is not likely to be a coincidence.

In 1998 Rudolph proceeded with another bombing of a clinic, this time in Alabama. In Birmingham Rudolph again used bombs that were engineered to cause damage to people. They were filled with nails and shrapnel that, upon detonation, flew out like a thousand supersharp bullets. One man, Robert "Sandy" Sanderson, a security guard, was killed on site. Another person, nurse Emily Lyon, lost an eye and sustained disfiguring amounts of shrapnel in her body. According to the FBI director, Rudolph's bombs "were carefully designed to the maximum extent to kill and maim and injure the innocent."[47]

In 2003 Eric Rudolph was captured outside a grocery store in rural North Carolina. Although he appeared to be foraging for food in the store's garbage dumpster, he was sporting clean shoes, freshly dyed and cut hair, and a relatively aloof attitude. He did not resist the rookie patrolman who apprehended and arrested him. Some have speculated that these details suggest he was not living the rugged life in the mountains as rumored but instead he was helped. If he was a harbored fugitive for five years, did he receive aid from random residents, or was it a network of supporters? Also, he confessed to having stashed 250 pounds of dynamite in four locations, "including a twenty-five-pound bomb across the road from the Army National Guard armory that served as the base for the FBI manhunt."[48] Was that stockpile of dynamite of his own making and for his use only? The FBI doesn't say. The leaderless resistance strategy worked. Only Eric Rudolph was pursued in relation to four bombings claimed in the name of the Army of God.[49]

After a plea bargain, Eric Rudolph is serving multiple consecutive life sentences with no chance of parole. He is also writing. The writings are posted on the Army of God website.

Prison Writings

Eric Rudolph's prison writings attest to the intersections of paramilitary lifestyle, supremacist ideas, and antiabortion zealotry that characterize his earlier life. His novel, published in 2013, imagines what someone like him might do in the twenty-first century. One nonfiction piece from 2014 addresses new strategic directions in antiabortion organizing. Both writings reflect the permutations of right-wing America in the new millennium. It seems that these texts were written not only to reflect the times but also to shape their movements.

The 2014 essay is titled "White Lies: Eugenics, Race, and Abortion."[50] Rudolph seems to have written this in response to a billboard campaign launched in 2010, the infamous campaign purporting that abortion is Black genocide that I mentioned in chapter 2. Billboards in Atlanta, Chicago, and New York claimed, "Black children are an endangered species." Rudolph opposes the antiabortion efforts that argue abortion targets the African American community. Most commenters on the billboard campaign understood it to be a scare tactic to divide the Black vote during the midterm elections of Obama's first term. Rudolph also realizes that it is an attempt to attract African Americans into the movement generally and during election years particularly. After an account of the history of eugenics, in which Rudolph exonerates Margaret Sanger as only an elitist and not a racist, his main message is to raise the alarm of demographic decline among whites. He spells this out with verifiable statistics.

America has the highest fertility rate among western nations, at 2.1 children per woman. But a closer look at these numbers reveals that America's relatively high fertility rate is due to its large non-white population. Look at whites alone, and their fertility rate is only slightly higher than their European cousins.

Switch to birth rates per 1,000 people, and we see the same disparity. The birth rate for black women in America is 14.7 per

1,000, as compared to 12.1 for whites. For Hispanic women, the birth rate is 17.1 per 1,000.

Couple these suicidal birth rates with an estimated two million Third World immigrants crossing our borders every year (some legal, others not), it's easy to see why America's white majority is swiftly becoming a minority. As recently as 1960, whites accounted for 87 percent of the U.S. population; blacks for only 10 percent; Hispanics for less than three percent. Fifty years later, these numbers look different. In the 2010 census, whites numbered 196.6 million, or 64 percent of the U.S. population; blacks rose to 13 percent; but the biggest increase came among Hispanics, who reached 50 million, or 16 percent. Two years later (2012), whites shrank to 62 percent; blacks up to 13.7; Hispanics to almost 19 percent.

America's white population is aging rapidly. Although still 62 percent of the population, only 52 percent of all babies under one year old are white. America's complexion is projected to grow much darker by 2050, when whites will be a minority at 45 percent; blacks up slightly to 14 percent; Hispanics are expected to reach 31 percent; and Asians will round it out at 10 percent. In short, white people face imminent extinction unless these trends are reversed.

Why is this happening? There are several causes, but demographers point to the short period between 1963 and 1973 as the tipping point, for in that decade both the "Pill" and legal abortion became widely available to western women.[51]

None of these impressive statistics takes into account infant and maternal mortality rates, which, as I pointed out in chapter 1, are suffered by African Americans the most. Nor do these statistics factor in *any* mortality rates at all. We need to consider how many people get killed by the police, or in the armed services, or in domestic violence, or in mass shootings—and how those issues affect some groups in the United States more than others. The Movement for Black Lives emerged to draw attention to these deadly disparities, as has the rich analyses based on research conducted by reproductive justice scholars. Efforts to shut down these lines of thinking serve to perpetuate the idea that Rudolph and others believe: that white women are not reproducing enough of the right kind of babies and, consequently, white Western society will end.

For all his dismissal of race or racism as motivating factors, Rudolph certainly seems steeped in racial concerns in his delineation of the decline of "Western" civilization and the foreboding "darker" complexion of America. It seems evident to me that Rudolph has updated his motivating concern about a "New World Order," a phrase that was (as I suggested earlier) in the 1990s often synonymous with the antisemitic fantasy of a Zionist Occupied Government (ZOG). ZOG's goal, according to white supremacist fantasy-fear, was to eliminate the white race, and aborting white babies was a step toward that goal.[52] Instead of blaming the ZOG, Rudolph in the twenty-first century is blaming a "liberal regime" and can claim that he is not a white supremacist, yet he equates the decimation of Western civilization and Christianity with racial birth rates. His remedy for staving off this eradication is the revolutionary Christian. The closing line in his essay on armed resistance to abortion is "The church militant is the only thing that can save the faith, and western civilization."[53]

If you were worried that people in prison don't have the opportunity to keep up with the outside world, that doesn't seem to be the case with Rudolph. His emphasis on demographics is plenty current. In those white supremacist circles that Rudolph says he doesn't belong to, the fear of "white genocide" is spelled out in the same demographic terms as Rudolph uses. History buffs and those in the know should recognize this reliance on the fear of white genocide. It is a replay of the idea of "race suicide" for whites, which circulated in American culture at the turn of the nineteenth century. At that time, like now, white people saw immigration as a threat to their "race." As we saw in the introduction (with the National Alliance supplement to daily newspapers), the idea of rejecting immigrants because "they can't make white babies" is based on the same contention that Rudolph implies: that we need more Western women to have more white babies. The National Alliance's response is to "send them [immigrants] back"; Rudolph's answer was to murder abortion providers. Both solutions answer one problem: the demographic demise of the white race and/as Western civilization.

Another spin on this perceived problem is decidedly antisemitic. The great replacement theory is a newer version of the old "race suicide" bogeyman. Based on a book published in 2012, the theory contends that white people will be demographically replaced by immigrants and Jews. The National Immigration Forum recognizes three main conventions of writings espousing a great replacement. First, it alarms people through a rhetoric of invasion, claiming that hordes of immigrants are arriving with the intention of overtaking the country. Second, allowing these hordes to enter is seen as a way for Democrats to obtain more votes at the election polls. Third, in many iterations of the replacement theory, Jewish elites are described as engineering the "flooding" of immigrants into the country. Each of these conventions relies on impressions but no statistical proof.[54]

The theory catches on because it resonates with nativist scare tactics that have been deployed before, as well as the old fear of the international Jew, sometimes nowadays referred to in a coded way as "globalists." The international Jew, not the Black man, became understood as white man's worst enemy in the 1970s, when various factions of white supremacists were striving to gain power and coherence. In response to the civil rights movement and to the nazification of the Klan, American supremacists reconsidered Black people as too mentally inferior to engineer anything and instead embraced the so-called international Jew as their priority problem. They saw people of color as dupes of the Jews.

Rudolph's writings suggest he subscribes to this final version of panic over demographic projections. In chastising the pro-life movement for arguing that Black people are the target of abortion-as-genocide, Rudolf is consistent with his argument that white people are demographically disappearing because of the advent of the birth control pill and the legalization of abortion. His recent writings have been updated. It's not the New World Order anymore. The thing to fear is now a demographic apocalypse for white people and Western civilization.

Another way Rudolph's prison writings are agonizingly current is in how he imagines new targets for revolutionary militants. In his 2013 novel, *All Enemies, Foreign and Domestic,* a transgender villain in a gay pride parade in San Francisco is the target for a pro-life patriot's fatal bomb. Rudolph's queer villain—a military officer (last name Fanning) who served in Afghanistan—is obviously based on Chelsea Manning. Fanning frames the protagonist, who greatly resembles Rudolph, of course, for murder. In killing off the transgender villain at a pride event, Rudolph's novel reflects the longstanding history of representing queers as deserving of violent death in fiction and film.[55] It more generally reflects the documented reality of how, despite increased visibility, "transgender and other gender-diverse people still face everyday discrimination" and "lack basic protections that cisgender people take for granted," resulting in discrepancies in employment, housing, healthcare, and safety.[56] Furthermore, as noted previously, the general demonization of transgender people has become the fastest-growing method by the right to instill panic, and hence a turnout at the polls. No doubt Rudolph has always been anti-LGTBQ, as his bombing of the lesbian bar in 1997 attests, but his novel squarely takes murderous aim at a transgender villain.

Another way in which the novel is noteworthy is its perpetuation of what historian Kathleen Belew calls the Vietnam story. This is a narrative that right-wing militants told themselves and others to justify paramilitary action in the United States. Blaming the federal government for supposedly preventing good American soldiers from defeating the communists in Vietnam, U.S. veterans were motivated to "bring the war home" and continue fighting the commies in the United States, according to Belew. In my 2002 book I make a similar case that antiabortion militants were inspired by and relied on the same story about Vietnam—"the feds didn't let us win." In particular, the man attributed with starting the Catholic "rescue" movement in the 1970s shifted his attention from protesting the war in Vietnam to protesting abortion because he felt that a female friend of his who had an abortion was behaving like his buddies who had PTSD from the war. But *she* never said she felt that way. By equating abortion with Vietnam, antiabortion militants redirected the accusation that U.S. soldiers were baby killers in the villages of Indochina. Instead of guys in fatigues being the baby killers, according to militants, it was the women who were terminating their pregnancies who should be considered baby killers.[57]

Rudolph's novel revives and updates the antiabortion version of the Vietnam story as one about Afghanistan. The novel's epigraph is a statement by Major Rusty Bradley from his memoir about serving in Afghanistan. The epigraph implicitly denigrates President Obama as commander in chief as it revives the idea that the only reason for military failure is incompetent or corrupt federal leadership, not the soldiers in the field. Regarding his time in Afghanistan, Bradley reflects, "I am asked if it was worth it all the time. If that question had been posed before 2008, I would have said yes. We were there to seek vengeance on behalf of the nation and to ensure that [Afghanistan] would never again become a staging area for terrorists. We had the full support of the White House and the administration. If that question was posed after 2008, I would say no. When your government does not let you win a war in which men sacrifice the greatest gift they have to offer, their lives and health, then something is very, very wrong."[58] The idea of (unwittingly or not) preventing soldiers from winning war is a staple from the Reagan era. It was popularized by the *Rambo* films, in which the title character played by Sylvester Stallone asks, "Do we get to win this time?"

Rudolph's novel features two characters—the main protagonist, Carson, and his uncle—who swap stories, sharing their perspectives on their time served in Afghanistan and Vietnam, respectively. The dialogues instill in the reader the idea that the federal government hinders "real" soldiers. The close relationship Carson enjoys with his uncle emerges in several warm and fuzzy father-son-like scenarios. This close sense of belonging and camaraderie is, according to Luke Mogelson, the reason U.S. veterans in the twenty-first century participate in paramilitary groups. Previous generations of veterans felt their government abandoned them by not providing strong military leadership in Vietnam, resulting in battlefield defeat, public humiliation, and psychological or physical damage. In contrast, today's veterans who served in Iraq and Afghanistan gravitate to disaffected militias not because they felt that strategic errors fouled them up. They are not angry because they didn't get to win, didn't achieve their military goal, as in the Vietnam era. They join far-right outfits because they want the camaraderie and crave the sense of loyalty shared among their soldier-brothers in an updated version of "the male fighting band" that served fascism in World War II. Once removed from the battlefield, the vets from twenty-first-century wars care less about the actual outcomes of the ongoing wars in which they fought than about the community they enjoyed and the pride of having served and sacrificed. Rudolph's novel puts these generations of veterans in conversation. It updates the Vietnam story for today's discharged soldier-reader who is often more attuned to conflict at home than abroad. Rudolph's title, *All Enemies, Foreign and Domestic*, clearly reflects this expansive view of warring.[59]

That phrase, "all enemies, foreign and domestic," is part of the Oath of Enlistment to which U.S. soldiers are sworn to uphold. It is the oath that white supremacist Louis Beam invoked when on trial for sedition. He successfully argued that he should not be held accountable for his part in building a "cohesive white power movement" aiming to overthrow the U.S. government because, as a veteran of the war in Vietnam, he believed "it was his duty to kill enemies, foreign and domestic."[60] It is this same oath for which the far-right group the Oath Keepers is named. Rudolph's novel sets out for men the same conversations and conclusions that characterize Beam's and the Oath Keepers' populist point of view: the real government is the people, so the federal government is not to be trusted; and the skills learned in armed forces training should be used on United States officials and citizens who are deemed enemies. Pairing Carson with his uncle at strategic points in the plot conveys this message about being a good man. The Oath Keepers was founded in 2009 by Elmer Stewart Rhodes, a lawyer and former paratrooper. In 2023 Rhodes was convicted of seditious conspiracy for his actions during the Capitol riot on January 6, 2021.

Rudolph's novel also presents us with a pair of wives who, through contrast with one another, exemplify what a real woman should be. At the outset of Rudolph's narrative Carson has a pregnant wife, Lydia, whose main mission is to save "bottom-feeding minnow[s] from those evil irrigation pumps." This frivolous environmentalist concern is a sign that Lydia does not have her priorities in order. Eventually she leaves Carson because she can't stand by her man when he is on trial for disobeying orders against torturing prisoners of war (which he did) and killing one of them (which he did not). Moreover, she terminates her perfectly healthy pregnancy in the eighth month. This side of Rudolph's story shows the reader what a bad woman is. It portrays third-trimester abortion as an easy elective. In reality there is nothing easy about terminating a late pregnancy. It is not easy for the woman or for the doctor, and it carries lots of medical risks. Abortions in the second and third trimesters are last-resort operations. But Rudolph portrays it as a thoughtless and vindictive choice for the immoral mother and a brutal killing of a son whose father would have loved him. To say that this depiction of abortion in the third trimester, a very rare occurrence, is medically inaccurate, sociologically misleading, and heavy-handed is to miss the point that it is, foremost, didactic. Rudolph is teaching his readers how a woman can be evil, vindictive, vain, and stupid.

In contrast to Lydia, one of the soldiers Carson served with has a widow, Kathy, who has two children. She questions none of Carson's motives and supports him unconditionally. It should come as no surprise that Rudolph describes her as "an Irish beauty" with "long strawberry blond hair and curves in all the proper places." The idealized whiteness of this wholesome and "proper" mother is very pronounced, as is her Catholic stoicism. Before Carson departs, in one scene, she "placed a crucifix in his palm and closed it. She kissed him lightly on the cheek. 'I'll pray that the blood of Jesus protects you, Captain.'"[61]

Indeed, it is her fateful letter that keeps Carson from committing suicide: "Hadn't been more than a week ago that he stuck that pistol in his mouth. If not for Kathy's letter, he'd have pulled the trigger for sure. Apparently, someone up there had plans for Bill Carson."[62] Those plans were to get revenge on Fanning, the transgender villain. When Carson told Kathy about how Fanning had framed him for murder, she tells him to forgive Fanning and let divine justice take care of it. To this, the narrator explains Kathy's perspective, which is sweet but ignorant: "Hers was a woman's view of the world: passive, oblivious to the realities that underpin her own existence, blind to the walls that surround her and protect her and the men with guns who kill to defend those walls."[63]

This line, and what follows, seems inspired by the 1992 film *A Few Good Men*. In that courtroom drama, Colonel Jessep (played unforgettably by Jack Nicholson) attempts to obliterate young JAG lawyer (played by Tom Cruise), who suspects that an enlisted man, Santiago, was murdered on Jessep's base. Jessep condescendingly addresses the lawyer trying to trap him:

Son, we live in a world that has walls, and those walls have to be guarded by men with guns. Who's gonna do it? You? . . . I have a greater responsibility than you can *possibly* fathom. You weep for Santiago, and you curse the Marines. You have that luxury. You have the luxury of not knowing what I know—that Santiago's death, while tragic, probably saved lives; and my existence, while grotesque and incomprehensible to you, saves lives. You don't want the truth because deep down in places you don't talk about at parties, you want me on that wall—you *need* me on that wall.

Rudolph's narration is similar in tone, word choice, and message: "Having spent the better part of his life guarding the wall, Carson had learned that forgiveness was a luxury reserved for those who live on the inside." In contrast to Kathy's naive view, or what Rudolph in another essay calls "milquetoast Christianity," Carson gives us a manly rendition of religious justice: "Fanning's crime was unforgivable. Letting it go wasn't an option."[64] Thus, in addition to sounding a lot like *A Few Good Men,* the dual affect of sentimentality and resentfulness functions to secure different roles for militant men and their oblivious women. When he returns from his murderous trip to San Francisco, Carson is welcomed without gushing emotions into Kathy's house and takes a seat at the head of the dinner table. Daddy is home. The world is restored.

That calm ending after the murderous bombings is how the novel helps Rudolph's readers to imagine their reward of familial peace, order, and filial respect after killing people. While that may be the case for soldiers who kill during wartime, Rudolph's novel promotes it for people like himself—domestic terrorists—whose killing of his own countrymen and -women is motivated by mere prejudices and conspiracist beliefs that have no basis in fact.

Rudolph's research for this novel must have been extensive. He had no actual experience of serving during war and was never deployed overseas. He was kicked out of the army for illegal drugs and/or insubordination after less than two years of serving in the states of Georgia and Kentucky. It was there that he learned, reportedly from a commander, how to make bombs, primarily out of found or cast-out materials.[65]

As a presumed survivalist, antisemite, and clinic bomber, Eric Rudolph exemplifies the intersection of paramilitary right-wing America, supremacist ideology, and antiabortion zealotry. His prison writings reveal an evolution of right-wing thought and targets from the 1990s to today.

Intersections, Encore: Paul deParrie's Absolutist Abolition

A contemporary of Eric Rudolph, Paul deParrie was also committed to opposing abortion and was steeped in antisemitism, nativism, and supremacism. He, too, had an overinflated sense of his own superiority as a Christian white man. While Rudolph was active in the southeast of the United States, with that crucial exception of his visit to Coeur d'Alene, deParrie was active in the Pacific Northwest, mainly Oregon. DeParrie's life is another example of how the white power, patriot militia, and antiabortion movements can intersect. Like Rudolph, deParrie wrote fiction and nonfiction.

Paul deParrie was not an assassin. So far as we know, he pulled no triggers and detonated no bombs. DeParrie moved in and out of far-right circles in Oregon, and his ability to incite and channel antiabortion, anti-government, and absolutist rage prefigured some of the most radical antiabortion groups and tactics today. As the internet was still relatively new in the 1990s, he invested a lot in print material to imagine and create a community that was as angry and uncompromising as he was. In addition to doxing clinic workers with wanted posters and the Nuremberg files website, deParrie was the editor of a magazine called *Life Advocate*. Advocates for Life Ministries was the Portland-based group that published the magazine. His publications from the 1990s promoted rationales for killing abortion providers. His publications at the turn of the millennium, from 1999 into the 2000s, featured abortion abolitionism. Abortion abolitionism rejects the pro-life stance as too soft, too lenient. Abortion abolitionists not only seek to criminalize abortion but also envision a Christian-based system of punishment for anyone who transgresses God's laws. Understanding the deeper history of abortion abolitionism exposes the entanglements of antiabortion militancy with that of other aspects of the far right. DeParrie, who died in 2006, wrote and published writings that legitimated antiabortion homicide and presaged today's abolitionist efforts to create a punitive Christian-based authoritarianism.

DeParrie was active with a variety of right-wing groups in the 1980s and 1990s. He was a member of the Oregon Citizens Alliance (OCA), a conservative Christian activist group that formed initially to challenge in the primary elections a Republican senator who wasn't conservative enough for their tastes. The group went on to oppose a nondiscrimination order that protected gay people from being fired for their sexual orientation in the state government, successfully repealing the executive order issued by the Oregon governor at the time. Buoyed by that statewide win, OCA sponsored a bill in 1990 to demand that minors notify parents if seeking an abortion, an effort that was defeated by Oregon voters. According to a researcher of far-right activity in the area, deParrie "was there at the OCA's most important functions and was often listed as a petition gatherer or one of the main signatories to different OCA initiatives." While he was honing his skills at legislative activism with the OCA, deParrie "also had a relationship with elements of what we call the Christian patriot movement, anti-Semitic tax protesters. Many of these people," the report clarifies, "are from more rural areas and are sort of brought into the White Supremacist movement by issues like opposition to taxation and land use planning laws, plus a host of other issues. Mr. deParrie has contributed to some of their publications. His books are often advertised in conspiracy newsletters."[66]

DeParrie was a force in right-wing print culture not only regionally. The books he authored included fiction—novels titled *The Haunt of Jackals* (1991) and *Blood upon the Rose* (1992)—as well as nonfiction titles such as *Unholy Sacrifices of the New Age* (1988), *The Rescuers* (1989), *Ancient Empires of the New Age* (1989), *Romanced to Death: The Sexual Seduction of American Culture* (1989), *Satan's Seven Schemes: An Overcomer's Guide to Spiritual Warfare* (1991), and *Dark Cures: Have Doctors Lost Their Ethics?* (1999). As these titles suggest, deParrie's writing deploys the same apocalyptic themes and gothic imagery that characterize so much antiabortion materials. His books depict women using the angel/devil dichotomy; they are either crass, stupid, and evil, or holy, clean, and pure. Physicians who offer abortions in his nonfiction and fiction writing are unethical, unclean, and un-American.

DeParrie also published books by other writers as editor of Advocates for Life Publications. These books were central to the discussions of how and why people could kill abortion providers. First, appearing in January 1994 was *A Time to Kill* by Michael Bray, who was convicted on charges of bombing a clinic. As mentioned in chapter 2, this text blamed a "testosterone deficiency" for the state of the world and encouraged men not to cower in their opposition to abortion. As previously mentioned, Bray borrows arguments from Catholic intellectual and University of Notre Dame professor Charles Rice, who himself had penned a think piece on the justifiable homicide of abortion providers. *A Time to Kill* provides theological, moral, and historical justifications for killing, and the timing of its appearance is important. It arrived in print after the first assassination of an abortion provider, Dr. David Gunn, in Florida, and after the first attempted assassination of Dr. George Tiller in Kansas in 1993. It precedes subsequent assassinations; after its publication in 1994, three reproductive health care workers were shot to death by abortion opponents.

As if to give more license to those considering lethal action against abortion providers, in January 1995 Advocates for Life published another book, *In Defense of Others: A Biblical Analysis and Apologetic on the Use of Force to Save Human Life,* by Cathy Ramey. Ramey was associate director of Advocates for Life Ministries, associate editor of *Life Advocate* magazine, and a "rescue"-style protester of local clinics. Internationally, she "co-organized the first rescue efforts in a former Iron Curtain country, Poland," in 1992 and was a delegate to the 1997 World Congress of Families held in Prague, in the Czech Republic. Ramey also "established and [was] director of the Christian Center for Bioethics," which had been "funded through Advocates for Life Ministries."[67]

The publication of Ramey's book coincided with the appearance of wanted posters produced by Advocates for Life at a January 1995 antiabortion rally in Washington, DC. These posters, titled "The Deadly Dozen," doxed abortion providers, accusing them of crimes against humanity and erasing their anonymity with accompanying photos. Later, in 1997, deParrie presented them to Neal Horsley for inclusion on his new website, the Nuremberg Files, thereby expanding into cyberspace the print media created by deParrie and Advocates for Life. By 1999 a lawsuit begun years earlier (in 1995) went to court, pitting the plaintiff, Planned Parenthood, against Advocates for Life Ministries and another, newer group, as well as fourteen individual antiabortionists, including Cathy Ramey and Michael Bray—but not deParrie or Horsley.[68] Planned Parenthood argued for the court and jury to consider the context of violence—including the murders and attempted murders of abortion providers and clinic workers, as well as the bombings and the "rescue" protests that were tantamount to harassment and stalking. Given that context, they argued, the "Deadly Dozen" wanted posters and their electronic versions on the Nuremberg Files constituted "clear threats" that did not merit First Amendment protection of free speech.

The jury believed Planned Parenthood. They were convinced that Advocates for Life Ministries was issuing "clear threats" by distributing their media. In 1999, Planned Parenthood won bigtime, and the doctors, nurses, and receptionists who daily helped people get their pap smears, birth control, and abortions breathed a sigh of relief that at least they were heard. They continued, however, to wear bulletproof vests and take other precautions. After all, Eric Rudolph was still at large, and who knew how many other bombers and snipers were lurking out there.

But for deParrie and the others at *Life Advocate,* the 1999 court decision was only a case of "smoke and mirrors" that constituted "Planned Parenthood's conspiracy to end free speech," as the title of an article claimed.[69] The article, which appeared in the March 1999 issue of *Life Advocate,* was a report on the ruling and was accompanied by a photograph. To illustrate how he felt gagged by the ruling, deParrie published next to this article a photo of himself with a mask covering his mouth, the mask barely covering his prominent nose. The cloth the mask was made from, which had stars and stripes, made it look like a little American flag, but deParrie wore it upside down to indicate a dire situation. When the U.S. flag is flown upside down on a flagpole it is military code and widely understood to be a distress signal. Although Advocates for Life Ministries was a defendant in the case, deParrie was not named personally. The cheeky photograph he published of himself by a report of the ruling suggests he is being silenced, yes, but it is more a sign of national distress than it is an effective muzzling of Paul deParrie.

Indeed, *Life Advocate*'s reporting of the 1999 trial and its outcome repeatedly emphasized the difficulty of prosecutors' attempts to reveal a conspiracy. The article dwells on details and circumstances in a way that assesses the effectiveness of leaderless resistance, the strategy that intends to cause damage presumed to be done by individuals unconnected to others. Key to prosecutors' effort to prove conspiracy was Neal Horsley's website, which displayed information on abortion providers that deParrie had provided. The website grew to include information about pro-choice politicians and advocates, who were thereby opened to antiabortion scrutiny and harassment. According to deParrie and Horsley, the intent for this was to "gather data" for a time in the future when abortion would again be criminalized and those who provided abortions would retroactively be named criminals. This visionary and punitive authoritarianism was spelled out on the website's home page: "Visualize Abortionists on Trial" now so that they can be punished in the future. But, according to the prosecutors, there was more happening than just gathering data. When one abortion provider was killed, Horsley did not take down that man's name but instead crossed it out. The name on the website appeared with a line drawn through it. In effect, the website was operating as a hit list. But that's not how *Life Advocate* saw it. *Life Advocate* reported:

> In fact, the Nuremberg Files website that presented such a distraction to the media was neither owned nor operated by any defendant in the lawsuit. None of the defendants so much as knew how to contact the owner. Another anti-abortionist, not a defendant, Paul deParrie would finally facilitate bringing in a man by the name of Neal Horsley. Horsley would testify in the trial that he alone made decisions about how his website was constructed and operated. While the lawsuit was filed in late 1995, Horsley testified that he had only created the now notorious website in late January 1997. Still, Planned Parenthood insisted a connection existed between the site and defendants, and news of the website permeated news stories.[70]

This description of the court case indicates that *Life Advocate* (and, by extension, its editor, Paul deParrie) was contemplating the limited success of leaderless resistance in the antiabortion movement. The whole point of leaderless resistance is to inflict damage and avoid the legal culpability of anyone associated with the presumed lone wolf. Because Horsley was not a named defendant in the lawsuit, his website—not he—"was also determined by the jury to be a 'true threat,'" in addition to the "Deadly Dozen" wanted posters. DeParrie was not a defendant either, but the judge "enjoined each and all defendants from republishing or distributing either of the two posters. Additionally, the judge named *Life Advocate* editor

Paul deParrie as an agent and ordered that he and all defendants were to turn over any copies of the posters in their possession." *Life Advocate* notes, "Last, since Planned Parenthood never sued the Nuremberg Files website and its owner, no order was forthcoming to hinder Neal Horsley from continuing to gather data on a future 'crimes against humanity' trial."[71]

Advocates for Life Ministries and its co-defendants lost this case. But by March 2001, the decision was reversed; the antiabortion defendants were judged not guilty of inciting violence. In May 2002, however, *that* decision was reversed by a "sharply divided" group of judges who decided the antiabortion materials *did* constitute true threats to physicians and clinic workers. Two months later a motion to rehear the case was denied. This meant that the original judgment for Planned Parenthood stood. Therefore, the Nuremberg Files website was prohibited from listing abortion providers in a way that constituted a hit list.[72]

But deParrie's take on the initial ruling is important to consider because it demonstrates the extremes he was prepared to go once he saw that Planned Parenthood couldn't prove a conspiracy. In the report on the ruling published in *Life Advocate,* deParrie was chagrined that he was implicated in the "clear threats" but recognized that he was not held accountable for them. Furthermore, deParrie recognized that prosecutors could not hold Horsley accountable for *anything.* They could not even prove a connection between Horsley and other antiabortionists, much less with the murderers of abortion providers or clinic workers. This apparently emboldened deParrie to become even more radical and go further to the right. Or, at least, the *Life Advocate*'s report on the court ruling coincided with a full-throttle rejection of the pro-life movement that was so reluctant to condone or aid lethal measures of protesting abortion.

In a note on "housekeeping" in the same issue of the magazine that reported on the ruling, deParrie breaks with the mainstream antiabortion movement in terms of the language he prefers. "We have decided on a couple of style changes in the pages of Life Advocate. First we will begin to capitalize the 'U' in Unborn because they are a 'class of people' like Blacks or Hispanics." The equation here effectively racializes the unborn as *another* "class of people" who are "like" but *not* part of Black or Hispanic communities; it suggests the Unborn is understood to be a class of white people. DeParrie continues his housekeeping: "Next, we have also decided to purge 'pro-life' from our own news stories in preference for 'anti-abortion.' The reason being that 'pro-life' has been diluted with the Shameless—er, Seamless Garment ideology (a Division of Pacifist Idolatry, Inc)." DeParrie here derides the largely Catholic idea that demands consistency in pro-life stances, so that one should argue not only for a prohibition of abortion, but also of the death penalty, for example. He is fed up with people who are pacifists and those who do not condone violent means to protest abortion.[73]

In his next issue of *Life Advocate* (May/June 1999), deParrie declares a full rejection of the pro-life moniker and announces the embrace of an abolitionist stance. Emboldened by the fact that Planned Parenthood could prove "clear threats" but could not tie those threats to all the people actually issuing them, deParrie is all the more disenchanted with the antiabortion groups who refuse to condone violence or call for it. He mocks and demeans appeals for anything less than absolutism, which implicitly includes using lethal force. He writes, "In coming issues, we will be bringing you material about our spiritual ancestors—The Abolitionists. These pieces should be encouraging and remind us not to be weary in well-doing. The Abolitionists did not succeed for many decades and it was those radicals who held the line of absolute principle—not the sniveling pragmatic fringe—who prevailed. So shall it be with Abortion Abolitionists—if we faint not and do not join the chorus for a kinder-and-gentler (to everyone except the babies), 'common ground' approach of the pro-lie movement."[74] While the appropriation of antislavery and African American history here is galling, equally so is deParrie's explicit aim to be "encouraging" to "radicals." Anything less is a false stance, a "pro-lie" rather than a pro-life movement. His disdain of a "kinder-and-gentler" stance mocked then-president George Herbert Walker Bush, who famously expressed desire for a "kinder and gentler" conservatism. DeParrie's anti-statist mockery, his explicit choices of language, and his implicit adherence to a leaderless resistance—all prefigure today's abortion authoritarian abolitionist movement and Make America Great Again populism.

By 2003, deParrie was publishing a magazine called *The Abortion Abolitionist*. Even more remarkable, deParrie demonstrates scarily accurate foresight of how antiabortion abolitionism would operate in the midst of public health crises, namely viral pandemics.

Volume 1, issue 2 of deParrie's *The Abortion Abolitionist* is the "SARS issue" (see figure 6 for an artist's rendering of the magazine cover). SARS refers to the viral respiratory illness outbreak that preceded COVID-19. On the cover of the magazine deParrie reused the photo of him wearing the upside-down American flag mask over his face, which had previously appeared with the aforementioned "Smoke and Mirrors" report in the March 1999 issue of *Life Advocate*. The mask that was initially meant to protest the supposed loss of free speech is now used to convey the futility of fight-

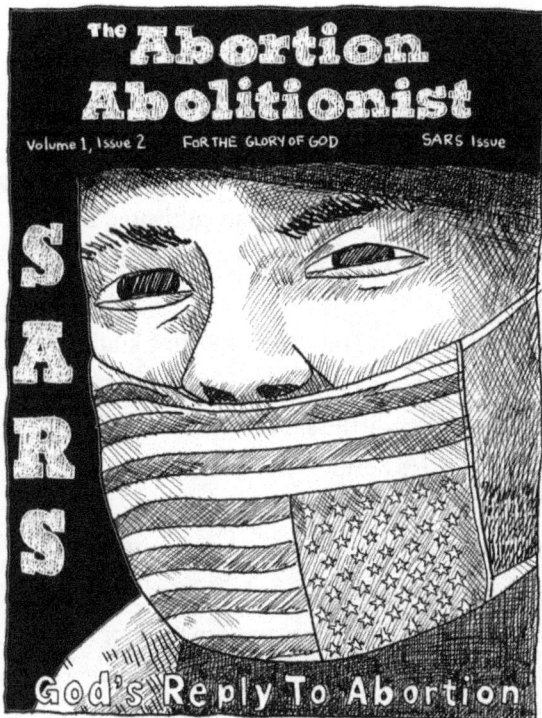

FIGURE 6. This line drawing of a 2003 cover of *The Abortion Abolitionist* features a photograph of Paul deParrie and prefigures the conspiracism surrounding the SARS COVID-19 pandemic as well as the idea of abolishing abortion. Drawing by author-illustrator Rachel Elliott, used with permission.

ing contagion because it is a judgment from God. The cover explicitly asserts that SARS is "God's reply to abortion." DeParrie's rationale appears to be that abortion is a sin, so God is punishing the world with a plague, or refusing to protect us from the plague. Some years earlier, amid discussions of stem cell research, deParrie issued a warning about the relationship between abortion and vaccines. The warning prefigures anti-vaccine conspiracism of the SARS scare of the early 2000s and the COVID-19 era later in the century. It also deploys the depravity narrative that was derived from antisemitic and gothic depictions of abortion as blood libel and would recirculate as the QAnon conspiracy theory of

Democrats as baby sacrificers. He writes, "A totally unprepared world is being spoon-fed cannibalism—again. The recent news that 'stem' cells are now viewed as a boon to medicine has wowed the public." DeParrie repeated a myth that stem cells are obtained through abortion procedures: "Careful readers will notice that these stem cells are taken from aborted babies and cultivated for cell lines much like the chicken pox vaccine. However, they still come from murder victims."[75]

DeParrie was frighteningly ahead of his time. The same kind of virus that causes COVID-19 circulated in the early 2000s as SARS, and deParrie met that threat in exactly the same way that authoritarian populists met COVID-19. He derides vaccinations as a purported means by which the elite medical establishment, enabled by the supposedly cannibalistic federal government, enjoys its life-prolonging medicine and, at the same time, curbs the individual rights of a certain "class of people," the white unborn who represent the real Christians and the real Americans. Here we have a man with a mask that he refuses to wear properly. His nose hangs out over it as a mockery of precaution, a defiance of both the safety measures for avoiding SARS and of the nation that will not protect the unborn, a "class of people." This is an early example of SARS-era populist sentiment that flourished amid a pandemic and then festered as an attack on democracy.

The title of deParrie's magazine—*Abortion Abolitionist*—appropriates anti-racist language and heritage in service to the plight of the white man, much like Created Equal. It also prefigures an absolutist approach to opposing abortion, which is to end it entirely by outlawing and punishing people, and not give in to the incrementalism of legal reform.

Most understandings of abortion abolitionism trace the ideas back to a group called Abolish Human Abortion, which started in 2011 in Oklahoma. Founded by young white men, Abolish Human Abortion was touted as the new vanguard in opposing abortion.[76] Its founders protested what they saw as an incremental-ist approach of undoing reproductive rights via regulatory legisla-tion. To challenge the pro-life establishment, Abolish Human Abortion unapologetically appropriated the historical plight of enslaved Africans in America and claimed to be pro-woman. Adopting the language of social justice as a means to thwart racial oppression, the campaign deployed a claim of abortion as Black genocide, invoking the historical trauma of people of color who have endured centuries of scientific and medical racism. As explored in chapter 2, the antiabortion movement had for years attempted to win support from African Americans with materials in different media, including comic books, video magazines, memes, so-called documentaries, campus tours, and bus tours. This race-based "scare tactic," as Kathryn Joyce has called it, becomes increasingly prominent when racial politics are impor-tant to electoral races.[77]

These racial and religious references to genocide, slavery, and the Holocaust are not mere comparisons.[78] Rather, they serve to tell a story of human atrocities that lead up to abortion as an apoca-lyptic culmination of human depravation.[79] Abolish Human Abortion embraced and perpetuated this narrative in claiming that "the abortion holocaust exceeds all previous atrocities practiced by the Western World." The result is a generic diminishment (if not erasure) of actual historical persecutions based on religion, race, sexuality, and gender. Moreover, abolishing abortion becomes an epic battle not against actual people as historical agents but a "war with the entire worldview that makes abortion legal in the first place." Thus, the AHA's home page declares, "Every age has its evils. Every age has its abolitionists." This declaration sounds like a tagline to a video game and casts the political battle over abortion as an apocalyptic narrative and generic vision quest to quash evil.[80]

In this theocratic vision quest, optics are all-important. In sharp contrast to their older counterparts who shame women with Bibles held aloft, AHA activists style themselves as progressive hipsters, posturing as cool big brothers to younger kids they recruit at high schools, which they consider to be the front lines of the abortion wars, not clinics. Their posters, memes, and websites rely on well-crafted graphic designs resembling the aesthetics of tattoos.

The AHA's historical arguments that compare the medical practice of abortion to the economic system of slavery are questioned even by some antiabortionists.[81] The group's use of visual artifacts from nineteenth-century abolitionist campaigns lends a veneer of historical authenticity to the comparison. Relying on pictorial assertion rather than historical fact of any relationship between antiabortion and antislavery campaigns, the AHA is deliberate in its choice of visual rhetoric.[82] Just like deParrie, AHA rejects the right-to-life approach because it is believed to invite incremental-ism instead of a commitment to act to end abortion—AHA states, "We are not pro-life." For example, one design created to comment on the explosive 2013 fight over Texas HB2 uses a tattoo-like aes-thetic and declares Fort Worth to be a "city of sin" and of "child sac-rifice," which is depicted by red blood streaming from one adult hand to another adult's palm (see figure 7). The design also features line drawings of both Democratic senator Wendy Davis and Republican governor Rick Perry flanking the AHA symbol, indict-

FIGURE 7. Equating abortion with "child sacrifice," Abolish Human Abortion opposes the term "pro-life" and uses a symbol conjoining the letters "A," "H," and "A," which appear to some as a white supremacist emblem.

ing them both in the gory hellscape pictured. The AHA thus rejects the soft-focus cuteness of baby images that populate "pro-life" materials. Instead of sentimental images, AHA designed a pictorial symbol that links the initials AHA in such a way that it resembles the newer incarnations of swastikas that are proliferating among white supremacist groups. The initials, assembled as a cross-hatched lightning bolt, resemble the German *Wolfsangel*.[83] To some, the AHA looks a lot like Nazism. The AHA's optics of appearing to be pro-Black, pro-woman, a radical upstart, and hipster cool are thus also read as white supremacist.

By updating and proliferating the racialized message that abortion is a matter of slavery and genocide, white advocates of abolishing abortion do not always specify which racial groups are the target of these imagined racial attacks. Contemporary antiabortionists have redesigned their look in ways that make them legible to a variety of factions of the right. They are similar to the polo-shirted, khakied alt-right who marched in the Unite the Right Rally of 2017 in Charlottesville. Those groups shunned the white robes of the KKK and recrafted Nazi symbols into updated iconography. Superficially, then, the AHA appears to be more progressive than its earlier counterparts. Especially in the age of social media, the control of optics determines whose narrative is replicated, read, followed, believed, and acted out. In other words, the control of optics determines whose news—fake or not—has the most impact.

In 2018 AHA launched what they call a "lobbying organization." Dubbed Free the States, it "exists to inform people of the power they possess to abolish abortion at the state level and to provide training and leadership to the growing abolitionist movement." It mirrors the Posse Comitatus groups of the 1970s and the patriot militia groups that emerged in the 1980s eschewing federal citizenship in favor of sovereign or state citizenship. Free the States touted the political strength of hyperlocalization. The racist resolve of states' rights –the rationale by which mid-twentieth-century Southerners fought for racial segregation—is easy to hear in "Free the States."[84]

By 2020 AHA/Free the States had become Abolitionists Rising, a nationwide organization still headquartered in Oklahoma. The idea of abortion abolitionism became more widespread and popular, expanding well beyond Oklahoma. According to Hannah Silver and Cloee Cooper, the leading organizations of the antiabortionist abolitionist movement include "End Abortion Now, an Arizona-based grassroots group of churches working to criminalize abortion"; the "Texas legal hub, Foundation to Abolish Abortion, which offers biblical principles and resources to state legislators to introduce abortion abolitionist bills nationwide"; and Operation Save America. The absolutist abolitionist faction of the antiabortion movement held their first national conference in Texas in 2020. This was about the same time that people protested en masse the police brutality that Derek Chauvin's murder of George Floyd illuminated. The coinciding of the flourishing of the Movement for Black Lives and the first convening of an antiabortion "abolitionist" movement comprised mostly of white people is a historical juxtaposition worthy to note. Perhaps a more telling measure of influence in this day and age: "Abolitionists Rising has more than 100,000 followers" on TikTok.[85]

Leaders of the antiabortion "abolitionist" movement argue against the homicide of physicians, bombings of clinics, and violence in general, yet they persist with the imagery that helps vigilantes imagine the dissolution of the unborn, of white people, of Christian Western civilization. Their materials recycle the apocalyptic themes and gothic imagery that demonize a very simple and safe medical procedure that individual people voluntarily choose as a nefarious systemic "child sacrifice" engineered by evildoers (who may or may not be human). Deploying that phrase—"child sacrifice"—repeatedly, leaders of the antiabortion abolitionist movement underscore and reemphasize conspiracy theories that have mutated over the decades. Abolitionists Rising organizer T. Russell Hunter says he wants to "get the culture to start seeing child sacrifice for what it is,"[86] but he fails to say who he presumes is benefiting from the supposed child sacrifice, just as those who claim abortion is genocide neglect to say who is supposedly benefiting from it or perpetuating it. "Child sacrifice" has become another way of appealing to a broad array of right-wing groups and individuals without having to reach consensus on what you're actually talking about. According to QAnon acolytes, "child sacrifice" alludes to a presumed "occult society of cannibalistic Satan worshippers, including Barack Obama, George Soros, the Clintons, and other liberal celebrities, [who were] ritualistically raping and devouring sacrificial children."[87] QAnon believers who participated in the January 6, 2021, attack on the Capitol contributed to the insurrection because, in the words of one sign, "the children cry out for justice" (see figure 8). One journalist ascribed the "meteoric rise of QAnon" to a "spiritual yearning of the faithful for the end of time."[88] A coinciding reason may be because American antiabortion materials since the nineteenth century have popularized the idea of children under attack by ghoulish women and doctors. Abolitionist leader Hunter and his group share gothic imagery and a sense of apocalyptic immediacy with other absolutists and militants.

Violent insurrection is not what the leaders of the antiabortion abolitionists say they want. Their goal is a sea change in American culture. "We affirm that civil government alone is instructed by God to systematically wield the sword against the evil-doer."[89] The emphasis on civil government is a rejection of federal government. Just as the Posse Comitatus and the Christian patriot militia movement saw their citizenship as beholden only to the local level of

FIGURE 8. A variation on the theme of abortion as child sacrifice that goes back to old antisemitic tales of blood libel, QAnon conspiracy theories about satanic rituals of killing children entered the Capitol with insurrectionists on January 6, 2021.

governance so, too, do the so-called abolitionists. Their goal is a wholesale cultural shift to a theocratic way of life in which those who provide or obtain abortions will be punished. Thus it was that on January 6, 2021, workers at abortion clinics across the nation were surprised not to have their usual protesters around. When they turned on the TV to watch the insurrection unfold, they recognized in the crowd the faces of those who usually were at their clinics.[90]

Among political strategies embraced by antiabortion abolitionists is one prescribed by erstwhile Trump advisor Steve Bannon. They aim for activists to "oust moderate Republicans and take control of state and county Republican parties."[91] The ordinances and laws they mean to encourage would, as we saw in chapter 1, entitle vigilant citizens to surveil family members and neighbors, and to criminalize not only abortions themselves but also those who seek, obtain, or provide them.

Paul deParrie is not alive to see what AHA, Free the States, and the broader antiabortion abolitionist movement are achieving. Neal Horsley, too, is dead. Yet now is the time that his imperative to "Visualize Abortionists on Trial" is getting easier to see. Many antiabortion abolitionists may never have heard of deParrie or Horsley or read the *Abortion Abolitionist* magazine, but they are de facto legacies devoted to authoritarian populism and a punitive Christian state that deParrie, and his various associates on the far right, envisioned.

Leaderless Then, Less Evasive Now

Militant men of the antiabortion movement have always mingled with supremacist ideas, absolutist mentalities, and paramilitary anti-statism. The historical trajectory from lone wolf bombers to abortion abolitionists suggests that leaderless resistance is a successful strategy. Individual incidents of antiabortion violence and homicide have been regarded as the work of individuals alone— apart from other abortion opponents and other far-right militants. However, primary writings authored by right-wing men like deParrie and Rudolph indicate a delighted commitment to leaderless resistance as practiced across a broad swath of right-wing militants. So long as these militants continue as individuals to wage war against their enemies, prosecutors are hard-pressed to prove conspiracy.

But evasion no longer seems to be a primary goal for these militants. Now we are in a different stage of militancy because supremacist ideologies and anti-statism have gone mainstream. Over the decades, the parallel and sometimes intersecting far-right movements have built an infrastructure of legal advocates, transnational support, vigilantes armed to the teeth, and major party protection. To continue to report on, study, and see far-right militants as separate groups inspired by niche causes is to ignore decades of shared tactics, mindsets, imagery, narratives, personnel, and goals. In many cases, as these chapters show and as the following conclusion will review, opposing abortion has flourished in and facilitated these intersections.

Conclusion

Locals and Kings

My years of researching violence at abortion clinics colored how I experienced the attack on the U.S. Capitol on January 6, 2021, and inspired me to revisit the relationships among right-wing movements, rhetoric, tactics, and personnel. Roughly a year after the insurrection, the Supreme Court that Donald Trump built eviscerated *Roe v. Wade* and the national standards for regulating abortion with the decision in the case of *Dobbs v. Jackson*. But the post-*Roe* landscape does not take us back to a pre-*Roe* era. We can't regain rights the way feminists and lawyers won them in the 1970s. *Dobbs* did not merely put us back at square one. We can't build reproductive rights back up, little by little. We cannot simply weather the storms and let time pass, trusting that the progressive work of history will repeat as a matter of course. Nor should we want to take such a passive posture. Such sentiment presumes that only reproductive rights were lost with the *Dobbs* decision. On the contrary, *Dobbs* didn't merely take away a constitutional right. It advanced strategic alignments and the synergy of what are usually regarded as separate political and social phenomena.

People committed to right-wing militancy, authoritarian populism, and white nationalism are often seen as lone wolves or as part of distinct political movements. Most academic study of patriot militias, antiabortionists, and white supremacists has made it seem that all these people stay in their own lanes. But as the previous chapters have shown, opposing abortion has flourished in and facilitated intersections among these militants and movements since long before their collusions and like-mindedness were made clear in events such as the insurrectionary attack on the Capitol. Opposing abortion has greased the wheels of these intersecting movements by providing:

- justifications for lying and spreading false information as a matter of defending Christ or Western civilization or the nation;
- stories derived from antisemitic myths about cannibalistic and/or satanic politicians and doctors who literally feed off of children, born and unborn;
- gothic imagery that helps white people envision the injury that they anticipate due to presumed demographic, political, and cultural demise;
- stories and images that tell white people that the result of demographic changes will be total subjugation and enslavement of them and that, therefore, absolutism is necessary;
- stories that help militants envision what revolutionary violence looks like and who their enemies, foreign and domestic, are;
- stories repackaging the Cold War–era equation of homosexuality with pedophilia as current moral panics over supposed transgender groomers and queer terrorists;
- stories that convince women that their sense of national belonging will be obliterated or enshrined depending on their maternal status;

- stories that convince military veterans that their combat skills need to be applied to moral and political disagreements at home, in the neighborhood, and at all levels of government;
- justifications for taking up arms against the federal government;
- imagined court battles that give readers a sense that they are being victimized systematically because of their political point of view;
- real court battles that define free speech in ways that make it compatible with incitement to violence and insurrection;
- stories and images that convince white Americans that their offspring are most endangered when in fact African American infant and maternal mortality rates are the highest;
- stories and images that appropriate African American history to convince Black people that they need to vote against politicians who otherwise might benefit their community;
- narratives that instill a sense of apocalyptic or revolutionary urgency that prepares people to expect or accelerate conflict that is all or nothing—a zero sum game in which everything can be either lost or gained;
- local and worldwide networks that help vigilante gunmen and bombers try to get away with murder;
- anti-travel policies that accelerate animosity and suspicion among neighbors and family members;
- nativist and reproducerist depictions of "invading" immigrants who supposedly make the wrong babies;
- punitive policies that criminalize people if they can't ensure the outcome of their pregnancies;
- laws like Texas's SB8 that effectively deputize the locals, offering rewards for turning in people who seek or help someone seeking an abortion.

These achievements of the antiabortion movement have compelled Americans to imagine scenarios in which white nationalism and right-wing populism seem to be the natural and inevitable responses. These stories, images, practices, and policies have primed Americans to accept and favor what once was deemed extreme. Moreover, as we have seen, antiabortion tactics, personnel, funds, and narratives have shaped campaigns overseas, contributing to a global rise of right-wing populism and authoritarianism. How have we come to a point where we must contend with an extremism in law and politics that is no longer seen as extreme?

I have some sense of how we got here, and in these chapters I hope I have shared my understanding in a helpful way. In chapters 1 and 2 I explained how white people opposing abortion claim victimhood not so much for the unborn as for themselves. White women are depicted worldwide as victims of abortion, seen as an evil global industry supposedly full of unethical doctors and clinic personnel who exploit patients sexually, financially, and mentally. An innovative corollary narrative is how women are victimized by transgender people, a new addition to the imagined rogues' gallery of evildoers attacking white women. What is a woman, according to these narratives of white victimhood? In diametrically opposing women from transgender people, such stories not only narrate cisgender white women as victims, but they also deny the very existence of transgender women, transmen, and any nonbinary or gender-divergent folks. Such stories don't just innocuously reflect a religious worldview. They effectively erase the personhood of those who are deemed objects rather than the speaking subject of the story. *What* is a woman? Their answer is that women are things—*whats*, not *whos*—that have no claim to human rights, or to personhood (much less equality) under the law.

White men are also claiming victim status, showing us images of themselves being castigated by frivolous, self-serving, angry women. They misrepresent actual procedures and the results of abortion because their goal is not merely convincing people that their religious point of view is worthy of consideration. Instead, men claiming victimhood feel entitled to hold court in public spaces, acting as arbiters of who and what can or can't be said, seen, or touched.

Such claims of victimhood feed a sense of entitlement to wage war. As chapters 3 and 4 make clear, antiabortion militants have become more radical over the past fifty years. These militant ranks include both women and men but are predominantly if not entirely white. The women have provided narratives that rehearse antisemitic conspiracy theories and paramilitary tactics of the Cold War, the Reagan Revolution, the Tea Party, and QAnon delusions. Each of the women's stories I examined has retained and recirculated an apocalyptic sense of inevitable, all-encompassing, and absolutist conflict that feeds right-wing populism. Mildred Jefferson wrote that physicians were social executioners. Joan Andrews inspired a group of "rescuers" who took no central orders but invaded clinics leaderlessly. For a fee, Norma McCorvey falsely testified about ghostly children who haunted her until she converted to a pro-life stance. Abby Johnson updated that clinic-to-Christian conversion story for a new generation, riding the fame and fortune it gave her all the way to the MAGA rally on January 6. Shelley Shannon contributed to *The Army of God Manual,* in which her preferred method of opposing abortion—gunning down people—became the prescribed parting shot, if you will, of the manual's declaration of war against the federal government.

That anti-statist approach emerged in the sometimes parallel, sometimes intersecting movements of the far right, as chapter 4 attests. Antiabortion militants embraced paramilitary tactics and supremacist ideologies as they emerged with the patriot militia and the white power movements throughout the 1970s, '80s, and '90s. Bomber Eric Rudolph exemplified this crossover, as did Paul deParrie. DeParrie's works as a writer and editor are extraordinary in showing us how much the antiabortion movement prefigured and facilitated the authoritarian impulses that throb throughout right-wing America today. He long ago pulled the veneer of moderation off pro-life politics. His work promoted an absolutist, Christian authoritarian stance. His and his abolitionist followers' endeavors to "visualize abortionists on trial" heralded the criminalization of both doctors and patients that we see now enacted by laws such as SB8. Indeed, the courts play a decisive role now more than ever. Two recent decisions from the Supreme Court in particular have profoundly shaped America's future.

In the summer of 2024, the U.S. Supreme Court issued its decision in *Trump v. United States*. A federal grand jury had indicted the former president for conspiring to overturn election results by spreading lies about election fraud. Trump's lawyers responded that he was immune from criminal prosecution. Many people thought that Trump's motion for the indictment to be dismissed was a frivolous lawsuit meant only to slow down the process until, ideally, after the 2024 election. But it turned out to have a much bigger impact.

The Supreme Court decision granted presidential immunity from criminal prosecution, meaning that any president could not be held accountable for breaking the law while he or she was attending to official business. It was a shocking decision. A fundamental idea undergirding the formation of the United States is that laws apply to everyone equally, regardless of wealth, race, or station. While we know that, in practice, laws are written and implemented by people whose biases are not always acknowledged, resulting in historical patterns of disadvantages and advantages, the *principle* of the rule of law is fundamental to democracy. The Supreme Court decision eroded this democratic foundation.

Disagreement from members of the Supreme Court whom Donald Trump did not appoint made no bones about it: "It makes a mockery of the principle, foundational to our Constitution and system of Government, that no man is above the law," Justice Sonia Sotomayor wrote. She warned:

> The relationship between the President and the people he serves has shifted irrevocably. In every use of official power, the President is now a king above the law. Never in the history of our Republic has a President had reason to believe that he would be immune from criminal prosecution if he used the trappings of his office to violate the criminal law. Moving forward, however, all former Presidents will be cloaked in such immunity. If the occupant of that office misuses official power for personal gain, the criminal law that the rest of us must abide will not provide a backstop. With fear for our democracy, I dissent.

The dramatic words were appropriate. This was an extremely erosive and antidemocratic decision. Moreover, it was on par with—and presaged by—the *Dobbs* decision from two years earlier in terms of unprecedented disregard for established norms and fundamental practices.

In its 2022 decision in *Dobbs v. Jackson Women's Health Organization,* the Supreme Court concluded that two key cases securing abortion rights, *Roe v. Wade* (1973) and *Planned Parenthood of Southeastern Pennsylvania v. Casey* (1992), had been wrongly decided. The effect was to demolish the national standards by which abortion had been regulated for nearly fifty years, allowing the states to set their own rules about who could terminate their pregnancy and when. By doing so, the Supreme Court flouted a basic norm of jurisprudence: the idea that justices arrive at legal decisions by understanding what came before, those conclusions from previous court cases that created precedents to follow. This basic norm is the doctrine of stare decisis. Legal scholars saw in *Dobbs* not only a decision against abortion but also a decision that thwarted the doctrine of stare decisis. This was not, experts contend, an unintentional consequence.

According to a *Harvard Law Review* article, the justices' anti-abortion efforts were "deployed to overcome the force of stare decisis in Dobbs—and may ultimately reshape the scope and substance of the Court's stare decisis analysis in future cases."[1] In other words, the Supreme Court is poised to more freely ignore established law. According to an article in the newsletter of the American Bar Association, the court's decision in *Dobbs* displayed "a nonchalance about the principle of *stare decisis* that could place all of the Court's constitutional precedents at potential risk: No matter the vintage of the precedent. No matter how ingrained that precedent has become in legal doctrine. No matter how thoroughly that precedent has set our societal expectations or shaped how we understand our rights and responsibilities. In short, after *Dobbs,* everything we think we know about the Constitution seems up for grabs and may be."[2]

Once again in American history, opposing abortion was doubly effective: it reduced an individual's right to terminate a pregnancy, and it advanced an antidemocratic agenda. *Dobbs* opened the door to authoritarian rule by announcing the Supreme Court's intention to no longer rely on established U.S. law. Two summers later, the court's decision in *Trump v. United States* invited presidents to become kings. Elected again in 2024, Trump appears poised to take up that invitation. In addition to the erosion of stare decisis and to the rule of law that the Supreme Court has issued since the third Trump-appointed justice joined the bench, the lower courts will also have an impact. Throughout his 2016–20 term, Trump appointed a historic number of judges, including a third of the justices on the Supreme Court as well as record numbers of judges on appellate courts and district courts.[3] Thirty percent of appellate judges are young Trump appointees, ensuring a conservative judiciary that will guide U.S. jurisprudence for decades. The resulting Republican influence over the lower courts contributes to an empowerment of federal judges and those "lesser magistrates" discussed in the introduction. Matthew Trewhella was not responsible for this empowerment and these appointments, but his rationale for focusing on the "lesser" and local officials became popular with MAGA strategists.

The street-preacher radical Trewhella—who in the 1990s was affiliated with the anti-government U.S. Taxpayers Party, called for forming militias, and supported killing physicians—has in recent years transformed into a suit-and-tie Republican. He is helping strategists focus on the locals to thwart anything they see as tyranny, including gun regulation, health mandates such as vaccinations and pandemic precautions, same-sex marriage, and legal abortion. This increased focus on the local will be paramount if accusations of electoral irregularity and fraud emerge in challenges to voting results. The local folks are encouraged to take the law into their own hands: "During a speech to the Waukesha GOP last year, Trewhella focused on how local officials were best positioned to safeguard" what they felt were "Americans' most cherished freedoms."[4] Echoing the posse comitatus idea that exalted the power of the county and was seen as extreme throughout the twentieth century, Trewhella contended that "the country is breaking apart. Counties are becoming important in the process. Counties may secede from one state and join an adjoining state as things break apart. Several adjoining counties may end up leaving a state and forming their own state." While Trewhella's power of prediction may prove negligible, his exaltation of local authority feeds the right-wing populism embraced by Republicans. Trewhella told his Republican audience, "You may have to do things in the future you're not authorized to do." In other words, they may have to break the law. The implication is that they should. Encouraging "the people" in positions of local authority to revolt against democratic procedures places a new emphasis on the local scene. It also dovetails with the emphasis on the local in fights over abortion.

Especially now that pills have become the typical way to end a pregnancy, antiabortionists can't achieve their goals by protesting at clinics or even by assassinating physicians. The location of abortion care has moved from *providers* in brick-and-mortar buildings to *patients* in the privacy of their own homes. More than 60 percent of abortions since *Dobbs* have been achieved by taking pills such as mifepristone and misoprostol. Self-managed abortion means you're the abortionist, so deParrie's and Horsley's old imperative to "visualize abortionists on trial" now has a new meaning that we see playing out in the criminalization and prosecution of people seeking to terminate pregnancy.[5]

Moreover, the imperative to "visualize" has emerged in the twenty-first century as a compulsion to imagine bodily subjugation at the hands of supposed enemies. The unborn, once depicted primarily as cute babies who needed rescuing, now most often appear as gory "American carnage." Antiabortion materials now promote the unborn as a sign of what you as an individual have escaped and what your future holds—torture, dismemberment, and dissolution. Unless you become a warrior in a populist push for Christian nationalism, you'll succumb to a bloody victimhood on the battlefields of American equality and white Western civilization. These antiabortion horror stories circulated gothic images and apocalyptic tales so much that Americans were primed to believe them not only in the context of imagining abortion but also in the context of imaging their own demise and that of their children.

In some especially horrifying situations, this compulsion to imagine children's demise has resulted in psychotic violence. Luke Mogelson, who suggests that we are living through a "shared psychosis," notes the example of a father who killed his own children because he was sure they had serpent DNA. The father killed his own children because he was afraid that they were going to grow up as monstrous lizard people. Another example Mogelson offers involves a mother drowning her three infants because she was paranoid about child sex trafficking. These parents' fears reflect the fears of Republicans who have been the target audience of conspiracy theories spread through social media: in a nationwide poll, a whopping 23 percent of Republicans agreed that "the government, media, and financial worlds in the U.S. are controlled by a group of Satan-worshipping pedophiles who run a global sex trafficking operation."[6]

But these ideas preceded social media. As I've shown, antiabortionists have perpetuated horror stories of bloody "slaughter" in "hell houses," depicting a purported "doctrine of demons" that supposedly calls for "child sacrifice." Whether we call such widespread fears a shared psychosis, a vast phantasm, mis- or dis-information, alternative facts, fake news, or lies, we can see these storms of horror as legacies of the antiabortion movement, deployed by all sorts of MAGA believers and right-wing strategists.

Right-wing strategists prevailed in the 2024 U.S. elections, not simply perpetuating a populist Make America Great Again movement but ushering in a MAGA state. We don't know which campaign promises and Republican proposals will be fulfilled, in what order, or at what pace.

Will Trump become king, as Sotomayor suggested he could? Indeed, President Trump's inaugural remarks in January 2025 presented him as divinely appointed as kings are said to be. Referring to the assassination attempt in Pennsylvania in July 2024, he said, "My life was saved for a reason. I was saved by God to make America great again." Shortly thereafter he issued a barrage of executive orders that rewarded and advanced the prejudices and predilections of his supporters, with little respect for the law or science. He called for an end to birthright citizenship, a move deemed unconstitutional, and ordered mass deportation. He also declared that the United States would recognize only "two sexes." The National Institutes of Health were commanded to cease communications and conferences. The president is already making commands like a king.[7]

Will the locals be further compelled to take matters into their own hands, as SB8 promotes and Trewhella predicted? Crucially, we don't know how much the second Trump administration will reward and rely on the heretofore anti-statist elements of right-wing America. Will the militias, white supremacists, and antiabortion militants partner with the new government? President Trump's immediate blanket pardon of those convicted of violent and seditious crimes committed on January 6, 2021, is a clear embrace of those people. So is his subsequent pardon of protesters prosecuted for blockading an abortion clinic. Will he deputize them to operate as extralegal fighting bands sent to enforce his commands alongside—or in opposition to—the police and the military? Whether or not any official deputization occurs, Trump's pardon has communicated an invitation to the locals, the "lesser magistrates," and those who consider themselves to be "the people." They are free to ignore the rule of law and act on his behalf again, as they did in the 2021 attack on the Capitol.[8]

Similarly, Elon Musk's appearance at the inaugural festivities bolstered the spirits of white supremacists. The multibillionaire Trump supporter addressed a crowd of revelers and gave two exuberant salutes. The gestures were widely regarded as fascist salutes used by a variety of white supremacists. Speculation about whether it was intentional or accidental ensued. But, as one report noted, "Musk's straight-armed gesture [was] embraced by right-wing extremists regardless of what he meant." Social media posts by white supremacists confirmed they were emboldened in the moment.[9] This physical gesture by Musk and Trump's presidential gesture of pardoning extremists who attacked the Capitol and abortion clinics were readily received as encouragements by the far right. With such straightforward support, they likely would again fight on behalf of Trump. Perhaps, however, given the Republicans' control of all branches of government, we may not see that kind of civilian combat again. Trump and the Republicans may not need it to ensure any authoritarian populist visions and white nationalist plans.

In 2021, I could not fathom that the insurrectionary violence I was watching would one day be called a "day of love" by Trump, the president-elect. In 2017, when I drove through the rain to see abortion foes try to shut down the last clinic in Kentucky, I kept pondering what their slogan "ignore *Roe*" meant. I didn't recognize then that it was part of a larger, growing impulse to ignore wholesale the rule of law. Twenty-five years ago, when I first started to research the antiabortion movement and traveled to Buffalo, New York, with a righteous band of feminists, I could not see what was coming. My activist friends couldn't either. We just knew something was up.

The young filmmaker who was with us on that 1999 trip to Buffalo became an award-winning documentarian whose work includes *American Insurrection*, the 2022 Frontline film about the January 6, 2021, attack on the Capitol. Another one who was with us became a reporter, then editor, for National Public Radio. A third became an award-winning choreographer and professor of dance, steeped in the politics of the body.

I just kept writing. I don't know if what you're reading now will become more—or less—relevant in the next twenty-five years. As we ride through the storms of this century, I'm hoping for less.

Acknowledgments

In January 2021, after listening to how I had watched the insurrection on January 6, Lynn Paltrow told me, "You're doing a webinar." I hate Zoom. I had been a hermit hiding away during the pandemic, so the webinars that ultimately resulted left me feeling vulnerable, but they also opened doors of collaboration that nourished this book. I thank Lynn for urging me to be brave, something she has done for hundreds of people throughout her career as a pioneer in legal advocacy that decenters abortion while fighting for reproductive rights. She has fostered activist and intellectual communities that seek a broader frame of analysis, and she has fought for clients caught in webs of unfair policing. One of the webinars Lynn asked me to participate in paired me with Loretta Ross, whom—like Lynn—I met in the 1990s. Loretta's work is legendary, and I've had the privilege of appearing with her on several panels over the years. As one of the founders of reproductive justice, she has been an inspiration. I also want to honor at the outset Chip Berlet, a third person I met in the 1990s. He taught me how to study right-wing politics and culture with humor and dedication. His lifelong commitment to democracy, his humility in research, and his precision in documentation have been awesome models. These three people have at different times been beacons for me, illuminating analytical frameworks and research practices that helped me write not only this book, but also the three preceding it. I am so grateful for their lifetimes of inspiring work.

This book would not have been possible without the support of the College of Arts and Sciences at University of Kentucky. In 2022 I was named University Research Professor, which came with money for research. In 2023 I became the Otis A. Singletary Chair in the Humanities, which also provided research funds. I thank our dean, Ana Franco-Watkins, for democratizing the process for selecting endowed chairs; the committee who selected me; and Ann Kingsolver for supporting me in this venture and ever since we both arrived at University of Kentucky in 2011. The funds from these two honors allowed me to hire graduate students. Kyle Eveleth, Kendall Sewell, and Daria Goncharova were outstanding research assistants at different times as I was writing this book. In 2024, the university granted me sabbatical leave, which gave me precious time away from teaching, without which I could not have written the book. I spell out all these supports to emphasize how crucial institutional investment like this is for all researchers, but especially for humanities scholars. Accessing the support would have been impossible without the conscientious administrative assistance of Michelle Del Toro, manager of the Department of Gender and Women's Studies, who makes everything run without fail. Colleagues in the department—Melissa Stein, Elizabeth Williams, Srimati Basu, Charlie Zhang, Frances Henderson, Anastasia Todd, Jenn Hunt, Aria Halliday, and Karen Tice—are so smart that I am inspired to produce good work that I hope approximates theirs. Our department's emphasis on transnational analysis helped me grow as a scholar; parts of this book are reprinted from "Opposing Abortion to Protect Women: Transnational Strategy Since the 1990s," which appeared in the Gender and the Rise of the Global Right issue of *Signs: Journal of Women in Culture and Society* 44, no. 3 (2019): 665–692. I am very grateful to be part of a vibrant research-oriented feminist department.

I am also deeply indebted to the Institute for the Study of Societal Issues at the University of California for providing in-kind support by hosting me as visiting scholar at the Berkeley Center for Right-Wing Studies during my sabbatical. Some insights in this book were first published in the center's "Right-Wing Studies: A Roundtable on the State of the Field," the inaugural issue of the *Journal of Right-Wing Studies*, 25–28. I am grateful to Deborah Lustig, Maxwell Vanderwarker, and Lawrence Rosenthal, the splendid director of the center, for a very productive spring 2024 semester. Larry Rosenthal and Carole Joffe have been staunch supporters of this project, and I am an intellectual beneficiary of them both. Others in California, namely Yvette Lindgren, Kristin Luker, and Grace Howard, were wonderful touchstones as I wrote that semester.

I am most grateful for my partner, graphic novelist Rachel Elliott, who held down the fort in Kentucky while I was on the West Coast. Rachel is otherwise my constant companion, and nobody knows how much fun we have together. When

I could not locate reproducible images, she offered to produce line drawings of the artifacts. We experienced two deaths while I was writing this book, and those losses showed me again how lucky I am to have Rachel's love. I am also grateful for her side of my family, the Elliotts—Jana, Rick, Kayo, David, Hannah, May, and Jack—for their support and understanding during the entire stressful span of 2023–24. During those months and always, Steve Waksman also was a reliable source of support and camaraderie; I am enormously grateful for our enduring friendship through fun and tough times. Speaking of tough, I celebrate my University of Kentucky colleagues who fought diligently to retain shared governance while I was in California, especially Akiko Takenaka and Molly Blasing. The facts that we didn't succeed and that the attacks on higher education keep coming are no reflection on your bravery, resolution, and worthiness.

For the shaping of the content and prosody of the book, I owe thanks to several scholarly communities and a great team of editors. Scholars who hosted me in Lausanne and Rome for international workshops on demographics and right-wing politics in fall 2023 and spring 2024 aided my study of populism. Thank you, Mattia Diletti, Oscar Mozzoleni, Marianna Griffini, Alberta Giorgi, and Carlos de la Torre. I'm grateful to Carlos and to his coeditors for allowing me to reprint some insights that appear in their book as "How Opposing Abortion Serves Populism" in *Still the Age of Populism? Re-examining Concepts and Theories,* edited by Amie Kreppel, Michael Bernhard, and Carlos de la Torre (Routledge, 2024), 117–27. I am also grateful to the international audience gathered by Alan Nadel for the Bavarian American Academy, and for Alan, who has always been a funny and intellectually engaged colleague at Kentucky. Journalists John Archibald, John Hammontree, and Becca Andrews were terrific interlocutors as we all shared research. I am also deeply grateful for Chelsea Ebin, a kindred queer spirit who brought me into conversation with a new generation of feminist scholars of right-wing studies. I appreciate Chelsea and her coeditors for allowing me to reprint portions of an article in their collection: "Created Equal but 'Equal in No Other Respect': Opposing Abortion to Protect Men," in *Male Supremacism in the United States: From Patriarchal Traditionalism to Misogynist Incels and the Alt-Right,* edited by Emily Carian, Alex DiBranco, and Chelsea Ebin (Routledge, 2022), 94–114. Mary Reynolds and Annie Wilkinson were also probing collaborators who helped shape my thinking on gender and authoritarianism; thank you for supporting my work in conjunction with the Women's Donor Network and Political Research Associates.

As for editors, Rickie Solinger nearly pounced when I mentioned I was thinking of writing a sort-of sequel to *Killing for Life*. I am grateful to her (and Arlene) for her generosity. She promoted the proposal at UC Press, and Naomi Schneider met with me several times to discuss how it fit in the Reproductive Justice Series. They also supported the project by hiring James J. Berg to coach me in creating a more personal voice. Jim, the extraordinary scholar/editor of Christopher Isherwood's work, coaxed me out of my vulnerability, analyzed the patterns of my academic writing, and with tough love helped me fashion a more narrative approach. It was wonderful to work with such an intellectually and politically astute editor. I also had the great fortune of Toby Beauchamp's insights on the manuscript. Toby was very kind to read my work at the beginning of the semester he was stepping into the role of department chair; thank you. I am also grateful for the legal expertise of Jessica Friedman, who read the book over for any lapses in judgment that could be mistaken for libel or invasion of privacy. The team at University of California Press is excellent; I'm especially grateful for Sharron Wood, the copyeditor, and Aline Dolinh, who wrangled everything. The book has benefited from guidance by all these people. Of course, any errors are solely mine.

I send a shout-out to reproductive justice advocates and social justice activists who over the years have shown great fortitude and ingenuity. I'm proud that our paths have crossed in one way or another, especially those I associate with that early career trip to Buffalo: Rosemary Candelario, Jacqueline Soohen, and Miranda Kennedy. I also hold close to my heart the *many* people who through the years organized and supported the Take Root Red States Reproductive Justice Conference, in both Oklahoma and Kentucky. There are now too many to list, and I'm thankful for all.

And, finally, *ciao* to Martha Mason. We saw a lot of each other while I was writing this book. What a year it was! Thanks for riding the waves of anticipation and grief with me, and for traveling *en famille avec moi, toujours votre soeur.* This one's for you.

Notes

Introduction

1. Thomas Novelly, "As Buffer Zone Debated, Courthouse the First Site of Week-Long Abortion Protests," *Courier-Journal* (Louisville, KY), July 24, 2017, www.courier-journal.com/story/news/local/2017/07/24/operation-save -america-begins-weeklong-abortion-protest-louisville/499502001/.

2. Dave Mistich, "'Appalachia Shaming' on Day 100," *100 Days in Appalachia,* April 30, 2017, www.100daysinappalachia.com/2017/04/appalachian- shaming-day-100-white-supremacist-rally-counter-protest-no-one-wanted/.

3. Ryan Lenz, "The Battle for Berkeley," *Hatewatch,* May 1, 2017, www .splcenter.org/hatewatch/2017/05/01/battle-berkeley-name-freedom -speech-radical-right-circling-ivory-tower-ensure-voice-alt.

4. Eric Goodman, "On the 19th of April," *Self,* April 1999, 111. See also Eyal Price, *Absolute Convictions* (New York: Henry Holt), 2006; Jon Wells, *Sniper: The True Story of Antiabortion Killer James Kopp* (New York: Harper Collins, 2008).

5. Carol Mason, *Killing for Life: The Apocalyptic Narrative of Pro-Life Politics* (Ithaca, NY: Cornell University Press, 2002).

6. andré douglas pond cummings and Steven A. Ramirez, "The Racist Roots of the War on Drugs and the Myth of Equal Protection for People of Color," *University of Arkansas at Little Rock Law Review* 44, no. 4 (2022), https:// lawrepository.ualr.edu/lawreview/vol44/iss4/1; Deborah Small, "The War on Drugs Is a War on Racial Justice," *Social Research* 68, no. 3 (2001): 896–903, www.jstor.org/stable/40971924.

7. Kathryn Joyce, "Deep State, Deep Church: How QAnon and Donald Trump Have Infected the Catholic Church," *Vanity Fair,* October 30, 2020, www.vanityfair.com/news/2020/10/how-qanon-and-trumpism-have -infected-the-catholic-church.

8. Leslie Reagan, *Dangerous Pregnancies: Mothers, Disabilities, and Abortion in America* (Berkeley: University of California Press), 2012.

9. Tina Vásquez, "How the Antiabortion Movement Fed the Capitol Insurrection," *Prism,* January 22, 2021, http://prismreports.org/2021/01/22/how-the-antiabortion-movement-fed-the-capitol-insurrection/; Molly Osborn, "Anti-Abortion Activist Abby Johnson Had Quite the Adventure at the Capitol Riot," *Jezebel,* January 12, 2021, www.jezebel.com/anti-abortion-activist-abby -johnson-had-quite-the-adven-1846043253; Carter Sherman, "Anti-Abortion Activists Were All Over the Capitol Riots," *Vice,* January 12, 2021; Abortion Access Front, "The Role Anti-Abortion Extremists Played in the Terrorism on Our Nation's Capitol," www.aafront.org/anti-abortion-extremists-at-capitol/.

10. Melinda Liu, "Inside the Anti-Abortion Underground," *Newsweek,* August 29, 1994, www.newsweek.com/inside-anti-abortion-underground-187894.

11. Matthew Trewhella, *The Doctrine of the Lesser Magistrates: A Proper Resistance to Tyranny and a Repudiation of Unlimited Obedience to Civil Government* (North Charleston, SC: CreateSpace Independent Publishing Platform, 2013).

12. Anna Rosensweig, "Whose Resistance Theory?," *Modern Language Quarterly* 83, no. 3 (September 2022): 335–48.

13. Karen McCally, "Why Is a 16th-Century Tradition Attracting Activists on the Christian Right?," University of Rochester NewsCenter, www.rochester .edu/newscenter/early-modern-resistance-theory-christian-right-544452/.

14. Rusty Thomas, "The Line Was Crossed—Where Do We Go from Here?," *Operation Save America,* May 25, 2017, www.operationsaveamerica .org/2017/05/25/4125/.

15. Rusty Thomas, "Open Letter to the Police in America," *Operation Save America,* July 19, 2016, www.operationsaveamerica.org/2016/07/19/press -release-open-letter-to-the-police-in-america/.

16. Satchel Walton and Cooper Walton, "KSP Training Slideshow Quotes Hitler, Advocates 'Ruthless' Violence," *Manual RedEye* (duPont Manual High School, Louisville, KY), October 30, 2020, https://manualredeye.com/90096 /news/local/police-training-hitler-presentation/.

17. Rosensweig, "Whose Resistance Theory?," 340–41.

18. Chip Berlet and Spencer Sunshine, "Rural Rage: The Roots of Right-Wing Populism in the United States," *Journal of Peasant Studies* 46, no. 3 (2019): 480–513.s

19. Karen Lee Ashcraft, *Wronged and Dangerous: Viral Masculinity and the Populist Pandemic* (Bristol: Bristol University Press, 2022), 68.

20. Ashcraft, *Wronged and Dangerous,* 68.

21. "What a Real President Was Like," *Washington Post,* November 13, 1988, www.washingtonpost.com/archive/opinions/1988/11/13/what-a-real-president-was-like/d483c1be-d0da-43b7-bde6-04e10106ff6c/.

22. Ella Myers, *The Gratifications of Whiteness: W.E.B. Du Bois and the Enduring Rewards of Anti-Blackness* (New York: Oxford, 2022); David R. Roediger, *The Wages of Whiteness: Race and the Making of the American Working Class* (New York: Verso, 1991).

23. Chip Berlet, "Collectivists, Communists, Labor Bosses, and Treason: The Tea Parties as Right-Wing Populist Counter-Subversion Panic," *Critical Sociology* 38, no. 4 (July 2012): 565–87.

24. Benedict Anderson, *Imagined Communities: Reflections on the Origin and Spread of Nationalism* (London: Verso, 2016).

25. Robert Chappell, "Racist Propaganda Appears in Madison, Middleton," *Madison 365,* October 5, 2020, https://madison365.com/racist-propoaganda-appears-in-madison-middleton/; Montse Ricossa, "Hateful Flyers in the Quad Cities," October 18, 2019, www.kwqc.com/content/news/Hateful-flyers-in-the-Quad-Cities-563424181.html.

26. Yotam Ophir et al., "Weaponizing Reproductive Rights: A Mixed-Method Analysis of White Nationalists' Discussion of Abortions Online," *Information, Communication & Society* 26, no. 11 (2022): 2186–2211.

27. Yvonne Lindgren, "Trump's Angry White Women: Motherhood, Nationalism, and Abortion," *Hofstra Law Review* 48, no. 1 (2019): 1–46, https://scholarlycommons.law.hofstra.edu/hlr/vol48/iss1/3.

28. Lindgren, "Trump's Angry White Women," 10 (italics in the original).

29. Lindgren, "Trump's Angry White Women," 10.

30. Lindgren, "Trump's Angry White Women," 4.

31. Lindgren, "Trump's Angry White Women," 37.

32. Chip Berlet and Matthew Lyons, *Right-Wing Populism in the United States: Too Close for Comfort* (New York: Guilford Press, 2000), 11–15.

33. I use the term "patriot" to refer to groups known as Christian patriots or patriot militias that emerged in the 1970s and became popular in the 1980s. These groups are not actually, in my mind, American patriots because they are antidemocratic, antiegalitarian, and usually anti-statist. Historically, they are part of the populist far right that envisions white supremacist and/or theocratic revolution obtained through paramilitary fighting, organizing society on the local (usually the county) level, and leaderless resistance to the federal government.

34. In *Killing for Life,* I explain kairotic time in relation to the writings of conservative Catholic activist L. Brent Bozell Jr. and his *Triumph* magazine, which explained that "kairos is the time of salvation." See chapter 5, "Making Time for America's Armageddon." More recently Jeff Sharlet described it as "movement time," a "sort of slow motion, sped up, outside of the flow of minutes and days, the temporal experience suggested by the Christian theological term *kairos.*" Sharlet, *The Undertow: Scenes from a Slow Civil War* (New York: Norton, 2023), 37.

35. Jill Lepore, *The Whites of Their Eyes: The Tea Party's Revolution and the Battle over American History* (Princeton, NJ: Princeton University Press, 2010), 16.

36. Alexandar Mihailovic, "Hijacking Academic Autonomy: Neo-Aryanism and Internet Expertise," in *Digital Media Strategies of the Far Right in Europe and the United States,* ed. Patricia Anne Simpson and Helga Druxes (London: Rowman & Littlefield, 2015), 89.

37. Anna Rosensweig, "Whose Resistance Theory?," 342.

38. Sharlet, *The Undertow.*

39. Carol Mason, "Opposing Abortion to Protect Women: Transnational Strategy since the 1990s," *Signs: Journal of Women in Culture and Society* 44, no. 3 (2019): 665–92.

40. Toby Beauchamp, *Going Stealth: Transgender Politics and U.S. Surveillance Practices* (Durham, NC: Duke University Press, 2018).

41. C. Mander, "Murder of Trans People Nearly Doubled," CBS News, www.cbsnews.com/news/transgender-community-murder-rates-everytown-for-gun-safety-report/.

42. The American Library Association reported that 2023 saw a 65 percent increase since the previous year of books targeted for censorship. Nearly half

of these were titles that represented stories by or about Black and Indigenous people, people of color, and/or LGBTQ lives. See American Library Association, "American Library Association Reports Record Number of Unique Book Titles Challenged in 2023," March 14, 2024, www.ala.org/news/2024/03 /american-library-association-reports-record-number-unique-book-titles. For details of librarians being fired, see Matt Bloom, "A Librarian Was Fired after Refusing to Ban Books," National Public Radio, January 2, 2024, www.npr.org/2024/01/02/1222566899/a-librarian-was-fired-after-refusing-to -ban-books-she-fought-back.

43. Daniel Dale, "Fact Check: Trump Falsely Claims Schools Are Secretly Sending Children for Gender-Affirming Surgeries," CNN, September 4, 2024, www.cnn.com/2024/09/04/politics/donald-trump-fact-check-children -gender-affirming-surgery/index.html.

44. I write about the distinction between right-to-life and pro-life in my 2002 book, noting the founding of the American Life League as an important development. "In dismissing the right-to-life approach, with all references to human rights and civil rights, the American Life League marks a change. The nuance of the word *life* shifts from indicating individual, singular, autonomous, and ultimately human life of 'the fetus' to indicate 'American life' as a collectivity—a national body created by God, operated by conservative principles, and symbolized by 'the unborn.'" See Mason, *Killing for Life*, 14–20.

45. Cynthia Miller-Idriss, *Hate in the Homeland: The New Global Far Right* (Princeton, NJ: Princeton University Press, 2020), 17–18.

1. Protecting Women from Abortion around the World

1. Srimati Basu, "Practicing Vulnerability—Men's Rights Activists, Embodiment and Appropriation," presented at the Center for South Asian Studies Lecture Series, University of Michigan, Ann Arbor, March 2019.

2. Dave Huber, "Professor Says It's Not about Free Speech," *College Fix*, April 19, 2023, www.thecollegefix.com/professor-says-its-not-about-free -speech-after-what-is-a-woman-is-painted-on-campus-rock/.

3. Jillian Flack and Molly Huffer, "It's Not about Free Speech," *Kent Wired*, April 18, 2023, https://kentwired.com/96504/latest-updates/its-not-about

-free-speech-members-of-the-lgbtq-community-speak-out-against-anti-trans-message-fusion-collab/.

4. The high infant and maternal mortality rates for Black people have been a sustained disparity in the United States for decades. See, for example, data from 1980 to 2013 in Laura Briggs, *How All Politics Became Reproductive Politics* (Berkeley: University of California Press, 2017), 133. For a cultural analysis of racial disparities in infant and maternal mortality, see Khiara M. Bridges, *Reproducing Race: An Ethnography of Pregnancy as a Site of Racialization* (Berkeley: University of California Press, 2011), especially 107–14.

5. C. Mander, "Murder of Trans People Nearly Doubled," CBS News, www.cbsnews.com/news/transgender-community-murder-rates-everytown-for-gun-safety-report/.

6. Carol Sanger, *About Abortion: Terminating Pregnancy in Twenty-First-Century America* (Cambridge, MA: Belknap Press of Harvard University Press, 2017).

7. Eighth Amendment of the Constitution Act 1983 (Ir.), www.irishstatutebook.ie/eli/1983/ca/8/enacted/en/html.

8. Ross Douthat, "The Irish Exception," *New York Times*, May 19, 2018, www.nytimes.com/2018/05/19/opinion/sunday/ireland-abortion-amendment.html.

9. Harriet Sherwood, "Remember Savita," *Guardian*, May 23, 2018.

10. Ed O'Loughlin, "As Irish Abortion Vote Nears, Fears of Foreign Influence Rise," *New York Times*, March 26, 2018, www.nytimes.com/2018/03/26/world/europe/ireland-us-abortion-referendum.html.

11. O'Loughlin, "As Irish Abortion Vote Nears."

12. Claire Provost and Lara Whyte, "Foreign and 'Alt-Right' Activists Target Irish Voters on Facebook ahead of Abortion Referendum," *Open Democracy*, April 25, 2018, www.opendemocracy.net/5050/claire-provost-lara-whyte/north-american-anti-abortion-facebook-ireland-referendum.

13. Protection of Life During Pregnancy Act 2013 (Act No. 35/2013) (Ir.), www.irishstatutebook.ie/eli/2013/act/35/enacted/en/print.

14. Lynn Morgan, "The Dublin Declaration on Maternal Health Care and Anti-Abortion Activism: Examples from Latin America," *Health and Human Rights Journal* 19, no. 1 (2017): 41–53.

15. Joer Dreweke, "Study Purporting to Show Link between Abortion and Mental Health Outcomes Decisively Debunked," Guttmacher Institute,

March 5, 2012, www.guttmacher.org/news-release/2012/study-purporting -show-link-between-abortion-and-mental-health-outcomes-decisively.

16. "Article That Critiques High-Profile Abortion Study Retracted," *Retraction Watch,* December 29, 2022, https://retractionwatch.com/2022/12/29/article -that-critiqued-high-profile-abortion-study-retracted/,

17. Americans United for Life, "Defending Life 2018," 471, https://aul.org /wp-content/uploads/2018/10/Defending-Life-2018.pdf.

18. Robin Marty, "Meet Joe Scheidler, Patriarch of the Anti-Abortion Movement," Political Research Associates, January 23, 2015, https://politicalresearch .org/2015/01/23/meet-joe-scheidler-patriarch-anti-abortion-movement; O'Loughlin, "As Irish Abortion Vote Nears."

19. Marty, "Meet Joe Scheidler."

20. Karissa Haugeberg, *Women against Abortion: Inside the Largest Moral Reform Movement of the Twentieth Century* (Urbana: University of Illinois Press, 2017).

21. Mark Crutcher, *Firestorm: A Guerrilla Strategy for a Pro-life America* (Denton, TX: Life Dynamics, 1992), 75.

22. Crutcher, *Firestorm,* 59.

23. Crutcher, *Firestorm,* 70.

24. Crutcher, *Firestorm,* 40.

25. Sarah MacDonald, "People Are Only Hearing Sterilised Version of Abortion, PLC Conference Hears," *CatholicIreland.net,* December 5, 2017, www.catholicireland.net/people-hearing-sterilised-version-abortion-plc -conference-hears/.

26. Human Life International Staff, "UPDATE: HLI Ireland Conference Forced to Move after Threats Rescheduled," *Human Life International,* September 22, 2017, www.hli.org/2017/09/venue-refuses-hosting-hli-event-after -receiving-threats/.

27. Cara Delay, "From the Backstreet to Britain: Women and Abortion Travel in Irish History," in *Travellin' Mama: Mothers, Mothering, and Travel,* ed. Charlotte Beyer, Janet MacLennon, Dorsia Smith Silva, and Marjorie Tesser (Bradford, ON: Demeter, 2019), 217–34.

28. Michele Rivkin-Fish, "Conceptualizing Feminist Strategies for Russian Reproductive Politics: Abortion, Surrogate Motherhood, and Family Support after Socialism," *Signs* 38, no. 3 (2013): 573.

29. Rivkin-Fish, "Conceptualizing Feminist Strategies"; Sonja Luehr-mann, "Innocence and Demographic Crisis: Transposing Post-Abortion Syndrome into a Russian Orthodox Key," in *A Fragmented Landscape: Abortion Governance and Protest Logics in Europe,* ed. Silvia De Zordo, Joanna Mishtal, and Lorena Anton (New York: Berghahn, 2016), 103–22.

30. Michele Rivkin-Fish, "Anthropology, Demography, and the Search for a Critical Analysis of Fertility: Insights from Russia," *American Anthropologist* 105, no. 2 (2003): 290.

31. Rivkin-Fish, "Anthropology, Demography, and the Search for a Critical Analysis of Fertility," 289, 293.

32. Rivkin-Fish, "Conceptualizing Feminist Strategies," 573; see also Rivkin-Fish, "Anthropology, Demography, and the Search for a Critical Analysis of Fertility."

33. Sophia Kishkovsky, "Russians Adopt U.S. Tactics in Opposing Abortion," *New York Times,* June 9, 2011, www.nytimes.com/2011/06/10/world /europe/10iht-abortion10.html.

34. Kishkovsky, "Russians Adopt U.S. Tactics."

35. Ilaria Parogni, "The Strategic Savvy of Russia's Growing Anti-Abortion Movement," *The Nation,* August 30, 2016, www.thenation.com/article/archive /the-strategic-savvy-of-russias-growing-anti-abortion-movement/.

36. Parogni, "The Strategic Savvy of Russia's Growing Anti-Abortion Movement"; Haugeberg, *Women against Abortion,* 45–49.

37. Hannah Levintova, "How U.S. Evangelicals Helped Create Russia's Anti-Gay Movement," *Mother Jones,* February 21, 2014, www.motherjones .com/politics/2014/02/world-congress-families-russia-gay-rights/; Hannah Levintova, "The World Congress of Families' Russian Network," *Mother Jones,* February 21, 2014, www.motherjones.com/politics/2014/02/world-congress -families-us-evangelical-russia-family-tree/.

38. Parogni, "The Strategic Savvy of Russia's Growing Anti-Abortion Movement."

39. Rivkin-Fish, "Conceptualizing Feminist Strategies," 585; see also Michele Rivkin-Fish, "Pronatalism, Gender Politics, and the Renewal of Family Support in Russia: Toward a Feminist Anthropology of 'Maternal Capital,'" *Slavic Review* 69, no. 3 (2010): 701–24.

40. Parogni, "The Strategic Savvy of Russia's Growing Anti-Abortion Movement."

41. HRC (Human Rights Campaign), "Exposed: The World Congress of Families," June 2015, https://assets2.hrc.org/files/assets/resources/Exposed TheWorldCongressOfFamilies.pdf, 12.

42. Kishkovsky, "Russians Adopt U.S. Tactics."

43. HRC, "Exposed," 13.

44. HRC, "Exposed," 14. See also Hannah Levintova, "Did Anti-Gay Evangelicals Skirt U.S. Sanctions on Russia?," *Mother Jones*, September 8, 2014, www.motherjones.com/politics/2014/09/world-congress-families-russia -conference-sanctions/

45. Jeffrey Mervis, "Crashing the Boards: Neuroscientist Maureen Condic Brings a Different Voice to NSF Oversight Body," *Science*, November 26, 2018, www.science.org/content/article/crashing-boards-neuroscientist-maureen -condic-brings-different-voice-nsf-oversight-body.

46. John Jalsevac, "Top Scientists Meet in Moscow, Tell Russian Government: Fetus Is Human; Ban Abortion," LifeSiteNews, July 15, 2015, www .lifesitenews.com/news/top-scientists-meet-in-moscow-tell-russian-government -fetus-is-human.-ban-a.

47. Parogni, "The Strategic Savvy of Russia's Growing Anti-Abortion Movement."

48. Parogni, "The Strategic Savvy of Russia's Growing Anti-Abortion Movement."

49. Maria Young, "Russia Gay Laws Cheered by US Conservatives," *Sputnik News*, March 8, 2013, https://sputniknews.com/analysis/20130803182557638 -Russia-Gay-Homosexuality-Laws-Cheered-by-US-Conservatives/.

50. Young, "Russia Gay Laws Cheered by US Conservatives."

51. Anton Shekhovtsov, *Russia and the Western Far Right: Tango Noir* (London: Routledge, 2018), 180.

52. J. Lester Feder and Alberto Nardelli, "This Anti-Abortion Leader Is Charged with Laundering Money from Azerbaijan," *Buzzfeed News*, April 26, 2017, www.buzzfeed.com/lesterfeder/this-anti-abortion-leader-is-charged -with-laundering-money.

53. Neil Datta, *Tip of the Iceberg: Religious Extremist Funders against Human Rights for Sexuality and Reproductive Health in Europe 2009-2018.* (Brussels: European Parliamentary Forum for Sexual and Reproductive Rights, 2021), 22.

54. Datta, *Tip of the Iceberg*, 32.

55. Christian Broadcasting Network (CBN), "Orthodox Priest Warns Europe Will Turn Muslim in 30 Years, Russia in 50," May 16, 2017, https://cbn.com /news/world/orthodox-priest-warns-europe-will-turn-muslim-30-years -russia-50; Middle East Media Research Institute (MEMRI), "Russian Orthodox Prelate Predicts: Europe Will Turn Muslim in 30 Years, Russia in 50," Special dispatch no. 6920, May 12, 2017, www.memri.org/reports/russian-orthodox -prelate -predicts-europe-will-turn-muslim-30-years-russia-50.

56. Pavel Chikov, "In the Name of God: Atheists in Russia under Fire," *Moscow Times,* May 18, 2017, https://themoscowtimes.com/articles/in-the -name-of-god-atheists-in-russia-under-fire-op-ed-58025.

57. Parogni, "The Strategic Savvy of Russia's Growing Anti-Abortion Movement."

58. HRC, "Exposed," 7.

59. Siân Norris, *Bodies Under Siege: How the Far-Right Attack on Reproductive Rights Went Global* (London: Verso, 2023), 74.

60. Neil Datta. *Tip of the Iceberg,* 82.

61. Luehrmann, "Innocence and Demographic Crisis," 115.

62. Carol Mason, *Killing for Life: The Apocalyptic Narrative of Pro-Life Politics* (Ithaca, NY: Cornell University Press, 2002), 16–17; Luehrmann, "Innocence and Demographic Crisis," 107.

63. Luehrmann, "Innocence and Demographic Crisis," 107; Mason, *Killing for Life,* 17–21; Sonja Luehrmann, "'God Values Intentions': Abortion, Expiation, and Moments of Sincerity in Russian Orthodox Pilgrimage," *Hau: Journal of Ethnographic Theory* 7, no. 1 (2017): 163–84; Carol Mason, "Minority Unborn," in *Fetal Subjects, Feminist Positions,* ed. Lynn Marie Morgan and Meredith W. Michaels (Philadelphia: University of Pennsylvania Press, 1999), 159–74.

64. Luehrmann, "Innocence and Demographic Crisis," 116.

65. Kishkovsky, "Russians Adopt U.S. Tactics."

66. Kristina Stoeckl and Dmitry Uzlaner, *The Moralist International: Russia in the Global Culture Wars* (New York: Fordham University Press, 2022), 134.

67. Stoeckl and Uzlaner, *The Moralist International,* 134.

68. Agnieszka Graff and Elzbieta Korolczuk, *Anti-Gender Politics in the Populist Moment* (New York: Routledge, 2022), 56.

69. Rosalind Petschesky, *Abortion and Women's Choice: The State, Sexuality, and Reproductive Freedom* (Boston: Northeastern University Press, 1984); Andrew Merton, *Enemies of Choice* (Boston: Beacon Press, 1981); Connie Paige,

The Right-to-Lifers: Who They Are, How They Operate, Where They Get Their Money (New York: Summit Books, 1983); Carol Mason, *Reading Appalachia from Left to Right: Conservatives and the 1974 Kanawha County Textbook Controversy* (Ithaca, NY: Cornell University Press, 2009).

70. Daniel K. Williams, *Defenders of the Unborn: The Pro-Life Movement before Roe v. Wade* (New York: Oxford University Press, 2016).

71. John Corrales, "Donald Trump Asks for Evangelicals' Support," *New York Times,* June 22, 2016, www.nytimes.com/2016/06/22/us/politics /donald-trump-asks-for-evangelicals-support-and-questions-hillary-clintons-faith.html.

72. Javier Corralis and Jacob Kiryk, "Homophobic Populism," in *Oxford Research Encyclopedia of Politics,* published online August 15, 2022, https://doi .org/10.1093/acrefore/9780198228637.012.2080.

73. At this writing in 2024, there are 658 anti-trans bills introduced, 45 of which have been passed into law. This number is "more than any other year on record. An unprecedented 80 bills are being considered at the federal level as the targeting of trans people increasingly moves to the national stage." The Trans Legislation Tracker is available at https://translegislation.com/.

74. TX SB8. 2021, Texas Senate Bill 8, 87th Legislative Session, regular session, https://capitol.texas.gov/tlodocs/87R/billtext/pdf/SB00008F.pdf.

75. Kate Zernicke, "States Aren't Waiting for the Supreme Court to Tighten Abortion Laws," *New York Times,* March 7, 2022.

76. Mason, *Killing for Life.*

77. Political Research Associates, "The Abortion Abolitionists with Cloee Cooper," *Inform Your Resistance,* https://politicalresearch.org/2023/09/14 /abortion-abolitionists-cloee-cooper; Carol Mason, "Opposing Abortion to Protect Women: Transnational Strategy Since the 1990s," *Signs: Journal of Women in Culture and Society* 44, no. 3 (2019): 665–92.

78. Heather Cox Richardson, "Letters from an American," September 1, 2023, https://heathercoxrichardson.substack.com/p/september-1-2023.

79. Zernicke, "States Aren't Waiting for the Supreme Court."

80. Kitchner quoted in Richardson, "Letters from an American."

81. Courtney Blackington, "Two Polish Women Died after Being Refused Timely Abortions. Many Poles Are Outraged—and Protesting," *Washington Post,* February 18, 2022, www.washingtonpost.com/politics/2022/02/18 /poland-abortion-protest/.

82. Alex Cocotas, "How Poland's Far-Right Government Is Pushing Abortion Underground," *Guardian*, November 30, 2017, www.theguardian.com /news/2017/nov/30/how-polands-far-right-government-is-pushing-abortion -underground.

83. Purvaja S. Kavattur, Somjen Frazer, Abby El-Shafei, et al., "The Rise of Pregnancy Criminalization: A Pregnancy Justice Report," Pregnancy Justice, 2023.

2. Vulnerable Guise and Racial Demise

1. Dustin Massengill, "UK Condemns Statements Made by Protesters on Campus," Fox 56 News, September 25, 2023, https://fox56news.com/news /local/uk-condemns-statements-made-by-protesters-on-campus/; Gavin Cooper, "No Matter How Offensive the Protests, We Must Support Free Speech on UK's Campus," *Lexington-Herald Leader*, September 28, 2023, www .kentucky.com/opinion/op-ed/article279882394.html.

2. Allison Jewell, "Students Rally for Administration Explanations amid Anti-Queer Protests," *Louisville Cardinal*, September 27, 2023, www.louisvillecardinal .com/2023/09/students-rally-for-administration-explanations-amid-anti-queer -protests/

3. Fallon Cross, "Protests on UofL and UK's Campus: Students Outraged," *Rambler*, October 11, 2023, https://transyrambler.com/2023/10/11/protests -on-uofl-and-uks-campus-students-outraged/.

4. Cynthia Miller-Idriss, *Hate in the Homeland: The New Global Far Right* (Princeton, NJ: Princeton University Press, 2020), 92–111.

5. Kristin Luker, *Abortion and the Politics of Motherhood* (Berkeley: University of California Press, 1984), 11.

6. Women of color and reproductive justice advocates have remarked on racist underpinnings of antiabortion work and other forms of reproductive control for decades, a primer for which is Loretta Ross and Rickie Solinger, *Reproductive Justice: An Introduction* (Berkeley: University of California Press, 2017). Scholars from many disciplines and journalists have documented connections among organized white supremacists and opposition to abortion. See, for example, Alex DiBranco, "The Long History of the Anti-Abortion Movement's Links to White Supremacists," *The Nation*, February 3, 2020, www .thenation.com/article/politics/anti-abortion-white-supremacy/. An early

analysis of the unborn as a signifier of a white future is my essay, Carol Mason, "Minority Unborn," in *Fetal Subjects, Feminist Positions*, ed. Lynn Morgan and Meredith Michaels (Philadelphia: University of Pennsylvania Press, 1999), 159–74. Later, as white supremacist fears of demographic demise grew more prominent in right-wing and conservative circles worldwide, scholars and watchdog groups recognized their proliferation, a summary of which is Agnieszka Graff, Ratna Kapur, and Suzanna Danuta Walters, "Introduction: Gender and the Rise of the Global Right," *Signs: Journal of Women in Culture and Society* 44, no. 3 (March 2019): 541–60, https://doi.org/10.1086/701152.

7. American Bible Society, *Stand in the Gap: A Sacred Assembly of Men*, Commemorative Edition New Testament (Nashville, TN: Thomas Nelson Publishers, 1997).

8. American Bible Society, *Stand in the Gap*.

9. Susan Faludi, *The Undeclared War against American Women* (New York: Crown, 1991).

10. Michael Bray, *A Time to Kill* (Portland, OR: Advocates for Life, 1994), 156.

11. Carol Mason, *Killing for Life: The Apocalyptic Narrative of Pro-Life Politics* (Ithaca, NY: Cornell University Press, 2002), 35.

12. Mason, *Killing for Life*; Patricia Baird-Windle and Eleanor J. Bader, *Targets of Hatred: Anti-Abortion Terrorism* (New York: Palgrave, 2001); Jennifer Jefferis, *Armed for Life: The Army of God and Anti-Abortion Terror in the United States* (Santa Barbara, CA: Praeger, 2011).

13. Jennifer L. Holland, *Tiny You: A Western History of the Anti-Abortion Movement* (Berkeley: University of California Press, 2020).

14. Mason, *Killing for Life*, 117.

15. Michelle Kelsey Kearl, "WWMLKD? Coopting the Rhetorical Legacy of Martin Luther King, Jr. and the Civil Rights Movement," *Journal of Contemporary Rhetoric* 8, no. 3 (2018): 184–99. Kearl makes this argument in relation to racism and sexism as she analyzes the Created Equal brochure (193).

16. Kearl, "WWMLKD?"; Shyrissa Dobbins-Harris, "The Myth of Abortion as Black Genocide: Reclaiming Our Reproductive Cycle," *National Black Law Journal* 26, no. 1 (2017): 86–127; Kathryn Joyce, "Abortion as Black Genocide," *Public Eye*, April 29, 2010, www.politicalresearch.org/2010/04/29/abortion-as-black-genocide-an-old-scare-tactic-re-emerges; Celeste Condit, *Decoding Abortion Rhetoric* (Champaign: University of Illinois Press, 1994); Karen

Newman, *Fetal Positions: Individualism, Science, Visuality* (Stanford, CA: Stanford University Press, 1996); Rosalind Petchesky, *Abortion and Woman's Choice: The State, Sexuality, and Reproductive Freedom* (Boston: Northeastern University Press, 1984); Mason, *Killing for Life*, 38–45.

17. Mason, *Killing for Life*, 43.

18. For refutations and examinations of the claim that abortion is genocide, see Kearl, "WWMLKD?"; Mason, *Killing for Life*, 38–45 and 114–29; Jessica Woolford and Andrew Woolford, "Abortion and Genocide: The Unbridgeable Gap," *Social Politics: International Studies in Gender, State and Society* 14, no. 1 (2007): 126–53. For refutations of the claim that abortion is Black genocide, see Dobbins-Harris, "The Myth of Abortion as Black Genocide,"; Ross and Solinger, "Reproductive Justice," 134–35; and the five-part video series *Abortion Conspiracy* by Stuart TV, the first installment of which analyzes the billboard campaign claiming Black babies are an "endangered species" due to abortion, YouTube video, posted November 8, 2010, www.youtube.com/watch?v=HndqGMNnqDg&t=25s.

19. Kearl, "WWMLKD?," 184.

20. Created Equal, "Our Story," www.createdequal.org/our-story/.

21. Kearl, "WWMLKD?," 196–99.

22. Kearl, "WWMLKD?," 197.

23. Kearl, "WWMLKD?," 197.

24. Created Equal, "One Question Stumps College Student," www.createdequal.org/outreach/.

25. Daniel Martinez HoSang and Joseph E. Lowndes, *Producers, Parasites, Patriots: Race and the New Right-Wing Politics of Precarity* (Minneapolis: University of Minnesota Press, 2019), 15.

26. HoSang and Lowndes, *Producers, Parasites, Patriots*, 15.

27. Barry Goldwater, *Conscience of a Conservative* (Shepherdsville, KY: Victor Publishing, 1960), 38 (italics in the original).

28. Goldwater, *Conscience of a Conservative*, 38.

29. Mark Harrington, "Social Justice Critical Theory and Christianity," *Radio Activist: The Mark Harrington Show*, December 31, 2020, https://createdequal.podbean.com/e/social-justice-critical-theory-and-christianity-are-they-compatible-the-mark-harrington-show-12-31-2020. The episode appears to have been originally broadcast on August 6, 2020, as seen here:

https://markharrington.org/live/social-justice-critical-theory-and-christianity-are-they-compatible/.

30. HoSang and Lowndes, *Producers, Parasites, Patriots,* 15.

31. Mark Harrington, "Top Ten Reasons Not to Support the Black Lives Matter Movement," *Radio Activist: The Mark Harrington Show,*" November 5, 2020, https://markharrington.org/live/top-ten-reasons-to-not-support-the-blacklivesmatter-movement-the-mark-harrington-show-11-05-2020/.

32. For relevant critiques of the billboards, see Zakiya Luna, "'Black Children Are an Endangered Species': Examining Racial Framing in Social Movements," *Sociological Focus* 51, no. 3 (2018): 238–51; Akiba Soloman, "Another Day, Another Race-Baiting Abortion Billboard," *Colorlines,* March 29, 2011, www.colorlines .com/articles/another-day-another-race-baiting-abortion-billboard; Michelle Goldberg, "Obama Billboard Shows Anti-Abortion Focus on African-Americans," *Daily Beast,* March 30, 2011, www.thedailybeast.com/obama-billboard-shows -anti-abortion-focus-on-african-americans; Sujatha Jesudason, "The Latest Case of Reproductive Carrots and Sticks: Race, Abortion and Sex Selection," *Scholar and Feminist Online* 9.1–9.2 (Fall 2010/Spring 2011), http://sfonline.barnard.edu /reprotech/jesudason_01.htm. Addressing these billboards as well as Ryan Bomberger's rhetoric is Lisa Guenther, "The Most Dangerous Place: Pro-Life Politics and the Rhetoric of Slavery," *Postmodern Culture* 22, no. 2 (2012), www .proquest.com/docview/2560063616/abstract/911A11D9171449200PQ/2.

33. Joyce, "Abortion as Black Genocide."

34. Malaika Jabali, "White People Are Killed by Cops Too. But That Doesn't Undermine Black Lives Matter, *Guardian,* July 16, 2020, www.theguardian .com/commentisfree/2020/jul/16/trump-police-abolition-black-americans. Another source recognizes that "relative to White victims, Black victims were overrepresented" in the number of people shot by police in a five-year period. See Julie A. Ward et al., "National Burden of Injury and Deaths from Shootings by Police in the United States, 2015–2020," *American Journal of Public Health* 114, no. 4 (2024): 387–97. See also Gabriel L. Schwartz and Jaquelyn L. Jahn, "Mapping Fatal Police Violence across U.S. Metropolitan Areas: Overall Rates and Racial/Ethnic Inequities, 2013–2017," *PLOS ONE* 15, no. 6: e0229686, https://doi.org/10.1371/journal.pone.0229686.

35. Daniel Geary, *Beyond Civil Rights: The Moynihan Report and Its Legacy* (Philadelphia: University of Pennsylvania Press, 2015).

36. See Kearl, "WWMLKD?," 192–96, for a comprehensive takedown of Created Equal's claims that abortion is ageism in her analysis of a Created Equal brochure.

37. Scott Krzych, "The Price of Knowledge: Hysterical Discourse in Anti-Michael Moore Documentaries," *Comparatist* 39 (2015): 80. See also Scott Krzych, *Beyond Bias: Conservative Media, Documentary Form, and the Politics of Hysteria* (New York: Oxford University Press, 2021).

38. Krzych, "The Price of Knowledge," 80–81.

39. Krzych, "The Price of Knowledge," 90.

40. Krzych, "The Price of Knowledge," 81.

41. Created Equal, "Jumbotron Campus Debut," www.youtube.com /watch?v=7Nbp6ewiLPU&feature=emb_logo.

42. Kearl, "WWMLKD?," 197.

43. Krzych, "The Price of Knowledge," 96.

44. Grace S. Chung, Ryan E. Lawrence, Kenneth A. Rasinski, et al., "Obstetrician-Gynecologists' Beliefs about When Pregnancy Begins," *American Journal of Obstetrics and Gynecology* 206, no. 2 (2012): e1–7, www.ajog.org /article/S0002-9378(11)02223-X/fulltext.

45. Created Equal, *Abortion: Doctrine of Demons,* www.createdequal.org /doctrine-of-demons.

46. Mason, *Killing for Life.*

47. Nazis used the idea of blood libel, a false allegation that Jews ritualistically use the blood of children, to promote antisemitism. United States Holocaust Memorial Museum, "Blood libel," *Holocaust Encyclopedia,* https:// encyclopedia.ushmm.org/content/en/article/blood-libel.

48. Mason, *Killing for Life,* 171–79.

49. Jessica Winter, "The Link Between the Capitol Riot and Anti-Abortion Extremism," *New Yorker,* March 11, 2021, www.newyorker.com/news/daily -comment/the-link-between-the-capitol-riot-and-anti-abortion-extremism.

50. Siân Norris, *Bodies Under Siege: How the Far-Right Attack on Reproductive Rights Went Global* (London: Verso, 2023), 47.

51. Norris, *Bodies Under Siege,* 73.

52. "The Christian Fright," *Harper's Magazine* 295, no. 1769 (October 1997): 20 ff; Harmon Leon, "Evangelical Haunted Houses Involve Much More Abortion than Normal Haunted House," *Vice,* November 1, 2013.

53. Karyn Valerius, "A Not-So-Silent Scream: Gothic and the US Abortion Debate," *Frontiers* 34, no. 3 (2013): 28.

54. Valerius, "A Not-So-Silent Scream," 28.

55. Valerius, "A Not-So-Silent Scream," 27

56. "Anti-Abortion Protest on Campus," *Kentucky Kernel,* October 19, 2017, video originally posted with editorial, "No Matter What You Say, Free Speech Belongs to Everyone," https://kykernel.com/37173/uncategorized/editorial-no-matter-what-you-say-free-speech-belongs-to-everyone/.

57. William David Hart, "Slaves, Fetuses, and Animals," *Journal of Religious Ethics* 42, no. 4 (December 2014): 661–90, https://doi.org/10.1111/jore.12077.

58. "Anti-Abortion Protest on Campus."

59. "Anti-Abortion Protest on Campus."

60. According to the 2018 Form 990 they submitted to the IRS, Created Equal reported revenue of more than a million dollars, and Harrington's salary was listed as $99,250. Reform America, Form 990 for fiscal year ending in 2018, obtained from https://projects.propublica.org/nonprofits/organizations/331097372.

61. Mason, *Killing for Life,* 174.

62. Silas Allen, "Anti-Abortion Group Sues," *Oklahoman,* January 29, 2013, https://oklahoman.com/article/3749938/anti-abortion-group-sues-oklahoma-state-university.

63. Loree Lewis, "Court Rules On Miller-Young Case," *Daily Nexus,* August 27, 2014, https://dailynexus.com/2014-08-27/court-rules-on-miller-young-case/.

64. Bill Roberts, "BSU, Anti-Abortion Group Settle Free Speech Lawsuit," *Idaho Statesman,* June 3, 2015, www.idahostatesman.com/news/local/education/boise-state-university/article40861854.html.

65. Kate Murphy, "Students Sue Miami University," *Cincinnati Inquirer,* December 1, 2017, www.cincinnati.com/story/news/2017/11/30/students-sue-miami-university-over-anti-abortion-protest/908549001/.

66. Rick Seltzer, "Cal State to Pay $240,000 to Settle Anti-Abortion Speaker Lawsuit," *Inside Higher Ed,* February 6, 2020, www.insidehighered.com/quicktakes/2020/02/06/cal-state-pay-240000-settle-anti-abortion-speaker-lawsuit.

67. Ryan Lenz, "The Battle for Berkeley," *Hatewatch,* May 1, 2017, www.splcenter.org/hatewatch/2017/05/01/battle-berkeley-name-freedom-speech-radical-right-circling-ivory-tower-ensure-voice-alt.

68. Richard Fausset and Allan Feuer, "Far-Right Groups Surge into National View in Charlottesville," *New York Times,* August 13, 2017, www.nytimes.com/2017/08/13/us/far-right-groups-blaze-into-national-view-in-charlottesville.html.

69. "Caught on Cam," Sinclair News, 16 KMJR Eugene, Oregon, July 10, 2014, https://nbc16.com/news/nation-world/caught-on-cam-pro-life-activists-confronted-attacked-by-woman.

70. "Ohio Woman Must Pay," *LifeSiteNews,* August 26, 2014, www.lifesitenews.com/news/ohio-woman-must-pay-80-after-attack-on-pro-lifers-assault-charge-dropped.

71. "Pro-Life Activists Confronted, Attacked on Camera," Fox News, July 11, 2014, https://video.foxnews.com/v/3669804665001.

72. "Fear, Fantasy and Feelings on the Far-Right," panel of the 2021 Joint Conference on Right-Wing Studies and Research on Male Supremacism, May 10, 2021, featured Sophie Bjork-James and Josefine Landberg, whose research and conversation inspired this insight.

3. Radicalization and Race in Women's Pro-Life Writing

1. Robyn Marasco, "Reconsidering the Sexual Politics of Fascism," *Historical Materialism,* June 25, 2021, www.historicalmaterialism.org/blog/reconsidering-sexual-politics-fascism.

2. Jeff Sharlet provides an in-depth discussion of Babbitt as martyr in *Undertow: Scenes from a Slow Civil War* (New York: Norton, 2023).

3. Jeff Sharlet, "January 6 Was Only the Beginning," *Vanity Fair,* June 22, 2022, www.vanityfair.com/news/2022/06/trump-ashli-babbitt-christians. See also Sharlet, *Undertow.*

4. Marasco, "Reconsidering the Sexual Politics of Fascism."

5. Joshua Prager, *The Family Roe: An American Story* (New York: W. W. Norton, 2021), 145.

6. Robert D. McFadden, "Kenneth C. Edelin, Doctor at Center of Landmark Abortion Case, Dies at 74," *New York Times,* December 30, 2013, www.nytimes.com/2013/12/31/us/kenneth-c-edelin-physician-at-center-of-landmark-abortion-case-dies-at-74.html.

7. Jennifer Donnally, "The Edelin Manslaughter Trial and the Anti-Abortion Movement," *Massachusetts Historical Review* 20 (2018): 1–32; Carol A.

Stabile, "The Traffic in Fetuses," in *Fetal Subjects, Feminist Positions*, ed. Lynn Morgan and Meredith W. Michaels (Philadelphia: University of Pennsylvania Press, 1999), 133–58, https://doi.org/10.9783/9781512807561-009; Prager, *The Family Roe*; McFadden, "Kenneth C. Edelin, Doctor at Center of Landmark Abortion Case, Dies at 74."

8. Mildred Jefferson is quoted in Joshua Prager, "The Groundbreaking and Complicated Life of Mildred Fay Jefferson," CNN Opinion, May 10, 2022, www.cnn.com/2022/05/10/opinions/abortion-pro-life-hero-mildred-fay -jefferson-prager/index.html.

9. Daniel K. Williams, *Defenders of the Unborn: The Pro-Life Movement before Roe v. Wade* (New York: Oxford University Press, 2016), 173.

10. John Warwick Montgomery, "The Fetus as a Person," *Human Life Review* 1, no. 2 (Summer 1975): 46.

11. Mildred Jefferson, "Faith on the Line in the New Civil War," *Lux in Tenebris* (Winter 1990), p. 10, MC 696, item F+D.3, Writings, Articles and essays, 1990–1992, Schlesinger Library, Radcliffe Institute, Harvard University, Cambridge, MA, https://hollisarchives.lib.harvard.edu/repositories/8/archival_ objects/3497126.

12. Karissa Haugeberg, *Women against Abortion: Inside the Largest Moral Reform Movement of the Twentieth Century* (Urbana: University of Illinois Press, 2017), 5.

13. Correspondence between Jefferson and Kivie Kaplan in 1962 suggests that she was not interested in joining the NAACP. Kaplan, a board member of the NAACP and member of the Social Action Commission of the Union of American Hebrew Congregations, was a friend who attempted to help Jefferson get placed in a hospital. He wrote to her when that attempt failed, lamenting that she was "still suffering from the problem of discrimination." He sent her two books and a report on his trip to the NAACP convention. Jefferson wrote back collegially, asking after Kaplan's family but not thanking him for the books. Despite their long-term friendship, she seemed to keep talk of the NAACP at arm's length. Mildred Jefferson, Letter to Daniel Federman, MD, MC 696, box 16, folder 9, Medical practice: Correspondence and related, 1952–1992, Schlesinger Library, Radcliffe Institute, Harvard University, Cambridge, MA, https://hollisarchives.lib.harvard.edu/repositories/8/archival_ objects/3497076.

14. Mildred Jefferson, letter dated June 7, 1989, MC 696, box 4, Personal correspondence, 1980–1989, Schlesinger Library, Radcliffe Institute, Harvard University, Cambridge, MA, https://hollisarchives.lib.harvard.edu/repositories/8/archival_objects/3497062.

15. Mildred Jefferson, press release, August 4, 2003, MC696, box 10, folder 9, Press releases, 1980–2010, Schlesinger Library, Radcliffe Institute, Harvard University, Cambridge, MA, https://hollisarchives.lib.harvard.edu/repositories/8/archival_objects/3497185.

16. Mildred Jefferson, memo to Brenda, June 14, 2001, MC696, box 10, folder 10, Press releases, 1980–2010, Schlesinger Library, Radcliffe Institute, Harvard University, Cambridge, MA.

17. Jefferson, memo to Brenda.

18. Janice M. Irvine describes depravity narratives in the context of opposing sex education. Depravity narratives became standard fare as conservative and right-wing protests focused on multiracial curricula and transgender rights. See Janice M. Irvine, *Talk about Sex: The Battles Over Sex Education in the United States* (Berkeley: University of California Press, 2002).

19. Paul Marx, *Confessions of a Prolife Missionary: The Journeys of Fr. Paul Marx* (Gaithersburg, MD: Human Life International, 1988), 80.

20. Marx, *Confessions of a Prolife Missionary,* 96.

21. Jefferson quoted in Haugeberg, *Women against Abortion,* 15.

22. Prager, *The Family Roe,* 114.

23. Prager, *The Family Roe,* 115.

24. Mary Ziegler, *Abortion and the Law in America: Roe v. Wade to the Present* (Cambridge: Cambridge University Press, 2020), 62.

25. The book is included among Jefferson's papers at the Schlesinger, MC 696, box 9, folder 10, subseries C, Right to Life Crusade, Inc., 1978–2010.

26. Carol Mason, *Killing for Life: The Apocalyptic Narrative of Pro-Life Politics* (Ithaca, NY: Cornell University Press, 2002), 10–14.

27. Haugeberg, *Women against Abortion,* 85.

28. Haugeberg, *Women against Abortion,* 82–83.

29. Joan Andrews, *You Reject Them, You Reject Me: The Prison Letters of Joan Andrews* (Brentwood, TN: Trinity Communications, 1988), 33–34 (brackets in the original).

30. Andrews, *You Reject Them, You Reject Me,* 21 (italics added).

31. Haugeberg, *Women against Abortion,* 91.

32. Randall A. Terry, *Accessory to Murder: The Enemies, Allies, and Accomplices to the Death of Our Culture* (Brentwood, TN: Wolgemuth & Hyatt, 1990), 139.

33. Terry, *Accessory to Murder,* 139.

34. Terry, *Accessory to Murder,* 227 (italics in the original).

35. Mason, *Killing for Life,* 24–25.

36. Evelyn A. Schlatter, *Aryan Cowboys: White Supremacists and the Search for a New Frontier, 1970–2000* (Austin: University of Texas Press, 2006), 104.

37. Schlatter, *Aryan Cowboys,* 103; Catherine McNicol Stock, *Rural Radicals: Righteous Rage in the American Grain* (Ithaca, NY: Cornell University Press, 2017); Chip Berlet and Matthew N. Lyons, *Right-Wing Populism in America: Too Close for Comfort* (New York: Guilford Press, 2000).

38. Daniel Martinez HoSang and Joseph E. Lowndes, *Producers, Parasites, Patriots: Race and the New Right-Wing Politics of Precarity* (Minneapolis: University of Minnesota Press, 2019), 47–71.

39. Chip Berlet and Carol Mason, "Swastikas in Cyberspace: How Hate Went Online," in *Digital Media Strategies of the Far Right in Europe and the United States,* ed. Patricia Anne Simpson and Helga Druxes (Lanham, MD: Lexington Books, 2015).

40. Kathleen Belew, "The Revolutionary Turn," chapter 5 of *Bring the War Home: The White Power Movement and Paramilitary America* (Cambridge, MA: Harvard University Press, 2018).

41. Haugeberg, *Women against Abortion,* 91.

42. Mason, *Killing for Life,* 179–86.

43. Nicole Youngman, "Jeeries Jubilee," *The Body Politic,* May/June 1998, 38.

44. Abby Johnson and Cindy Lambert, *Unplanned: The Dramatic True Story of a Former Planned Parenthood Leader's Eye-Opening Journey across the Life Line* (Carol Stream, IL: Tyndale House Publishers, 2014); Paul Saurette and Kelly Gordon, *The Changing Voice of the Anti-Abortion Movement* (Toronto: University of Toronto Press, 2015), 179–80.

45. Amanda Marcotte, "The Earth-Shaking Abortion That Never Happened," *Slate,* January 7, 2010, https://slate.com/human-interest/2010/01/the-earth-shaking-abortion-that-never-happened.html.

46. Karyn Valerius, "A Not-So-Silent Scream: Gothic and the US Abortion Debate," *Frontiers: A Journal of Women Studies* 34, no. 3 (2013): 27–47.

47. Johnson and Lambert, *Unplanned,* 121, 137.

48. Johnson and Lambert, *Unplanned,* 114.

49. Johnson and Lambert, *Unplanned*, 138.

50. Johnson and Lambert, *Unplanned*, 139.

51. Johnson and Lambert, *Unplanned*, 244.

52. Lawrence Rosenthal, *Empire of Resentment: Populism's Toxic Embrace of Nationalism* (New York: The New Press, 2020), 7.

53. Rosenthal, *Empire of Resentment*, 10.

54. Nate Blakeslee, "Sorting Fact from Fiction in the Story of Pro-Life Celebrity Abby Johnson," *Texas Monthly,* April 16, 2019, www.texasmonthly.com/news-politics/fact-fiction-pro-life-celebrity-abby-johnson-unplanned/.

55. Benjamin Siegel and Ivan Pereira, "Former Planned Parenthood Employee Abby Johnson's Anti-Abortion Comments under Scrutiny after Graphic RNC Speech," ABC News, August 25, 2020, https://abcnews.go.com/Politics/planned-parenthood-employee-abby-johnsons-anti-abortion-comments/story?id=72609833.

56. Haugeberg, *Women against Abortion*, 123.

57. Christina Nifong, "Anti-Abortion Violence Defines 'Army of God,'" *Christian Science Monitor,* February 4, 1998.

58. Haugeberg, *Women against Abortion*, 127.

59. Jennifer Jefferis recognizes that an epilogue added in 1992 "introduced the justification for attacking human beings." See her *Armed for Life: The Army of God and Anti-Abortion Terror in the United States* (Santa Barbara, CA: Praeger, 2011).

60. "The Declaration," in *The Army of God Manual,* www.armyofgod.com/AOGsel7.html.

61. "Recommended Reading Sources," Appendix F, in *The Army of God Manual.*

62. Haugeberg, *Women against Abortion*, 119.

63. Haugeberg, *Women against Abortion*, 129.

64. Haugeberg, *Women against Abortion*, 129.

65. Haugeberg, *Women against Abortion*, 137.

66. *The Army of God Manual*, 48.

67. Haugeberg, *Women against Abortion*, 108.

68. Jefferis, *Armed for Life*, 30.

69. Robert Spitzer, "The NRA's Journey from Marksmanship to Political Brinkmanship," *The Conversation,* February 23, 2018, https://theconversation.com/the-nras-journey-from-marksmanship-to-political-brinkmanship-92160.

Amid an epidemic of mass shootings, the NRA's power may be waning. See Charles D. Phillips, "The Politics of Firearm Safety: An Emerging New Balance of Power," *American Journal of Public Health* 108, no. 7 (July 2018): 868–70, https://doi.org/10.2105/AJPH.2018.304462.

70. Haugeberg, *Women against Abortion*, 137.

71. Jefferson Robbins, "Report: Released Abortion-Clinic Terrorist to Take Up Residence in Douglas County," *Source One News* (Quincy, Washington), November 9, 2018, www.yoursourceone.com/columbia_basin/report-released -abortion-clinic-terrorist-to-take-up-residence-in-douglas-county/article_ 366ae798-e46f-11e8-94fa-5bcd716e1561.html.

72. In 2016 both the media and Donald Trump perpetuated the idea that 52 percent of white women voted for him. This figure was based on faulty exit polls and has since been debunked. The more reliable statistic for how many white women supported Trump for president is 47 percent. See Molly Ball, "Donald Trump Didn't Really Win 52% of White Women in 2016," *Time,* October 18, 2018, https://time.com/5422644/trump-white-women-2016/.

73. Abby Johnson proudly posted about her participation in the Jericho March on Facebook on December 12, 2020: www.facebook.com/abbyjohnsonprolife /photos/a.671232512886825/3854801071196604/?type=3.

74. Anti-Defamation League, "Pro-Trump Rallies in DC Attract Extremists and Erupt into Violence," December 13, 2020, www.adl.org/resources/blog /pro-trump-rallies-dc-attract-extremists-erupt-violence.

75. Anti-Defamation League, "Pro-Trump Rallies in DC Attract Extremists."

76. The message was posted on Abby Johnson's Twitter account on January 3, 2021, https://twitter.com/AbbyJohnson/status/1345903843570233351.

77. Zachary Petrizzo, "Ali Alexander Flirts with Q in Telegram Rant about '17,'" *Daily Dot,* February 16, 2021, www.dailydot.com/debug/ali-alexander -qanon-telegram/.

4. Lone Wolves, Abortion Abolitionists, and the Men Who Penned Them

1. Interview by Becca Andrews, John Hammontree, and John Archibald with Carol Mason, November 13, 2023.

2. Regarding McVeigh's phone calls, see George Michael, *Lone Wolf Terror and the Rise of Leaderless Resistance* (Nashville, TN: Vanderbilt University Press,

2012), 40. On his ties to the white power movement, see Kathleen Belew, *Bring the War Home: The White Power Movement and Paramilitary America* (Cambridge, MA: Harvard University Press, 2018), 214–15.

3. Chip Berlet and Matthew N. Lyons, *Right-Wing Populism in America: Too Close for Comfort* (New York: Guilford Press, 2000), 17.

4. Tina Vásquez, "How the Anti-Abortion Movement Fed the Capitol Insurrection," *Prism,* January 22, 2021, http://prismreports.org/2021/01/22/how-the-antiabortion-movement-fed-the-capitol-insurrection/.

5. Andrew Macdonald [William Pierce], *The Turner Diaries,* 2nd ed. (New York: Barricade Books, 1978, 1980).

6. Jean Raspail, *The Camp of the Saints,* 4th American ed. (Petoskey, MI: Social Contract Press, 1987).

7. Tom Burghardt, "State Citizenship: Patriot Ties to White Supremacists and Neo-Nazis," *Body Politic* 5, no. 6 (June/July 1995): 12–18; Ann Bower and Valerie Finkelman, "Militia Men: Herb Philbrick in Camouflage," *Body Politic* 5, no. 6 (June/July 1995): 6–11; Evelyn A. Schlatter, *Aryan Cowboys: White Supremacists and the Search for a New Frontier, 1970-2000* (Austin: University of Texas Press, 2006); Catherine McNicol Stock, *Rural Radicals: Righteous Rage in the American Grain* (Ithaca, NY: Cornell University Press, 1996).

8. Rick Perlstein, *The Invisible Bridge: The Fall of Nixon and the Rise of Reagan* (New York: Simon and Schuster, 2014), 307.

9. Carol Mason, *Reading Appalachia from Left to Right: Conservatives and the 1974 Kanawha County Textbook Controversy* (Ithaca, NY: Cornell University Press, 2009).

10. Belew, *Bring the War Home,* 205.

11. For a first-person analysis of the events in 1979, see Sally Bermanzohn, *Through Survivor's Eyes: From the Sixties to the Greensboro Massacre* (Nashville, TN: Vanderbilt University Press, 2011). Scholars have noted how the massacre paralleled in strategy and impact the 2017 vehicular homicide of Heather Heyer in Charlottesville, Virginia, during the Unite the Right rally. See Tiffany Packer, "Guns, Torches and Badges: The 1979 Greensboro Massacre, the Charlottesville Unite the Right Rally, and the Lasting Impacts of Racial Violence on Black and Anti-Racist Communities," *Souls* 22, nos. 2–4 (2020): 141–59, https://doi.org/10.1080/10999949.2021.2003625.

12. Martin Lee, *The Beast Reawakens* (Boston: Little, Brown, 1997), 35.

13. Mary Ziegler, *Abortion and the Law in America: Roe v. Wade to the Present* (Cambridge: Cambridge University Press, 2020), 65–66.

14. Mary Ziegler, *Dollars for Life: The Anti-Abortion Movement and the Fall of the Republican Establishment* (New Haven, CT: Yale University Press, 2022), 41; Michael Sean Winters, *God's Right Hand: How Jerry Falwell Made God a Republican and Baptized the American Right* (New York: Harper Collins, 2019).

15. Ziegler, *Abortion and the Law in America*, 59–60.

16. Ziegler, *Dollars for Life*.

17. Belew, *Bring the War Home*, 116.

18. *White Power Report* (January 1977), 36, Wilcox Collection of Contemporary Political Movements, Spencer Research Library, University of Kansas.

19. Belew, *Bring the War Home*, 120–21, 144–45. Belew's book overlooks the importance of Dietz. The Liberty Bell Network was named after Dietz's print magazine, *The Liberty Bell,* and its first "posts" were items reprinted from the magazine. Moreover, the dial-up number that was advertised as the way to access the Liberty Bell Network was a 304 number, the area code for West Virginia, where Dietz—not Beam or Metzger—was located. See Chip Berlet and Carol Mason, "Swastikas in Cyberspace: How Hate Went Online," in *Digital Media Strategies of the Far Right in Europe and the United States,* ed. Patricia Anne Simpson and Helga Druxes (Lanham, MD: Lexington Books, 2015), 21–37.

20. Mason, *Reading Appalachia from Left to Right*, 57–89.

21. There are many critiques of the film. According to Mary Ziegler, it was the film's emphasis on fetal pain that was significant (*Abortion and the Law in America*, 77). According to Karyn Valerius, the film adhered to narrative conventions of portraying abortion in gothic terms; see her "A Not-So-Silent Scream: Gothic and the US Abortion Debate," *Frontiers: A Journal of Women Studies* 34, no. 3 (2013). The apocalyptic tone of the film is emphasized in my early work, Carol Mason, *Killing for Life: The Apocalyptic Narrative of Pro-Life Politics* (Ithaca, NY: Cornell University Press, 2002), 20. Contemporary analyses of the film noted how it portrayed the abortion as if the woman were not there; the erasure of women and their experiences is key among feminist critiques of *The Silent Scream* and of the visual politics of antiabortion propaganda in general.

22. For a discussion of how arguments from these particular groups changed throughout the decade, consider Ziegler, *Abortion and the Law in America*.

23. For a full account of Crutcher's *Firestorm* as a soi-disant "guerrilla strategy" that reflects leaderless resistance, see Mason, *Killing for Life,* 47–68.

24. For a full discussion of Charles Rice's argument and discussions of abortion as justifiable homicide, see Mason, *Killing for Life,* 68–71.

25. Belew, *Bring the War Home,* 196; Schlatter, *Aryan Cowboys.*

26. Belew, *Bring the War Home,* 205–6.

27. Belew, *Bring the War Home,* 236.

28. Lawrence Rosenthal, *Empire of Resentment: Populism's Toxic Embrace of Nationalism* (New York: The New Press, 2020), 36–39.

29. Rosenthal, *Empire of Resentment,* 70.

30. Rosenthal, *Empire of Resentment,* 6.

31. Judith Butler, *Who's Afraid of Gender?* (New York: Farrar, Straus and Giroux, 2024), 7.

32. Foundation for European Progressive Studies, *Gender As Symbolic Glue: The Position and Role of Conservative and Far Right Parties in the Anti-Gender Mobilizations in Europe,* ed. Eszter Kováts and Maari Põim (Budapest: Foundation for European Progressive Studies in cooperation with Friedrich-Ebert -Stiftung, 2015).

33. Tony Horwitz, "Run, Rudolph, Run: How the Fugitive Became a Folk Hero," *New Yorker,* March 15, 1999, 46–52.

34. Douglas Reichert Powell, *Endless Caverns: An Underground Journey into the Show Caves of Appalachia* (Durham: North Carolina University Press, 2018), 56.

35. Online communication distributed by Deja News, posted March 19, 1998; Mason, *Killing for Life,* 30.

36. James Ridgeway, *Blood in the Face: The Ku Klux Klan, Aryan Nations, Nazi Skinheads, and the Rise of a New White Culture* (New York: Thunder's Mouth Press, 1990), 113.

37. Eric Rudolph, "Racism," www.armyofgod.com/EricRudolphRacism .html.

38. Online communication distributed by Deja News, posted March 19, 1998; Mason, *Killing for Life,* 30.

39. Michael, *Lone Wolf Terror and the Rise of Leaderless Resistance,* 48.

40. Rudolph, "Racism."

41. Eric Rudolph, "A Time of War: Is Armed Resistance to Abortion Morally Justified?," November 2018, www.armyofgod.com/PacifismChristian1.pdf.

42. Southern Poverty Law Center, "Deborah Rudolph Speaks Out about Her Former Brother-in-Law, Olympic Park Bomber Eric Rudolph," *Intelligence Report*, November 29, 2001, www.splcenter.org/fighting-hate/intelligence -report/2001/deborah-rudolph-speaks-out-about-her-former-brother-law -olympic-park-bomber-eric-robert.

43. Online communication distributed by Deja News, posted March 19, 1998; Mason, *Killing for Life*, 30.

44. Southern Poverty Law Center, "Deborah Rudolph Speaks Out."

45. "FBI Witness Interview—Rhodes, Maura and Rhodes, Edward, March 6, 1998," Law enforcement records of Eric Rudolph Case / New Woman All Women Clinic, File Number 2246.2.7, Birmingham Public Library, Alabama. Thanks to Catherine Oseas Champion, head of the Archive Department at the Birmingham Public Library, and to John Hammontree, John Archibald, and Becca Andrews for verifying this information.

46. Southern Poverty Law Center, "Aryan Nations Leader Richard Girnt Butler in Final Days of Life," *Intelligence Report*, September 15, 1998, www .splcenter.org/fighting-hate/intelligence-report/1998/aryan-nations-leader -richard-girnt-butler-final-days-life.

47. Southern Poverty Law Center, "Eric Rudolph Charged in Bombings," *Intelligence Report*, December 15, 1998, www.splcenter.org/fighting-hate /intelligence-report/1998/eric-rudolph-charged-bombings.

48. Belew, *Bring the War Home*, 233.

49. Federal Bureau of Investigation, "Eric Rudolph," www.fbi.gov/history /famous-cases/eric-rudolph.

50. Eric Rudolph, "White Lies: Eugenics, Race, and Abortion," December 2014, www.armyofgod.com/EricRudolphWhiteLiesEugenicsAbortionand Racism2.pdf.

51. Rudolph, "White Lies."

52. Belew, *Bring the War Home*, 159.

53. Rudolph, "A Time of War."

54. National Immigration Forum, "The 'Great Replacement' Theory, Explained," https://immigrationforum.org/wp-content/uploads/2021/12 /Replacement-Theory-Explainer-1122.pdf.

55. Vito Russo, *The Celluloid Closet: The Homosexual in the Movies* (New York: Harper and Row, 1987).

56. S. Atwood, Thekla Morgenroth, and Kristina R. Olson, "Gender Essentialism and Benevolent Sexism in Anti-Trans Rhetoric," *Societal Issues and Policy Review* 18 (2024): 172.

57. For a full discussion of abortion and Vietnam, see Mason, *Killing for Life,* 10–15.

58. Eric Rudolph, *All Enemies, Foreign and Domestic,* www.armyofgod.com /EricRudolphEnemies1.pdf.

59. Luke Mogelson, *The Storm Is Here: An American Crucible* (New York: Penguin Press, 2022), 206–12. For a description of the historical precedent of these fight clubs in the context of twentieth-century fascism, see Lawrence Rosenthal, "The Male Fighting Band," in Yiannis Gabriel, *Organizations in Depth: The Psychanalysis of Organizations* (Thousand Oaks, CA: Sage Publications, 1999):18–23.

60. Belew, *Bring the War Home,* 173.

61. Rudolph, *All Enemies, Foreign and Domestic,* 50.

62. Rudolph, *All Enemies, Foreign and Domestic,* 141.

63. Rudolph, *All Enemies, Foreign and Domestic,* 145.

64. Rudolph, *All Enemies, Foreign and Domestic,* 145.

65. Jennifer Jefferis, *Armed for Life: The Army of God and Anti-Abortion Terror in the United States* (Santa Barbara, CA: Praeger, 2011), 38.

66. "Promoting Dignity," interview with Jonathan Mazzochi, *Body Politic* 5, no. 6 (June/July 1995): 19–23.

67. Life Advocate, "Cathy Ramey, Associate Editor," www.lifeadvocate .org/bio/cathy/biocathy.htm.

68. *Planned Parenthood of the Columbia/Willamette, Inc. v. American Coalition of Life Activists,* 290 F.3d 1058 (9th Cir. 2002).

69. "Smoke and Mirrors: Planned Parenthood's Conspiracy to End Free Speech," *Life Advocate* 13, no. 5 (March/April 1999), www.lifeadvocate .org/3_99/cover_s.htm.

70. "Smoke and Mirrors."

71. "Smoke and Mirrors."

72. Seth D. Berlin, "Are the Nuremberg Files and 'Wanted' Posters Protected Advocacy or Unprotected Threat?," *Communications Lawyer: The Journal of Media, Information, and Communications Law* 20, no. 2 (Summer 2002): 1, 26–35. See also Joshua Azriel, "The Internet and Hate Speech: An Examina-

tion of the Nuremberg Files Case," *Communication Law and Policy* 10, no. 4 (Autumn 2005): 477–98.

73. Paul deParrie, "The Editors Eye," *Life Advocate* 13, no. 5 (March/April 1999), www.lifeadvocate.org/3_99/e_eye.htm.

74. Paul deParrie, "The Editors Eye," *Life Advocate* 13, no. 6 (June 1999), www.lifeadvocate.org/5_99/e_eye.htm.

75. Paul deParrie, "Potpourri (or Niggling Things Revisited)," *Life Advocate* 13, no. 4 (January/February 1999), www.lifeadvocate.org/1_99/comment.htm.

76. Irin Carmon, "Meet the Rebels of the Anti-Abortion Movement," MSNBC, March 8, 2014, www.msnbc.com/melissa-harris-perry/meet-the -rebels-the-anti-abortion-movement-msna281321.

77. Kathryn Joyce, "Abortion as Black Genocide." *Public Eye,* April 29, 2010, www.politicalresearch.org/2010/04/29/abortion-as-black-genocide-an-old -scare-tactic-re-emerges.

78. Mason, *Killing for Life,* 118–27.

79. Mason, *Killing for Life,* 114–18.

80. Abolish Human Abortion (AHA), "International Coalition of Aboli- tionist Societies," http://abolishhumanabortion.com/international-coalition- of-abolitionist-societies/.

81. Jonathon Van Maren, "How Abolish Human Abortion Gets History Wrong," Canadian Centre for Bio-ethical Reform, January 15, 2014, www .endthekilling.ca/blog/2014/01/15/how-abolish-human-abortion-gets -history-wrong.

82. Abolish Human Abortion (AHA), "What Is the AHA Symbol For?," June 14, 2012. https://blog.abolishhumanabortion.com/p/abolitionists- identify.html. The same discussion has been republished under the heading "Light Up the Darkness," https://abolishhumanabortion.com/light-up-the -darkness/.

83. OllieGarkey, "Is an Anti-Choice Group Using a Nazi Symbol?," *Daily Kos,* July 9, 2012, www.dailykos.com/stories/2012/7/9/1107487/-Is-an-Anti -Choice-group-using-a-Nazi-Symbol.

84. Cloee Cooper and Hannah Silver, "101: Abortion Abolition," October 26, 2023, Political Research Associates, https://politicalresearch.org/2023/10 /26/101-abortion-abolitionists.

85. Cooper and Silver, "101: Abortion Abolition."

86. Heidi Beedle, "The Army of Gideon: Anti-Abortion Activism in Wichita," *Colorado Times Recorder,* March 8, 2023, https://coloradotimesrecorder.com/2023/03/the-army-of-gideon-anti-abortion-activism-in-wichita/52248/.

87. Mogelson, *The Storm Is Here,* 138.

88. Mogelson, *The Storm Is Here,* 142.

89. Hunter's document "The Norman Statement" is quoted in Beedle, "The Army of Gideon." The full text of the statement is at https://abolitionistsrising.com/norman-statement/.

90. Tina Vásquez, "How the Anti-Abortion Movement Fed the Capitol Insurrection."

91. Cooper and Silver, "101: Abortion Abolition."

Conclusion

1. Melissa Murray and Katherine Shaw, "*Dobbs* and Democracy," *Harvard Law Review* 137, no. 3 (January 2024): 729–807, https://harvardlawreview.org/print/vol-137/dobbs-and-democracy/.

2. Len Niehoff, "Unprecedented Precedent and Original Originalism: How the Supreme Court's Decision in Dobbs Threatens Privacy and Free Speech Rights," *Communications Lawyer* 29, no. 2 (Summer 2024), www.americanbar.org/groups/communications_law/publications/communications_lawyer/2023-summer/unprecedented-precedent-and-original-originalism/.

3. Shira A. Scheindlin, "Trump's Judges Will Call the Shots for Years to Come," *Guardian,* October 25, 2021, www.theguardian.com/commentisfree/2021/oct/25/trump-judges-supreme-court-justices-judiciary. "The numbers tell a clear story. There are a total of 816 active federal judges comprising the supreme court, the 13 appellate courts, and 91 district courts. In just one term Trump was able to appoint 28% of those judges due to past and continuing vacancies. Most importantly, he appointed 33% of America's nine supreme court justices and 30% of the appellate judges. The vast majority of his appointments were white males—not one of his 54 appellate judges is Black. But what really stands out is the age of his appointees. The average age of his appellate judges was 47 (five years younger than those selected by Barack Obama). Six of those were in their 30s, and 20 were under 45. By contrast, of the 55 appellate judges picked by Obama—in eight years, not four—none were in their 30s and only six were younger than 45."

4. Phoebe Petrovich, "The Gospel of Matthew Trewhella: How a Militant Anti-Abortion Activist Is Influencing Republican Politics," ProPublica, July 10, 2024, www.propublica.org/article/matthew-trewhella-pastor-activist-republican -politics.

5. Jeanne Flavin, *Our Bodies, Our Crimes: The Policing of Women's Reproduction in America* (New York: New York University Press, 2008); Lynn M. Paltrow and Jeanne Flavin, "Arrests of and Forced Interventions on Pregnant Women in the United States, 1973–2005: Implications for Women's Legal Status and Public Health," *Journal of Health, Politics, Policy, and Law* 38, no. 2 (April 2013): 299–343; Michele Goodwin, *Policing the Womb: Invisible Women and the Criminalization of Motherhood* (Cambridge: Cambridge University Press, 2020); Grace E. Howard, *The Pregnancy Police: Conceiving Crime, Arresting Personhood* (Berkeley: University of California Press, 2024).

6. Luke Mogelson, *The Storm Is Here: An American Crucible* (New York: Penguin Press, 2022), 314.

7. "Donald Trump's Second Inaugural Speech, Annotated," *New York Times*, January 20, 2025, www.nytimes.com/interactive/2025/01/20/us/trump-inauguration-speech-annotated.html; Selena Simmons-Duffin, "National Institutes of Health Cancel Scientific Meetings after Trump Directives," National Public Radio, January 23, 2025, www.npr.org/transcripts/nx-s1 -5272398; Zolan Kanno-Youngs, Michael D. Shear, and Noah Weiland, "Trump's Executive Orders: Reversing Biden's Policies and Attacking the 'Deep State,'" *New York Times*, January 20, 2025.

8. Alan Feuer, "Trump Grants Sweeping Clemency to All Jan. 6 Rioters," *New York Times*, January 20, 2025; Chris Cameron, "Trump Pardons Anti -Abortion Activists Who Blockaded Clinic," *New York Times,* January 23, 2025.

9. Bernard Condon, "Musk's Straight-Arm Gesture Embraced by Right-Wing Extremists Regardless of What He Meant," Associated Press, January 21, 2025, https://apnews.com/article/musk-gesture-salute-antisemitism -0070dae53c7a73397b104ae645877535.

Works Cited

Abolish Human Abortion (AHA). "International Coalition of Abolitionist Societies." 2017. http://abolishhumanabortion.com/international-coalition-of-abolitionist-societies/ (site discontinued).

———. "What Is the AHA Symbol For?" June 14, 2012. https://blog.abolishhumanabortion.com/p/abolitionists-identify.html. The same discussion has been republished under the heading "Light Up the Darkness," https://abolishhumanabortion.com/light-up-the-darkness/.

Abortion Access Front. "The Role Anti-Abortion Extremists Played in the Terrorism on Our Nation's Capitol." www.aafront.org/anti-abortion-extremists-at-capitol/.

Allen, Silas. "Anti-Abortion Group Sues." *Oklahoman,* January 29, 2013. https://oklahoman.com/article/3749938/anti-abortion-group-sues-oklahoma-state-university.

American Bible Society. *Stand in the Gap: A Sacred Assembly of Men.* Commemorative Edition New Testament. Nashville, TN: Thomas Nelson Publishers, 1997.

American Library Association. "American Library Association Reports Record Number of Unique Book Titles Challenged in 2023." March 14, 2024. www.ala.org/news/2024/03/american-library-association-reports-record-number-unique-book-titles.

Americans United for Life. "Defending Life 2018." https://aul.org/wp-content/uploads/2018/10/Defending-Life-2018.pdf.

Anderson, Benedict. *Imagined Communities: Reflections on the Origin and Spread of Nationalism.* London: Verso, 2016.

Andrews, Joan. *You Reject Them, You Reject Me: The Prison Letters of Joan Andrews*. Brentwood, TN: Trinity Communications, 1988.

"Anti-Abortion Protest on Campus." *Kentucky Kernel*, October 19, 2017. Video originally posted with editorial, "No Matter What You Say, Free Speech Belongs to Everyone." https://kykernel.com/37173/uncategorized /editorial-no-matter-what-you-say-free-speech-belongs-to-everyone/.

Anti-Defamation League. "Pro-Trump Rallies in DC Attract Extremists and Erupt into Violence." December 13, 2020. www.adl.org/resources/blog /pro-trump-rallies-dc-attract-extremists-erupt-violence.

The Army of God Manual. www.armyofgod.com/AOGsel7.html.

"Article That Critiques High-Profile Abortion Study Retracted." *Retraction Watch*, December 29, 2022. https://retractionwatch.com/2022/12/29 /article-that-critiqued-high-profile-abortion-study-retracted/.

Ashcraft, Karen Lee. *Wronged and Dangerous: Viral Masculinity and the Populist Pandemic*. Bristol: Bristol University Press, 2022.

Atwood, S., Thekla Morgenroth, and Kristina R. Olson. "Gender Essentialism and Benevolent Sexism in Anti-Trans Rhetoric." *Societal Issues and Policy Review* 18 (2024): 171–93.

Azriel, Joshua. "The Internet and Hate Speech: An Examination of the Nuremberg Files Case." *Communication Law and Policy* 10, no. 4 (Autumn 2005): 477–98.

Baird-Windle, Patricia, and Eleanor J. Bader. *Targets of Hatred: Anti-Abortion Terrorism*. New York: Palgrave, 2001.

Ball, Molly. "Donald Trump Didn't Really Win 52% of White Women in 2016." *Time*, October 18, 2018. https://time.com/5422644/trump-white -women-2016/.

Basu, Srimati. "Practicing Vulnerability—Men's Rights Activists, Embodiment and Appropriation." Presented at the Center for South Asian Studies Lecture Series, University of Michigan, Ann Arbor, March 2019.

Beauchamp, Toby. *Going Stealth: Transgender Politics and U.S. Surveillance Practices*. Durham, NC: Duke University Press, 2018.

Beedle, Heidi. "The Army of Gideon: Anti-Abortion Activism in Wichita." *Colorado Times Recorder*, March 8, 2023. https://coloradotimesrecorder .com/2023/03/the-army-of-gideon-anti-abortion-activism-in-wichita /52248/.

Belew, Kathleen. *Bring the War Home: The White Power Movement and Paramilitary America.* Cambridge, MA: Harvard University Press, 2018.

Berlet, Chip. "Collectivists, Communists, Labor Bosses, and Treason: The Tea Parties as Right-Wing Populist Counter-Subversion Panic." *Critical Sociology* 38, no. 4 (July 2012): 565–87.

Berlet, Chip, and Matthew N. Lyons. *Right-Wing Populism in America: Too Close for Comfort.* New York: Guilford Press, 2000.

Berlet, Chip, and Carol Mason. "Swastikas in Cyberspace: How Hate Went Online." In *Digital Media Strategies of the Far Right in Europe and the United States,* edited by Patricia Anne Simpson and Helga Druxes. Lanham, MD: Lexington Books, 2015.

Berlet, Chip, and Spencer Sunshine. "Rural Rage: The Roots of Right-Wing Populism in the United States." *Journal of Peasant Studies* 46, no. 3 (2019): 480–513.

Berlin, Seth D. "Are the Nuremberg Files and 'Wanted' Posters Protected Advocacy or Unprotected Threat?" *Communications Lawyer: The Journal of Media, Information, and Communications Law* 20, no. 2 (Summer 2002): 1, 26–35.

Bermanzohn, Sally. *Through Survivor's Eyes: From the Sixties to the Greensboro Massacre.* Nashville, TN: Vanderbilt University Press, 2011.

Bjork-James, Sophie, and Josefine Landberg. "Fear, Fantasy and Feelings on the Far-Right." Panel of the 2021 Joint Conference on Right-Wing Studies and Research on Male Supremacism, May 10, 2021.

Blackington, Courtney. "Two Polish Women Died after Being Refused Timely Abortions. Many Poles Are Outraged—and Protesting." *Washington Post,* February 18, 2022. www.washingtonpost.com/politics/2022/02/18/poland-abortion-protest/.

Blakeslee, Nate. "Sorting Fact from Fiction in the Story of Pro-Life Celebrity Abby Johnson." *Texas Monthly,* April 16, 2019. www.texasmonthly.com/news-politics/fact-fiction-pro-life-celebrity-abby-johnson-unplanned/.

"Blood libel." *Holocaust Encyclopedia.* https://encyclopedia.ushmm.org/content/en/article/blood-libel.

Bloom, Matt. "A Librarian Was Fired after Refusing to Ban Books." National Public Radio, January 2, 2024. www.npr.org/2024/01/02/1222566899/a-librarian-was-fired-after-refusing-to-ban-books-she-fought-back.

Bower, Ann, and Valerie Finkelman. "Militia Men: Herb Philbrick in Camouflage." *Body Politic* 5, no. 6 (June/July 1995): 6–11.

Bray, Michael. *A Time to Kill.* Portland, OR: Advocates for Life, 1994.

Bridges, Khiara M. *Reproducing Race: An Ethnography of Pregnancy as a Site of Racialization.* Berkeley: University of California Press, 2011.

Briggs, Laura. *How All Politics Became Reproductive Politics.* Berkeley: University of California Press, 2017.

Burghardt, Tom. "State Citizenship: Patriot Ties to White Supremacists and Neo-Nazis." *Body Politic* 5, no. 6 (June/July 1995): 12–18.

Butler, Judith. *Who's Afraid of Gender?* New York: Farrar, Straus and Giroux, 2024.

Cameron, Chris. "Trump Pardons Anti-Abortion Activists Who Blockaded Clinic." *New York Times,* January 23, 2025.

Carmon, Irin. "Meet the Rebels of the Anti-Abortion Movement." MSNBC, March 8, 2014. www.msnbc.com/melissa-harris-perry/meet-the-rebels -the-anti-abortion-movement-msna281321.

"Caught on Cam." Sinclair News, 16 KMJR, Eugene, Oregon, July 10, 2014. https://nbc16.com/news/nation-world/caught-on-cam-pro-life-activists -confronted-attacked-by-woman.

Chappell, Robert. "Racist Propaganda Appears in Madison, Middleton." *Madison 365,* October 5, 2020. https://madison365.com/racist-propaganda -appears-in-madison-middleton/.

Chikov, Pavel. "In the Name of God: Atheists in Russia under Fire." *Moscow Times,* May 18, 2017. https://themoscowtimes.com/articles/in-the-name -of-god-atheists-in-russia-under-fire-op-ed-58025.

Christian Broadcasting Network (CBN). "Orthodox Priest Warns Europe Will Turn Muslim in 30 Years, Russia in 50." May 16, 2017. https://cbn.com /news/world/orthodox-priest-warns-europe-will-turn-muslim-30-years -russia-50.

"The Christian Fright." *Harper's Magazine* 295, no. 1769 (October 1997): 20 ff.

Chung, Grace S., Ryan E. Lawrence, Kenneth A. Rasinski, John D. Yoon, and Farr A. Curlin. "Obstetrician-Gynecologists' Beliefs about When Pregnancy Begins." *American Journal of Obstetrics and Gynecology* 206, no. 2 (2012): e1–7. www.ajog.org/article/S0002-9378(11)02223-X/fulltext.

Cocotas, Alex. "How Poland's Far-Right Government Is Pushing Abortion Underground." *Guardian,* November 30, 2017. www.theguardian.com

/news/2017/nov/30/how-polands-far-right-government-is-pushing
-abortion-underground.

Condit, Celeste. *Decoding Abortion Rhetoric*. Champaign: University of
Illinois Press, 1994.

Condon, Bernard. "Musk's Straight-Arm Gesture Embraced by Right-Wing
Extremists Regardless of What He Meant." Associated Press, January 21,
2025. https://apnews.com/article/musk-gesture-salute-antisemitism
-0070dae53c7a73397b104ae645877535.

Cooper, Cloee, and Hannah Silver. "101: Abortion Abolition." Political
Research Associates, October 26, 2023. https://politicalresearch.org/2023
/10/26/101-abortion-abolitionists.

Cooper, Gavin. "No Matter How Offensive the Protests, We Must Support
Free Speech on UK's Campus." *Lexington-Herald Leader,* September 28,
2023. www.kentucky.com/opinion/op-ed/article279882394.html.

Corrales, John. "Donald Trump Asks for Evangelicals' Support." *New York
Times,* June 22, 2016. www.nytimes.com/2016/06/22/us/politics/donald-
trump-asks-for-evangelicals-support-and-questions-hillary-clintons
-faith.html.

Corralis, Javier, and Jacob Kiryk. "Homophobic Populism." In *Oxford
Research Encyclopedia of Politics*. Published online August 15, 2022. https://
oxfordre.com/politics/display/10.1093/acrefore/9780190228637.001
.0001/acrefore-9780190228637-e-2080.

Created Equal. *Abortion: Doctrine of Demons*. www.createdequal.org/doctrine
-of-demons.

———. "Jumbotron College Campus Debut." www.youtube.com/watch?v=
7Nbp6ewiLPU&feature=emb_logo.

———. "One Question Stumps College Student." www.createdequal.org
/outreach/ (page discontinued).

———. "Our Story." https://www.createdequal.org/our-story/.

Cross, Fallon. "Protests on UofL and UK's Campus: Students Outraged."
Rambler, October 11, 2023. https://transyrambler.com/2023/10/11/protests
-on-uofl-and-uks-campus-students-outraged/.

Crutcher, Mark. *Firestorm: A Guerrilla Strategy for a Pro-Life America*. Denton,
TX: Life Dynamics, 1992.

cummings, andré douglas pond, and Steven A. Ramirez. "The Racist Roots of
the War on Drugs and the Myth of Equal Protection for People of Color."

University of Arkansas at Little Rock Law Review 44, no. 4 (2022). https://lawrepository.ualr.edu/lawreview/vol44/iss4/1.

Dale, Daniel. "Fact Check: Trump Falsely Claims Schools Are Secretly Sending Children for Gender-Affirming Surgeries." CNN, September 4, 2024. www.cnn.com/2024/09/04/politics/donald-trump-fact-check-children-gender-affirming-surgery/index.html.

Datta, Neil. *Tip of the Iceberg: Religious Extremist Funders against Human Rights for Sexuality and Reproductive Health in Europe 2009-2018*. Brussels: European Parliamentary Forum for Sexual and Reproductive Rights, 2021.

Delay, Cara. "From the Backstreet to Britain: Women and Abortion Travel in Irish History." In *Travellin' Mama: Mothers, Mothering, and Travel,* edited by Charlotte Beyer, Janet MacLennon, Dorsia Smith Silva, and Marjorie Tesser, 217-34. Bradford, ON: Demeter, 2019.

deParrie, Paul. "The Editors Eye." *Life Advocate* 13, no. 5 (March/April 1999). www.lifeadvocate.org/3_99/e_eye.htm.

———. "The Editors Eye." *Life Advocate* 13, no. 6 (May/June 1999). www.lifeadvocate.org/5_99/e_eye.htm.

———. "Potpourri (or Niggling Things Revisited)." *Life Advocate* 13, no. 4 (January/February 1999). www.lifeadvocate.org/1_99/comment.htm.

DiBranco, Alex. "The Long History of the Anti-Abortion Movement's Links to White Supremacists." *The Nation,* February 3, 2020. www.thenation.com/article/politics/anti-abortion-white-supremacy/.

Dobbins-Harris, Shyrissa. "The Myth of Abortion as Black Genocide: Reclaiming Our Reproductive Cycle." *National Black Law Journal* 26, no. 1 (2017): 86-127.

"Donald Trump's Second Inaugural Speech, Annotated." *New York Times,* January 20, 2025. www.nytimes.com/interactive/2025/01/20/us/trump-inauguration-speech-annotated.html.

Donnally, Jennifer. "The Edelin Manslaughter Trial and the Anti-Abortion Movement." *Massachusetts Historical Review* 20 (2018): 1-32.

Douthat, Ross. "The Irish Exception." *New York Times,* May 19, 2018. www.nytimes.com/2018/05/19/opinion/sunday/ireland-abortion-amendment.

Dreweke, Joerg. "Study Purporting to Show Link between Abortion and Mental Health Outcomes Decisively Debunked." Guttmacher Institute, March 5, 2012. www.guttmacher.org/news-release/2012/study-purporting-show-link-between-abortion-and-mental-health-outcomes-decisively.

Eighth Amendment of the Constitution Act 1983 (Ir.), http://www
.irishstatutebook.ie/eli/1983/ca/8/enacted/en/html.

Faludi, Susan. *Backlash: The Undeclared War against American Women*. New
York: Crown, 1991.

Fausset, Richard, and Allan Feuer. "Far-Right Groups Surge into National
View in Charlottesville." *New York Times*, August 13, 2017. www.nytimes
.com/2017/08/13/us/far-right-groups-blaze-into-national-view-in
-charlottesville.html.

Feder, J. Lester, and Alberto Nardelli. "This Anti-Abortion Leader Is Charged
with Laundering Money from Azerbaijan." *Buzzfeed News*, April 26, 2017.
www.buzzfeed.com/lesterfeder/this-anti-abortion-leader-is-charged
-with-laundering-money.

Federal Bureau of Investigation. "Eric Rudolph." www.fbi.gov/history
/famous-cases/eric-rudolph.

Feuer, Alan. "Trump Grants Sweeping Clemency to All Jan. 6 Rioters." *New
York Times*, January 20, 2025.

Flack, Jillian, and Molly Huffer. "It's Not about Free Speech." *Kent Wired*,
April 18, 2023. https://kentwired.com/96504/latest-updates/its-not
-about-free-speech-members-of-the-lgbtq-community-speak-out
-against-anti-trans-message-fusion-collab/.

Flavin, Jeanne. *Our Bodies, Our Crimes: The Policing of Women's Reproduction
in America*. New York: New York University Press, 2008.

Foundation for European Progressive Studies. *Gender As Symbolic Glue: The
Position and Role of Conservative and Far Right Parties in the Anti-Gender
Mobilizations in Europe*, edited by Eszter Kováts and Maari Põim.
Budapest: Foundation for European Progressive Studies in cooperation
with Friedrich-Ebert-Stiftung, 2015.

Geary, Daniel. *Beyond Civil Rights: The Moynihan Report and Its Legacy*.
Philadelphia: University of Pennsylvania Press, 2015.

Goldberg, Michelle. "Obama Billboard Shows Anti-Abortion Focus on
African-Americans." *Daily Beast*, March 30, 2011. www.thedailybeast
.com/obama-billboard-shows-anti-abortion-focus-on-african
-americans.

Goldwater, Barry. *Conscience of a Conservative*. Shepherdsville, KY: Victor
Publishing, 1960.

Goodman, Eric. "On the 19th of April." *Self*, April 1999, 111.

Goodwin, Michele. *Policing the Womb: Invisible Women and the Criminalization of Motherhood*. Cambridge: Cambridge University Press, 2020.

Graff, Agnieszka, Ratna Kapur, and Suzanna Danuta Walters. "Introduction: Gender and the Rise of the Global Right." *Signs: Journal of Women in Culture and Society* 44, no. 3 (March 2019): 541–60. https://doi.org/10.1086/701152.

Graff, Agnieszka, and Elzbieta Korolczuk. *Anti-Gender Politics in the Populist Moment*. New York: Routledge, 2022.

Guenther, Lisa. "The Most Dangerous Place: Pro-Life Politics and the Rhetoric of Slavery." *Postmodern Culture* 22, no. 2 (2012). www.proquest.com/docview/2560063616/abstract/911A11D917144920PQ/2.

Harrington, Mark. "Social Justice Critical Theory and Christianity." *Radio Activist: The Mark Harrington Show,* December 31, 2020. https://createdequal.podbean.com/e/social-justice-critical-theory-and-christianity-are-they-compatible-the-mark-harrington-show-12-31-2020; the episode appears to have been originally broadcast on August 6, 2020, as seen here: https://markharrington.org/live/social-justice-critical-theory-and-christianity-are-they-compatible/.

———. "Top Ten Reasons Not to Support the Black Lives Matter Movement." *Radio Activist: The Mark Harrington Show*, November 5, 2020. https://markharrington.org/live/top-ten-reasons-to-not-support-the-blacklivesmatter-movement-the-mark-harrington-show-11-05-2020/.

Hart, William David. "Slaves, Fetuses, and Animals." *Journal of Religious Ethics* 42, no. 4 (December 2014): 661–90. https://doi.org/10.1111/jore.12077.

Haugeberg, Karissa. *Women against Abortion: Inside the Largest Moral Reform Movement of the Twentieth Century*. Urbana: University of Illinois Press, 2017.

Holland, Jennifer L. *Tiny You: A Western History of the Anti-Abortion Movement*. Berkeley: University of California Press, 2020.

Horwitz, Tony. "Run, Rudolph, Run: How the Fugitive Became a Folk Hero." *New Yorker,* March 15, 1999, 46–52.

HoSang, Daniel Martinez, and Joseph E. Lowndes. *Producers, Parasites, Patriots: Race and the New Right-Wing Politics of Precarity*. Minneapolis: University of Minnesota Press, 2019.

Howard, Grace E. *The Pregnancy Police: Conceiving Crime, Arresting Personhood*. Berkeley: University of California Press, 2024.

HRC (Human Rights Campaign). "Exposed: The World Congress of Families." June 2015. https://assets2.hrc.org/files/assets/resources /ExposedTheWorldCongressOfFamilies.pdf.

Huber, Dave. "Professor Says It's Not about Free Speech." *College Fix*, April 19, 2023. www.thecollegefix.com/professor-says-its-not-about-free-speech -after-what-is-a-woman-is-painted-on-campus-rock/.

Human Life International Staff. "UPDATE: HLI Ireland Conference Forced to Move after Threats Rescheduled." *Human Life International*, September 22, 2017. www.hli.org/2017/09/venue-refuses-hosting-hli-event-after -receiving-threats/ (page discontinued).

Irvine, Janice M. *Talk about Sex: The Battles Over Sex Education in the United States*. Berkeley: University of California Press, 2002.

Jabali, Malaika. "White People Are Killed by Cops Too. But That Doesn't Undermine Black Lives Matter." *Guardian*, July 16, 2020. www.theguardian .com/commentisfree/2020/jul/16/trump-police-abolition-black-americans.

Jalsevac, John. "Top Scientists Meet in Moscow, Tell Russian Government: Fetus Is Human; Ban Abortion." LifeSiteNews, July 15, 2015. www .lifesitenews.com/news/top-scientists-meet-in-moscow-tell-russian -government-fetus-is-human.-ban-a.

Jefferis, Jennifer. *Armed for Life: The Army of God and Anti-Abortion Terror in the United States*. Santa Barbara, CA: Praeger, 2011.

Jefferson, Mildred. Mildred Jefferson Papers. Schlesinger Library, Radcliffe Institute, Harvard University, Cambridge, MA.

Jesudason, Sujatha. "The Latest Case of Reproductive Carrots and Sticks: Race, Abortion and Sex Selection." *Scholar and Feminist Online* 9.1–9.2 (Fall 2010 /Spring 2011). http://sfonline.barnard.edu/reprotech/jesudason_01.htm.

Jewell, Allison. "Students Rally for Administration Explanations amid Anti-Queer Protests." *Louisville Cardinal*, September 27, 2023. www .louisvillecardinal.com/2023/09/students-rally-for-administration -explanations-amid-anti-queer-protests/.

Johnson, Abby, and Cindy Lambert. *Unplanned: The Dramatic True Story of a Former Planned Parenthood Leader's Eye-Opening Journey across the Life Line*. Carol Stream, IL: Tyndale House Publishers, 2014.

Joyce, Kathryn. "Abortion as Black Genocide." *Public Eye*, April 29, 2010. www.politicalresearch.org/2010/04/29/abortion-as-black-genocide -an-old-scare-tactic-re-emerges.

———. "Deep State, Deep Church: How QAnon and Donald Trump Have Infected the Catholic Church." October 30, 2020. www.vanityfair.com /news/2020/10/how-qanon-and-trumpism-have-infected-the-catholic -church.

Kanno-Youngs, Zolan, Michael D. Shear, and Noah Weiland. "Trump's Executive Orders: Reversing Biden's Policies and Attacking the 'Deep State.'" *New York Times,* January 20, 2025.

Kavattur, Purvaja S., Somjen Frazer, Abby El-Shafei, et al. "The Rise of Pregnancy Criminalization: A Pregnancy Justice Report." Pregnancy Justice, 2023.

Kearl, Michelle Kelsey. "WWMLKD? Coopting the Rhetorical Legacy of Martin Luther King, Jr. and the Civil Rights Movement." *Journal of Contemporary Rhetoric* 8, no. 3 (2018): 184–99.

Kishkovsky, Sophia. "Russians Adopt U.S. Tactics in Opposing Abortion." *New York Times,* June 9, 2011. www.nytimes.com/2011/06/10/world /europe/10iht-abortion10.html.

Krzych, Scott. *Beyond Bias: Conservative Media, Documentary Form, and the Politics of Hysteria.* New York: Oxford University Press, 2021.

———. "The Price of Knowledge: Hysterical Discourse in Anti–Michael Moore Documentaries." *Comparatist* 39 (2015): 80.

Lee, Martin. *The Beast Reawakens.* Boston: Little, Brown, 1997.

Lenz, Ryan. "The Battle for Berkeley." *Hatewatch,* May 1, 2017. www .splcenter.org/hatewatch/2017/05/01/battle-berkeley-name-freedom -speech-radical-right-circling-ivory-tower-ensure-voice-alt.

Leon, Harmon. "Evangelical Haunted Houses Involve Much More Abortion than Normal Haunted House." *Vice,* November 1, 2013.

Lepore, Jill. *The Whites of Their Eyes: The Tea Party's Revolution and the Battle over American History.* Princeton, NJ: Princeton University Press, 2010.

Levintova, Hannah. "Did Anti-Gay Evangelicals Skirt U.S. Sanctions on Russia?" *Mother Jones,* September 8, 2014. www.motherjones.com /politics/2014/09/world-congress-families-russia-conference -sanctions/.

———. "How U.S. Evangelicals Helped Create Russia's Anti-Gay Movement." *Mother Jones,* February 21, 2014. www.motherjones.com/politics/2014/02 /world-congress-families-russia-gay-rights/.

———. "The World Congress of Families' Russian Network." *Mother Jones,*
February 21, 2014. www.motherjones.com/politics/2014/02/world
-congress-families-us-evangelical-russia-family-tree/.

Lewis, Loree. "Court Rules On Miller-Young Case." *Daily Nexus,* August 27,
2014. https://dailynexus.com/2014-08-27/court-rules-on-miller-young
-case/.

Life Advocate. "Biography: Cathy Ramey, Associate Editor." www
.lifeadvocate.org/bio/cathy/biocathy.htm.

Lindgren, Yvonne. "Trump's Angry White Women: Motherhood, Nationalism,
and Abortion." *Hofstra Law Review* 48, no. 1 (2019): 1–46. https://
scholarlycommons.law.hofstra.edu/hlr/vol48/iss1/3.

Liu, Melinda. "Inside the Anti-Abortion Underground." *Newsweek,* August 29,
1994. www.newsweek.com/inside-anti-abortion-underground-187894.

Luehrmann, Sonja. "'God Values Intentions': Abortion, Expiation, and
Moments of Sincerity in Russian Orthodox Pilgrimage." *Hau: Journal of
Ethnographic Theory* 7, no. 1 (2017): 163–84.

———. "Innocence and Demographic Crisis: Transposing Post-Abortion
Syndrome into a Russian Orthodox Key." In *A Fragmented Landscape:
Abortion Governance and Protest Logics in Europe,* edited by Silvia De
Zordo, Joanna Mishtal, and Lorena Anton, 103–22. New York: Berghahn,
2016.

Luker, Kristin. *Abortion and the Politics of Motherhood.* Berkeley: University of
California Press, 1984.

Luna, Zakiya. "'Black Children Are an Endangered Species': Examining
Racial Framing in Social Movements." Sociological Focus 51, no. 3 (2018):
238–51.

Macdonald, Andrew [William Pierce]. *The Turner Diaries.* 2nd ed. New York:
Barricade Books, 1978, 1980.

MacDonald, Sarah. "People Are Only Hearing Sterilised Version of Abortion,
PLC Conference Hears." *CatholicIreland.net,* December 5, 2017. www
.catholicireland.net/people-hearing-sterilised-version-abortion-plc
-conference-hears/.

Mander, C. "Murder of Trans People Nearly Doubled." CBS News. www
.cbsnews.com/news/transgender-community-murder-rates-everytown
-for-gun-safety-report/.

Marasco, Robyn. "Reconsidering the Sexual Politics of Fascism." *Historical Materialism,* June 25, 2021. www.historicalmaterialism.org/blog /reconsidering-sexual-politics-fascism.

Marcotte, Amanda. "The Earth-Shaking Abortion That Never Happened." *Slate,* January 7, 2010. https://slate.com/human-interest/2010/01/the -earth-shaking-abortion-that-never-happened.html.

Marty, Robin. "Meet Joe Scheidler, Patriarch of the Anti-Abortion Movement." Political Research Associates, January 23, 2015. https:// politicalresearch.org/2015/01/23/meet-joe-scheidler-patriarch-anti -abortion-movement.

Marx, Paul. *Confessions of a Prolife Missionary: The Journeys of Fr. Paul Marx.* Gaithersburg, MD: Human Life International, 1988.

———. *The Death Peddlers: War on the Unborn.* Minneapolis, MN: Saint John's University Press, 1972.

Mason, Carol. "Created Equal but 'Equal in No Other Respect': Opposing Abortion to Protect Men." In *Male Supremacism in the United States: From Patriarchal Traditionalism to Misogynist Incels and the Alt-Right,* edited by E. Carian, A. DiBranco, and C. Ebin, 94–114. New Jersey: Routledge, 2022.

———. *Killing for Life: The Apocalyptic Narrative of Pro-Life Politics.* Ithaca, NY: Cornell University Press, 2002.

———. "Minority Unborn." In *Fetal Subjects, Feminist Positions,* edited by Lynn Marie Morgan and Meredith W. Michaels, 159–74. Philadelphia: University of Pennsylvania Press, 1999.

———. "Opposing Abortion to Protect Women: Transnational Strategy since the 1990s." *Signs: Journal of Women in Culture and Society* 44, no. 3 (2019): 665–92.

———. *Reading Appalachia from Left to Right: Conservatives and the 1974 Kanawha County Textbook Controversy.* Ithaca, NY: Cornell University Press, 2009.

Massengill, Dustin. "UK Condemns Statements Made by Protesters on Campus." Fox 56 News, September 25, 2023. https://fox56news.com/news /local/uk-condemns-statements-made-by-protesters-on campus/.

McCally, Karen. "Why Is a 16th-Century Tradition Attracting Activists on the Christian Right?" University of Rochester NewsCenter. www.rochester .edu/newscenter/early-modern-resistance-theory-christian-right-544452/.

McFadden, Robert D. "Kenneth C. Edelin, Doctor at Center of Landmark Abortion Case, Dies at 74." *New York Times,* December 30, 2013. www .nytimes.com/2013/12/31/us/kenneth-c-edelin-physician-at-center-of -landmark-abortion-case-dies-at-74.html.

Merton, Andrew. *Enemies of Choice.* Boston: Beacon Press, 1981.

Mervis, Jeffrey. "Crashing the Boards: Neuroscientist Maureen Condic Brings a Different Voice to NSF Oversight Body." *Science,* November 26, 2018.

Michael, George. *Lone Wolf Terror and the Rise of Leaderless Resistance.* Nashville, TN: Vanderbilt University Press, 2012.

Middle East Media Research Institute (MEMRI). "Russian Orthodox Prelate Predicts: Europe Will Turn Muslim in 30 Years, Russia in 50." Special dispatch no. 6920, May 12, 2017. www.memri.org/reports/russian -orthodox-prelate-predicts-europe-will-turn-muslim-30-years -russia-50.

Mihailovic, Alexandar. "Hijacking Academic Autonomy: Neo-Aryanism and Internet Expertise." In *Digital Media Strategies of the Far Right in Europe and the United States,* edited by Patricia Anne Simpson and Helga Druxes. London: Rowman & Littlefield, 2015.

Miller-Idriss, Cynthia. *Hate in the Homeland: The New Global Far Right.* Princeton, NJ: Princeton University Press, 2020.

Mistich, Dave. "'Appalachia Shaming' on Day 100." *100 Days in Appalachia,* April 30, 2017. www.100daysinappalachia.com/2017/04/appalachian -shaming-day-100-white-supremacist-rally-counter-protest-no-one- wanted/.

Mogelson, Luke. *The Storm Is Here: An American Crucible.* New York: Penguin Press, 2022.

Montgomery, John Warwick. "The Fetus as a Person." *Human Life Review* 1, no. 2 (Summer 1975).

Morgan, Lynn. "The Dublin Declaration on Maternal Health Care and Anti-Abortion Activism: Examples from Latin America." *Health and Human Rights Journal* 19, no. 1 (2017): 41–53.

Moyers, Bill D. "What a Real President Was Like." *Washington Post,* November 13, 1988. www.washingtonpost.com/archive/opinions /1988/11/13/what-a-real-president-was-like/d483c1be-d0da-43b7 -bde6-04e10106ff6c/.

Murphy, Kate. "Students Sue Miami University." *Cincinnati Inquirer,* December 1, 2017. www.cincinnati.com/story/news/2017/11/30/students -sue-miami-university-over-anti-abortion-protest/908549001/.

Murray, Melissa, and Katherine Shaw. "*Dobbs* and Democracy." *Harvard Law Review* 137, no. 3 (January 2024): 729–807. https://harvardlawreview.org /print/vol-137/dobbs-and-democracy/.

Myers, Ella. *The Gratifications of Whiteness: W. E. B. Du Bois and the Enduring Rewards of Anti-Blackness.* New York: Oxford, 2022.

National Immigration Forum. "The 'Great Replacement' Theory, Explained." https://immigrationforum.org/wp-content/uploads/2021/12/Replacement -Theory-Explainer-1122.pdf.

Newman, Karen. *Fetal Positions: Individualism, Science, Visuality.* Stanford, CA: Stanford University Press, 1996.

Niehoff, Len. "Unprecedented Precedent and Original Originalism: How the Supreme Court's Decision in Dobbs Threatens Privacy and Free Speech Rights." *Communications Lawyer* 29, no. 2 (Summer 2024). www .americanbar.org/groups/communications_law/publications /communications_lawyer/2023-summer/unprecedented-precedent -and-original-originalism/.

Nifong, Christina. "Anti-Abortion Violence Defines 'Army of God.'" *Christian Science Monitor,* February 4, 1998.

Norris, Siân. *Bodies Under Siege: How the Far-Right Attack on Reproductive Rights Went Global.* London: Verso, 2023.

Novelly, Thomas. "As Buffer Zone Debated, Courthouse the First Site of Week-Long Abortion Protests." *Courier-Journal* (Louisville, KY), July 24, 2017. www.courier-journal.com/story/news/local/2017/07/24/operation -save-america-begins-weeklong-abortion-protest-louisville/499502001/.

"Ohio Woman Must Pay." LifeSiteNews, August 26, 2014. www.lifesitenews .com/news/ohio-woman-must-pay-80-after-attack-on-pro-lifers-assault -charge-dropped.

OllieGarkey, "Is an Anti-Choice Group Using a Nazi Symbol?" *Daily Kos,* July 9, 2012. www.dailykos.com/stories/2012/7/9/1107487/-Is-an-Anti-Choice -group-using-a-Nazi-Symbol.

O'Loughlin, Ed. "As Irish Abortion Vote Nears, Fears of Foreign Influence Rise." *New York Times,* March 26, 2018. www.nytimes.com/2018/03/26 /world/europe/ireland-us-abortion-referendum.html.

Ophir, Yotam, Meredith L. Pruden, Dror Walter, Ayse D. Lokmanoglu, Catherine Tebaldi, and Rui Wang. "Weaponizing Reproductive Rights: A Mixed-Method Analysis of White Nationalists' Discussion of Abortions Online." *Information, Communication & Society* 26, no. 11 (2022): 2186–2211.

Osborn, Molly. "Anti-Abortion Activist Abby Johnson Had Quite the Adventure at the Capitol Riot." *Jezebel*, January 12, 2021. www.jezebel.com /anti-abortion-activist-abby-johnson-had-quite-the-adven-1846043253.

Packer, Tiffany. "Guns, Torches and Badges: The 1979 Greensboro Massacre, the Charlottesville Unite the Right Rally, and the Lasting Impacts of Racial Violence on Black and Anti-Racist Communities." *Souls* 22, nos. 2–4 (2020): 141–59. https://doi.org/10.1080/10999949.2021.2003625.

Paige, Connie. *The Right-to-Lifers: Who They Are, How They Operate, Where They Get Their Money.* New York: Summit Books, 1983.

Paltrow, Lynn M., and Jeanne Flavin. "Arrests of and Forced Interventions on Pregnant Women in the United States, 1973–2005: Implications for Women's Legal Status and Public Health." *Journal of Health, Politics, Policy, and Law* 38, no. 2 (April 2013): 299–343.

Parogni, Ilaria. "The Strategic Savvy of Russia's Growing Anti-Abortion Movement." *The Nation*, August 30, 2016. www.thenation.com/article /archive/the-strategic-savvy-of-russias-growing-anti-abortion -movement/.

Perlstein, Rick. *The Invisible Bridge: The Fall of Nixon and the Rise of Reagan.* New York: Simon and Schuster, 2014.

Petchesky, Rosalind. *Abortion and Women's Choice: The State, Sexuality, and Reproductive Freedom.* Boston: Northeastern University Press, 1984.

Petrizzo, Zachary. "Ali Alexander Flirts with Q in Telegram Rant about '17.'" *Daily Dot*, February 16, 2021. www.dailydot.com/debug/ali-alexander -qanon-telegram/.

Petrovich, Phoebe. "The Gospel of Matthew Trewhella: How a Militant Anti-Abortion Activist Is Influencing Republican Politics." ProPublica, July 10, 2024. www.propublica.org/article/matthew-trewhella-pastor -activist-republican-politics.

Phillips, Charles D. "The Politics of Firearm Safety: An Emerging New Balance of Power." *American Journal of Public Health* 108, no. 7 (July 2018): 868–70. https://doi.org/10.2105/AJPH.2018.304462.

Political Research Associates. "The Abortion Abolitionists with Cloee Cooper." *Inform Your Resistance*. https://politicalresearch. org/2023/09/14/abortion-abolitionists-cloee-cooper.

Powell, Douglas Reichert. *Endless Caverns: An Underground Journey into the Show Caves of Appalachia*. Durham: North Carolina University Press, 2018.

Prager, Joshua. *The Family Roe: An American Story*. New York: W. W. Norton, 2021.

———. "The Groundbreaking and Complicated Life of Mildred Fay Jefferson." CNN Opinion, May 10, 2022. www.cnn.com/2022/05/10/opinions /abortion-pro-life-hero-mildred-fay-jefferson-prager/index.html.

Price, Eyal. *Absolute Convictions*. New York: Henry Holt, 2006.

"Pro-Life Activists Confronted, Attacked on Camera." Fox News, July 11, 2014. https://video.foxnews.com/v/3669804665001.

"Promoting Dignity." Interview with Jonathan Mazzochi. *Body Politic* 5, no. 6 (June/July 1995): 19–23.

Provost, Claire, and Lara Whyte. "Foreign and 'Alt-Right' Activists Target Irish Voters on Facebook ahead of Abortion Referendum." *Open Democracy*, April 25, 2018. www.opendemocracy.net/5050/claire-provost-lara-whyte /north-american-anti-abortion-facebook-ireland-referendum.

Raspail, Jean. *The Camp of the Saints*. 4th American ed. Petoskey, MI: Social Contract Press, 1987.

Reagan, Leslie. *Dangerous Pregnancies: Mothers, Disabilities, and Abortion in America*. Berkeley: University of California Press, 2012.

Richardson, Heather Cox. "Letters from an American." September 1, 2023. https://heathercoxrichardson.substack.com/p/september-1-2023.

Ricossa, Montse. "Hateful Flyers in the Quad Cities." October 18, 2019. www .kwqc.com/content/news/Hateful-flyers-in-the-Quad-Cities-563424181.html.

Ridgeway, James. *Blood in the Face: The Ku Klux Klan, Aryan Nations, Nazi Skinheads, and the Rise of a New White Culture*. New York: Thunder's Mouth Press, 1990.

Rivkin-Fish, Michele. "Anthropology, Demography, and the Search for a Critical Analysis of Fertility: Insights from Russia." *American Anthropologist* 105, no. 2 (2003).

———. "Conceptualizing Feminist Strategies for Russian Reproductive Politics: Abortion, Surrogate Motherhood, and Family Support after Socialism." *Signs* 38, no. 3 (2013).

———. "Pronatalism, Gender Politics, and the Renewal of Family Support in Russia: Toward a Feminist Anthropology of 'Maternal Capital.'" *Slavic Review* 69, no. 3 (2010): 701–24.

Robbins, Jefferson. "Report: Released Abortion-Clinic Terrorist to Take Up Residence in Douglas County." *Source One News* (Quincy, Washington), November 9, 2018. www.yoursourceone.com/columbia_basin/report -released-abortion-clinic-terrorist-to-take-up-residence-in-douglas -county/article_366ae798-e46f-11e8-94fa-5bcd716e1561.html.

Roberts, Bill. "BSU, Anti-Abortion Group Settle Free Speech Lawsuit." *Idaho Statesman,* June 3, 2015. www.idahostatesman.com/news/local /education/boise-state-university/article40861854.html.

Roediger, David R. *The Wages of Whiteness: Race and the Making of the American Working Class.* New York: Verso, 1991.

Rosensweig, Anna. "Whose Resistance Theory?" *Modern Language Quarterly* 83, no. 3 (September 2022): 335–48.

Rosenthal, Lawrence. *Empire of Resentment: Populism's Toxic Embrace of Nationalism.* New York: The New Press, 2020.

———. "The Male Fighting Band." In Yiannis Gabriel, *Organizations in Depth: The Psychanalysis of Organizations,* 182–83. Thousand Oaks, CA: Sage Publications, 1999.

Ross, Loretta, and Rickie Solinger. *Reproductive Justice: An Introduction.* Berkeley: University of California Press, 2017.

Rudolph, Eric. *All Enemies, Foreign and Domestic.* 2017. www.armyofgod.com /EricRudolphEnemies1.pdf.

———. "Racism." www.armyofgod.com/EricRudolphRacism.html.

———. "A Time of War: Is Armed Resistance to Abortion Morally Justified?" November 2018. www.armyofgod.com/PacifismChristian1.pdf.

———. "White Lies: Eugenics, Race, and Abortion." December 2014. www .armyofgod.com/EricRudolphWhiteLiesEugenicsAbortionandRacism2.pdf.

Russo, Vito. *The Celluloid Closet: The Homosexual in the Movies.* New York: Harper and Row, 1987.

Sanger, Carol. *About Abortion: Terminating Pregnancy in Twenty-First-Century America.* Cambridge, MA: Belknap Press of Harvard University Press, 2017.

Saurette, Paul, and Kelly Gordon. *The Changing Voice of the Anti-Abortion Movement.* Toronto: University of Toronto Press, 2015.

Scheindlin, Shira A. "Trump's Judges Will Call the Shots for Years to Come."
    Guardian, October 25, 2021. www.theguardian.com/commentisfree/2021
    /oct/25/trump-judges-supreme-court-justices-judiciary.
Schlatter, Evelyn A. *Aryan Cowboys: White Supremacists and the Search for a
    New Frontier, 1970–2000.* Austin: University of Texas Press, 2006.
Schwartz, Gabriel L., and Jaquelyn L. Jahn. "Mapping Fatal Police Violence
    across U.S. Metropolitan Areas: Overall Rates and Racial/Ethnic
    Inequities, 2013–2017." *PLOS ONE* 15, no. 6 (2020): e0229686.
Seltzer, Rick. "Cal State to Pay $240,000 to Settle Anti-Abortion Speaker
    Lawsuit." *Inside Higher Ed,* February 6, 2020. www.insidehighered.com
    /quicktakes/2020/02/06/cal-state-pay-240000-settle-anti-abortion
    -speaker-lawsuit.
Sharlet, Jeff. "January 6 Was Only the Beginning." *Vanity Fair,* June 22, 2022.
    www.vanityfair.com/news/2022/06/trump-ashli-babbitt-christians.
———. *The Undertow: Scenes from a Slow Civil War.* New York: Norton, 2023.
Shekhovtsov, Anton. *Russia and the Western Far Right: Tango Noir.* London:
    Routledge, 2018.
Sherman, Carter. "Anti-Abortion Activists Were All Over the Capitol Riots."
    Vice, January 12, 2021.
Sherwood, Harriet. "Remember Savita." *Guardian,* May 23, 2018.
Siegel, Benjamin, and Ivan Pereira. "Former Planned Parenthood Employee
    Abby Johnson's Anti-Abortion Comments under Scrutiny after Graphic
    RNC Speech." ABC News, August 25, 2020. https://abcnews.go.com
    /Politics/planned-parenthood-employee-abby-johnsons-anti-abortion
    -comments/story?id=72609833.
Simmons-Duffin, Selena. "National Institutes of Health Cancel Scientific
    Meetings after Trump Directives." National Public Radio, January 23,
    2025. www.npr.org/transcripts/nx-s1-5272398.
Small, Deborah. "The War on Drugs Is a War on Racial Justice." *Social Research*
    68, no. 3 (2001): 896–903. http://www.jstor.org/stable/40971924.
"Smoke and Mirrors: Planned Parenthood's Conspiracy to End Free Speech."
    Life Advocate 13, no. 5 (March/April 1999). www.lifeadvocate.org/3_99
    /cover_s.htm.
Soloman, Akiba. "Another Day, Another Race-Baiting Abortion Billboard."
    Colorlines, March 29, 2011. www.colorlines.com/articles/another-day-
    another-race-baiting-abortion-billboard.

Southern Poverty Law Center. "Aryan Nations Leader Richard Girnt Butler in
Final Days of Life." *Intelligence Report*, September 15, 1998. www.splcenter
.org/fighting-hate/intelligence-report/1998/aryan-nations-leader-richard
-girnt-butler-final-days-life.
———. "Deborah Rudolph Speaks Out about Her Former Brother-in-Law,
Olympic Park Bomber Eric Rudolph." *Intelligence Report*, November 29,
2001. www.splcenter.org/fighting-hate/intelligence-report/2001
/deborah-rudolph-speaks-out-about-her-former-brother-law-olympic
-park-bomber-eric-robert.
———. "Eric Rudolph Charged in Bombings." *Intelligence Report*, December
15, 1998. www.splcenter.org/fighting-hate/intelligence-report/1998/eric-
rudolph-charged-bombings.
Spitzer, Robert. "The NRA's Journey from Marksmanship to Political Brinks-
manship." *The Conversation*, February 23, 2018. https://theconversation
.com/the-nras-journey-from-marksmanship-to-political-brinkmanship
-92160.
Stabile, Carol A. "The Traffic in Fetuses." In *Fetal Subjects, Feminist Positions*,
edited by Lynn Morgan and Meredith W. Michaels, 133–58. Philadelphia:
University of Pennsylvania Press, 1999.
Stock, Catherine McNicol. *Rural Radicals: Righteous Rage in the American
Grain*. Ithaca, NY: Cornell University Press, 2017.
Stoeckl, Kristina, and Dmitry Uzlaner. *The Moralist International: Russia in the
Global Culture Wars*. New York: Fordham University Press, 2022.
Terry, Randall A. *Accessory to Murder: The Enemies, Allies, and Accomplices
to the Death of Our Culture*. Brentwood, TN: Wolgemuth & Hyatt, 1990.
Thomas, Rusty. "Open Letter to the Police in America." *Operation Save
America*, July 19, 2016. www.operationsaveamerica.org/2016/07/19
/press-release-open-letter-to-the-police-in-america/.
———. "The Line Was Crossed—Where Do We Go from Here?" *Operation
Save America*, May 25, 2017. www.operationsaveamerica.org/2017/05
/25/4125/.
Trans Legislation Tracker. https://translegislation.com/.
Trewhella, Matthew. *The Doctrine of the Lesser Magistrates: A Proper Resistance
to Tyranny and a Repudiation of Unlimited Obedience to Civil Government*.
North Charleston, SC: CreateSpace Independent Publishing Platform,
2013.

Valerius, Karyn. "A Not-So-Silent Scream: Gothic and the US Abortion Debate." *Frontiers: A Journal of Women Studies* 34, no. 3 (2013): 27–47.

Van Maren, Jonathon. "How Abolish Human Abortion Gets History Wrong." Canadian Centre for Bio-ethical Reform, January 15, 2014. www.endthekilling.ca/blog/2014/01/15/how-abolish-human-abortion-gets-history-wrong.

Vásquez, Tina. "How the Anti-Abortion Movement Fed the Capitol Insurrection." *Prism,* January 22, 2021. http://prismreports.org/2021/01/22/how-the-antiabortion-movement-fed-the-capitol-insurrection/

Veznor, Tad. "What's Next after End of Decades-Long Keillor–MPR Relationship?" *Twin Cities Pioneer Press,* December 6, 2017. www.twincities.com/2017/12/06/whats-next-after-end-of-decades-long-keillor-mpr-relationship/.

Walton, Satchel, and Cooper Walton. "KSP Training Slideshow Quotes Hitler, Advocates 'Ruthless' Violence." *Manual RedEye* (duPont Manual High School, Louisville, KY), October 30, 2020. https://manualredeye.com/90096/news/local/police-training-hitler-presentation/.

Ward, Julie A., et al., "National Burden of Injury and Deaths from Shootings by Police in the United States, 2015-2020." *American Journal of Public Health* 114, no. 4 (2024): 387.

Wells, Jon. *Sniper: The True Story of Anti-Abortion Killer James Kopp.* New York: Harper Collins, 2008.

"What a Real President Was Like." *Washington Post,* November 13, 1988. www.washingtonpost.com/archive/opinions/1988/11/13/what-a-real-president-was-like/d483c1be-d0da-43b7-bde6-04e10106ff6c/.

Williams, Daniel K. *Defenders of the Unborn: The Pro-Life Movement before Roe v. Wade.* New York: Oxford University Press, 2016.

Winter, Jessica. "The Link Between the Capitol Riot and Anti-Abortion Extremism." *New Yorker*, March 11, 2021. www.newyorker.com/news/daily-comment/the-link-between-the-capitol-riot-and-anti-abortion-extremism.

Winters, Michael Sean. *God's Right Hand: How Jerry Falwell Made God a Republican and Baptized the American Right.* New York: Harper Collins, 2019.

Woolford, Jessica, and Andrew Woolford. "Abortion and Genocide: The Unbridgeable Gap." *Social Politics: International Studies in Gender, State and Society* 14, no. 1 (2007): 126–53.

Young, Maria. "Russia Gay Laws Cheered by US Conservatives." *Sputnik News,*
March 8, 2013. https://sputniknews.com/analysis/20130803182557638
-Russia-Gay-Homosexuality-Laws-Cheered-by-US-Conservatives/.

Youngman, Nicole. "Jeeries Jubilee." *The Body Politic,* May/June 1998.

Zernicke, Kate. "States Aren't Waiting for the Supreme Court to Tighten
Abortion Laws." *New York Times,* March 7, 2022.

Ziegler, Mary. *Abortion and the Law in America: Roe v. Wade to the Present.*
Cambridge: Cambridge University Press, 2020.

———. *Dollars for Life: The Anti-Abortion Movement and the Fall of the
Republican Establishment.* New Haven, CT: Yale University Press, 2022.

Index

ableism, 9

ABMAL campaign, 98

Abolish Human Abortion (AHA), 197–201, 204

Abolitionists Rising, 201–2

abortion: abortion rights, 9, 46, 50, 63, 110, 129, 213–14; decriminialization of, 7, 19, 50, 52, 77, 117. *See also* antiabortion movement; *Roe v. Wade*

abortion abolitionists: in 1970s, 152–57; in 1980s, 157–59; in 1990s, 159–65; about, 186; child sacrifice conspiracy theory, 146, 198–203; goal of, 202–3; January 6 US Capitol attack and, 151; organizations of, 197–201, 204; political strategies of, 203–4; Rudolph and, 151, 161. *See also* antiabortion abolitionist movement; deParrie, Paul; Hunter, T. Russell

The Abortion Abolitionist (periodical), 194–96, 204

Abortion: A Doctrine of Demons (film) (Created Equal), 89–90, 93–94

Abortion and the Politics of Motherhood (Luker), 75

abortion clinic workers: depictions of, 91, 162, 186; harassment of, 117, 130, 192; killings of, 5, 13–14, 77–78, 144, 160–62, 186, 189; support for, 3

abortion rights, 9, 46, 50, 63, 110, 129, 213–14

Accessory to Murder (Terry), 116, 123

Advocates for Life Ministries, 141, 188, 189, 190, 192

Alexander, Ali, 147

Alliance Defending Freedom (organization), 98–99

Allred, Gloria, 128

alt-right: Berkeley protests (2017), 2, 10, 99; Unite the Right rally, 10, 200. *See also* far right; white nationalism; white supremacists

American Birth Control League, 112

American Insurrection (2022 documentary) (Rowley), 220

American Life League (ALL) (organization), 31, 156, 229n44

Americans United for Life (AUL), 48–49, 54, 57, 157, 160
Andrews, Joan, 117–26, 136, 138, 147, 211. *See also* Terry, Randall
antiabortion abolitionist movement, 201–4. *See also* abortion abolitionists
antiabortion messaging: AHA and, 197–201, 204; deParrie and, 162, 185–96, 204, 212, 216; signage, 5–7
antiabortion militancy: in 1980s, 157–59; in 1990s, 116; *The Army of God Manual* and, 137, 159–61; *Firestorm* (Crutcher), 50, 160–61; January 6 US Capitol attack and, 10–11, 151; strategies of, 204–5; violence and, 9, 157–59, 161, 211. *See also* violence
antiabortion movement: in 1970s, 156–57; in 1980s, 157–59; in 1990s, 159–65; Christians and, 110; crossover of, 5, 31, 141, 158, 185–204, 212; far-right groups and, 31, 163, 212, 218; gender and, 30; global aspects of, 53–61, 162–63; McCorvey and, 127–30, 147; militia movement and, 77, 137, 161; populism and, 69, 210, 212, 218; pro-woman rhetoric and, 49; race and, 25, 75–76, 91, 104, 109, 110, 137, 197; radicalization of, 109; white nationalism and, 210; white supremacists and, 161; World Congress of Families (WCF) and, 162. *See also* antiabortion abolitionist movement; antiabortion messaging; antiabortion militancy; Jefferson, Mildred

antiabortion rescue movement: in 1970s, 179; in 1980s, 157–59; in 1990s, 159–65; about, 1–2; as apocalyptic war, 122–24, 147; protests, 188–89; race and, 117–18; Shannon and, 136. *See also* Andrews, Joan; Operation Rescue (organization); Operation Save America (organization); Ramey, Cathy
Anti-Defamation League, 146
anti-government militants, 3, 8, 77, 124, 146, 163, 185, 215
antisemitism: abortion opposition and, 61, 103, 113; Aryan Nations and, 126; blood libel myth, 90, 91, 195, 208, 240n47; conspiracy theories and, 168, 177, 211; far-right militants and, 114, 150, 163, 167, 171, 172, 176, 185; as historical prejudice, 79; Paul Marx and, 128; of tax protesters, 187
anti-statism: antiabortion movement and, 8, 9, 194; anti-vaccination movement and, 8; far-right militants and, 77, 212, 218; as mainstream, 204; paramilitary, 204; patriot (term usage) and, 125, 228n33; radicalization and, 33–34; terrorism and, 34, 109, 125–26, 137. *See also* anti-government militants
anti-vaccination movement, 7–9, 17, 80, 167, 195–96, 215
Antonov, Anatoly, 58–59
apocalyptic messaging: abortion opposition and, 9, 26–27, 66, 76–77; anti-vaccination movement and, 8; crossover of, 9; fundamentalism and, 33–34, 109;

Carlson, Allan, 57, 58–59

Carter administration, 163

"Caught on Cam" news spot, 99–103

censorship, 228n42

Centennial Park bombing, 171–72

Center for Bioethical Reform (CBR), 79

The Changing Voice of the Anti-Abortion Movement (Saurette and Gordon), 49

Charlottesville car attack, 10, 248n11

Chauvin, Derek, 201

child sacrifice. *See* satanic child sacrifice conspiracy theories

Christians: BLM and, 83–84; Christian conservatives, 78, 83, 84; Christian nationalism, 10, 61; conspiracy theories and, 113; Defensive Action Statement and, 15; evangelicals, 62–63, 145; fundamentalism, 133–34; McCorvey and, 127–30; populism and, 17, 62–64; *Roe v. Wade* and, 16; transgender issues and, 29; white Christian men as under attack, 75, 99, 104; World Congress of Families (WCF), 53–59. *See also* Andrews, Joan; Created Equal (organization); Johnson, Abby; McCorvey, Norma; Shannon, Shelley

civil rights movement, 80–82

Clinton, Hillary, 77, 90, 129, 145, 202

Closed (Scheidler), 49, 137

Cold War conspiracism, 33, 109–16, 146, 162, 208, 211

Coleman, Priscilla, 48, 49, 51

Columbine High School shooting, 4

common culture, 18, 19

Commonwealth v. Kenneth Edelin, 109–10

Concerned Women for America (organization), 54

Condic, Maureen, 55–56

The Conscience of a Conservative (Goldwater), 82–83

Cooper, Cloee, 201

Corrales, Javier, 63–64

Coulter, Ann, 99

Council on Biblical Manhood and Womanhood, 29

COVID-19 pandemic, 8, 17, 167, 194–96. *See also* anti-vaccination movement

Created Equal (organization): antiabortion protest on campus, 94–99; brochures, 237n15; "Caught on Cam" news spot, 100–103, 104; *Doctrine of Demons* (film), 89–94; fiscal information, 241n60; racial and religious assumptions of, 79–85; right-wing victimhood and, 103–4; videos of, 85–89; visual politics of, 33, 76, 196. *See also* Harrington, Mark

Crutcher, Mark, 49–50, 98, 160–61

Dangerous Pregnancies (Reagan), 9

Daubenmire, Dave, 11

Davis, Wendy, 198

The Death Peddlers (Marx), 113–14, 116

Defensive Action Statement, 14–15, 161

Delay, Cara, 51

deParrie, Paul, 34, 141, 162, 185–96, 204, 212, 216

DeSantis, Ron, 17

Dietz, George, 158
Dobbs v. Jackson, 34, 68, 70, 207, 213–15, 216
A Doctrine of Demons. See Abortion: A Doctrine of Demons (film) (Created Equal)
The Doctrine of the Lesser Magistrates (Trewhella), 14–15, 17, 27–28, 69
Drayer, Seth, 102
Dublin Declaration on Maternal Healthcare, 47–48
Duey, Randy, 170

Edelin, Kenneth, 109–10
Eighth Amendment (Ireland), 45–46, 47, 49, 51
elites: of abortion industry, 21; Democratic elites, 90, 91; of federal government, 20–21, 150; Hollywood elites, 90, 114; Jewish elites, 177; of medical establishmen, 196; populist view of, 17–19, 63, 134
End Abortion Now (organization), 201
Equal Rights Amendment, 62
Estes, Chad, 11
Evans, Derrick, 11
Expectant Mother Care, 47
extremism: antiabortion extremism, 66–67; Goldwater on, 14; in law and politics, 210; supremacist extremism, 170–73; Trewhella on, 13–14. *See also* Rudolph, Eric

Faludi, Susan, 76
Falwell, Jerry, 62
far right: in 1970s, 152–57; in 1980s, 157–59; in 1990s, 159–65; in

2000s, 165–66; in 2010s, 166–67; in 2020s, 167–68; antiabortion movement and, 31, 34; anti-statism and, 212; crossover of, 5, 151; defined, 31; federal government and, 150; gaslighting by, 12–13; patriot (term usage) and, 228n33; populism and, 31, 64; rhetoric of, 124; umbrella organizations and, 124. *See also* abortion abolitionists; alt-right; deParrie, Paul; January 6 US Capitol attack; Rudolph, Eric
feminism, 25, 42, 59, 76, 101, 111–12, 207, 249n21
Firestorm (Crutcher), 50, 160–61
Floyd, George, 168, 201
Flynn, Michael, 17, 146
Focus on the Family (organization), 54
For Life (organization), 56
Foundation to Abolish Abortion (organization), 201
Freedom of Choice Act, 143
Freemen Militia, 141
Free the States (organization), 200–201, 204
Fugitive Slave Act of 1850, 68

gender issues: anti-genderism, 61–65; anti-transgenderism, 65–66
Genocide Awareness Project, 78–79, 98
German measles (rubella) vaccine, 9
Goldwater, Barry, 14, 82–83
Graff, Agnieszka, 61
Greensboro Massacre, 155, 248n11
Griffin, Michael, 78, 127
Gunn, David, 14, 127, 188

164; police and, 16–17, 84, 239n34; Ruby Ridge standoff, 163–64; at Unite the Right rally, 10; Waco siege, 3, 164; "The Warrior Mindset" (slideshow), 16–17; white supremacists, 124. *See also* Andrews, Joan; antiabortion militancy; Army of God; *The Army of God Manual*; January 6 US Capitol attack; McVeigh, Timothy; Rudolph, Eric; Shannon, Shelley

Volontè, Luca, 57

Waco siege, 3, 164
waiting periods, 53
Walsh, Matt, 39–44
War on Drugs (program), 7–8
warrior narrative: Andrews and, 117–24, 126; Babbitt and, 107–9; Jefferson and, 109–16; Johnson and, 130–36; McCorvey and, 127–30; in pro-life writing, 107; racial aspects of, 33, 107; Shannon and, 136–45; victims in, 20, 28, 33; War on Poverty and, 125; "The Warrior Mindset," 16–17; white Christian men as under attack, 75–76. *See also* race; radicalization
Weaver family, 3, 163–64
Webb, Bill, 96–97
white nationalism: about, 22; antiabortion movement and, 21, 23–25, 30, 109, 208, 210; crossover of, 5, 13, 208; growing prevalence

of, 10; imagery used by, 22–23. *See also* alt-right; McVeigh, Timothy
white supremacists: crossover of, 5, 11, 27, 34, 161; far-right and, 31; of global right, 57; imagery used by, 22–23; Pikeville recruitment show, 2, 10. *See also* Ku Klux Klan; Patriot Front; Unite the Right rally
women: Black women, 43–44, 87–88, 109–16, 147, 174–75, 243n13; demonstrators claim as property, 72–76; in Ireland, 32, 45–49, 51–52, 70; right-wing attention on, 44; in Russia, 32, 45, 52–61, 70, 162; transgender issues and, 43; "What Is a Woman?" program, 39–44, 61, 210
Women against Abortion (Haugeberg), 49, 117
Women for America First, 107, 108, 146
Won by Love (McCorvey), 127–29, 131
World Congress of Families (WCF), 32, 53–59, 162, 188

Yiannopoulos, Milo, 99
Young Americans for Freedom, 40
You Reject Them, You Reject Me (Andrews), 120–21
Youth Defence (Irish organization), 49

Ziegler, Mary, 49, 116, 157, 249n21
Zionist Occupied Government (ZOG), 176

Founded in 1893,
UNIVERSITY OF CALIFORNIA PRESS
publishes bold, progressive books and journals
on topics in the arts, humanities, social sciences,
and natural sciences—with a focus on social
justice issues—that inspire thought and action
among readers worldwide.

The UC PRESS FOUNDATION
raises funds to uphold the press's vital role
as an independent, nonprofit publisher, and
receives philanthropic support from a wide
range of individuals and institutions—and from
committed readers like you. To learn more, visit
ucpress.edu/supportus.

www.ingramcontent.com/pod-product-compliance
Lightning Source LLC
Chambersburg PA
CBHW020830270326
41928CB00006B/485